NAKSHI KANTHA OF BENGAL

NAKSHI KANTHA

OF

BENGAL

SILA BASAK

GYAN PUBLISHING HOUSE
NEW DELHI - 110002

Nakshi Kantha of Bengal

ISBN : 81-212-0895-5

Published in 2007 in India by
Gyan Publishing House,
5, Ansari Road, Daryaganj, New Delhi-110002
Phones : 23282060, 23261060
Fax : (011) 23285914
E-mail : books@gyanbooks.com
Website : www.gyanbooks.com

Translated by : Sumanta Sen

Laser Type-setting by : Shagun Graphics, Delhi
Processing by : Guru ji Colour Scan, Delhi
Printed at : Jaina Offset Press, Delhi

My daughter
Sudeshna – Mili
and
two grandsons
Subhechha – Prince
Rebanta – Raj

Preface

The nakshi kantha is among those artistic creations that are truly Bengali in nature. The coverlet, for instance, may be an item of domestic use all over the world but no where else is it so finely embroidered, even taking into account the designed clothes made by such North American communities as the Navaho or the Hopi.

The art of kantha stitching has been kept alive for centuries by the women of Bengal who with their thread and needle have given expression for generations to their emotions. Like Saju in Jasimuddin's poem *Nakshi Kanthar Maath*, they have always told their life-story, their happiness, their pain, through the kanthas they made and continue to make.

I was drawn towards the nakshi kantha while visiting villages in Bangladesh in connection with another project. As my survey progressed I came into contact with numerous ordinary people and was overwhelmed by their hospitality. I am grateful to all of them. In Chittagong I had to spend a night with a family and was astonished to find a specimen of my subject in the bed. The next morning it was given to me as a gift.

The project would not have got off the ground but for the help and encouragement that I received from many. The names that need to be mentioned are, Anisuzzaman, Fazle Hasan Abed, the late Probhas Sen and Late Basanta Choudhury. Md. Saidur, Chandrasekhar Saha, Mohin Khan, Pallab Sengupta, Manas Mazumdar, Debkumar Gangopadhyaya, Late Arun Kumar Chattopadhyaya, Late Tarapada Santra, Sujit Dutta, Indranath Mazumdar, Leena Sarabhai, Jyotindra Jain, D.S. Mehta, Tofail Ahmed, Sayyada R. Ghuznavi, Ashraf Siddiqui, Biswanath Roy, Bishwanath Sarkar, Wakil Ahmed, Syed Mahbub Alam, Shamsuzzaman Khan, Indrajit Chowdhury, Suraya Rahman, Sunil Chandra Basak. I shall remain indebted to them for ever.

Amitendranath Tagore helped me with the permission to photograph a kantha collected by Abanindranath Tagore and the Tripura Government helped me see eleven kanthas which had been collected by Dinesh Chandra Sen and which are in its museum at Agartala. My heartfelt thanks to all of them. I am also grateful to photographers like Sibnath Biswas, Tarun Mistri, Md. Wahiduzzaman Roni, Milan Biswas and Farooq Helal. My daughter Sudeshna (Mili) and son-in-law Sumit (Joy) were the two pillars of constant support and help. The keen interest of my two nephew Parichay and Avinandan provided me the encouragement to complete the book fast. And finally, I must name Subhechha (Prince) and Rebanta (Raj)—my two grandsons, but for whose pleasant company, I could not have complete this book with satisfaction.

Sept. 28, 2006

Kolkata700031, India

Sila Basak

Contents

Acknowledgements

Abdul Khalek, Asish Chakravorty, Asish Pradhan
Academy of Fine Arts, Kolkata
Acharya Jogeshchandra Purakriti Sangrahasala, Bishnupur
AEDTA, Paris
Akshoy Kumar Maitreya and Raja Rajaram
Collection, North Bengal University, Siliguri
Ananda Publishers Pvt. Ltd. Kolkata
Anandniketan Kirtishala, Bagnan, Howrah
Anath Nath Das, Animesh Sen Gupta, Anita Das
Archana Roy, Arnab Basu, R.K. Tiwari, Arya Dasgupta
Asma Begum, U. Das, Ishtiaque Hassan, A. Roy
Asutosh Museum, University of Calcutta
Bangiya Sahitya Parishad, Kolkata
Bangladesh Loka O Karushilpa Foundation,
Bangladesh National Museum, Dhaka
Banglaghar Loka O Karushilpa Sangraha
Banya Bandopadhyaya, Bijan Mandal, Bipradas Palit
Bharabi Mukhopadhyaya, Manimala Dutta, Mohiuddin Ahmed
Birla Academy of Art and Culture, Kolkata
Chhanda Basu, Janak Jhankar Narjari, Zakiul Huq
Chittagong University Museum
Crafts Museum, New Delhi
Department Library
Durgaram Bhattacharya, Debashish Gayen
Folk Tradition Collection, Bangla Academy, Dhaka
Government Industrial and Commercial
Gurusaday Museum, Joka
Hossain, Shyamal Sahu, Shyamalkanti Chakravorti, Satinath Pal
Indian Museum, Kolkata
Jeenat Mahrukh Banu, Jyotsna, Gupta
Jnanranjan Haldar, Tokyo Hasegawa
Kala Bhavan, Visqa Bharati, Santiniketan
Karuangan, Kolkata
Kolkata University's Central and Bengali
Kripamoy Acharya, Chayan Islam, Chittaranjan Dasgupta
Manash Pan, Manik Sengupta, Mazharul Islam Toru

Mithila Museum, Nigata, Japan
Mridula Sarkar (Bandopadhyaya), Momen Chowdhury
Mukhopadhyaya, Lily Islam
Museum, Kolkata
Naresh Bandopadhyaya, Niranjan Goswami, Niru Shamsun Nahar
National Institute of Design, Ahmedabad
National Library, Kolkata
National Museum, New Delhi
Parag Rakshit, Prodyot Ghosh, Prasanta Chowdhury
Philadelphia Museum of Art, USA
Pratisthan, Dhaka
Premenda Mazumdar, Fazlur Rahman, Banaphool Chattopadhyay
Rabindra Bhavan, Viswa Bharati, Santiniketan
Ramkrishna Mission Institute Of Culture, Kolkata
Regional Design and Technical Development Centre, Kolkata
Rinku Bandhopadhyaya, Lalit mohan
Sambhu Nath Ghosh, Santi Dasgupta, Shamsul
Sarabhai Foundation, Calico Museum of Textiles, Ahmedabad
Satyajit Chowdhury, Sandip Mullick, Sudipta Rakshit
Selina Hossain, Stasi Bomento, Swapan Mazumdar, Himadri Ghosh
Shreyas Foundation, Shreyas Folk Museum, Ahmedabad
Sonargaon Hotel, Dhaka
Sonargaon, Narayanganj
State Archaelogical Museum, Kolkata
Sunandan Bandopadhyaya, Subhadra Bhattacharya
Sundarban Anchalik Sangrahasala, South 24 Paraganas
Tapankanti Mukhopadhyaya, Dilip Dasgupta
The University Press Limited, Dhaka
The Victoria and Albert Museum, London
Tripura Government Museum, Agartala
Victoria Memorial Hall, Kolkata

Photo Credits

A E D T A, Paris 8
Acharya Jagdish Chandra Collection, Bishnupur 131
Akshoy Kumar Maitreya and Raja Rajaram Collection, North Bengal University, Siliguri 132
Amina Begum, North 24 Parganas 68, 137
Amitendranath Tagore, Kolkata 52
Amiyabala Sarkar, Burdwan 98
Anandaniketan Kirtishala, Bagnan, Howrah 33, 97, 174, 180, 317
Anima Saha, Hooghly 91, 126
Anita Sarkar, Murshidabad 110
Arong, Dhaka 49, 66, 71-2, 78, 85, 89, 145, 211, 286, 336
Arun Nag, Santiniketan 81
Ashok Kumar Kundu, Kolkata 17
Asim Mondal, Kalyani 163
Asutosh Museum, Calcutta University 19, 40, 114, 298-313
Bangladesh Loka O Karushilpa Foundation, Sonargaon, Narayanganj 5, 26, 29, 34, 67, 177, 263, 268, 277, 285, 320, 322-25, 338-40, 343-49, 354-57
Bangladesh National Museum, Dhaka 55, 70, 103, 334
Behari Lal — Kavyasangrah, Calcutta University, 1964, (Collected by Bangiya Sahitya Parishad, Kolkata 178
Brojeswar Das, Orissa 96
Chandrasekhar Saha, Dhaka 25
Chittagong University Museum, Chittagong 278
Crafts Museum, New Delhi 10, 12, 50, 56-9, 65, 82, 94, 140, 150, 153, 164, 172, 175-76, 328, 350-53
Dineshchandra Sen, Kolkata 13, 100
Folk Tradition Collection, Bangla Academy, Dhaka 168, 169, 171, 233-34
Government Industrial & Commercial Museum, Kolkata 30, 134, 142
Gurusaday Museum, Joka 31, 41, 45, 53, 92, 99, 108, 123 146-49, 151, 157, 159, 165, 181, 197, 229-31, 242, 246-47, 251, 326, 332
Indian Museum, Kolkata 1, 62-3, 243, 252, 272
Indranath Mazumdar, Santiniketan 28
Jahanara Abedin, Dhaka 54, 235, 248-49, 264-67 271, 273, 279, 288, 290-91, 293, 316, 319, 321, 349
Jindhuprabha Devi, Dhaka 360
Jyotindra Jain, New Delhi 60
Jyotsna Gupta, Kolkata 79-80, 109
Kala Bhavan, Viswa Bharati, Santiniketan 6, 9, 11, 61, 156, 231, 238-41
Maya Mukherjee, Agartala 342
Md. Saidur, Dhaka 35-37, 44, 107, 111, 121, 124-25, 130, 133, 250, 269
Mithila Museum, Nigata, Japan 93, 167
Moitryee Ghoshal, North 24 Parganas 105
Moitryee Sen, Kolkata 88, 95
Museum of Folklore Dept. Kalyani University, Kalyani, Nadia 39, 102, 117
National Museum, New Delhi 18, 116, 184, 254, 257, 260, 262, 295-97, 331, 334
Nilima Pakhira, Hoogly 84
Philadelphia Museum of Art, USA

73, 1964-184-10 74, 1968-184-5 75, 1968-184-8 76, 1968-184-6	Kanthas of Faridpur, East Pakistan (Now Bangladesh), Doneted by Stella Kramrisch

Prasant and Geeta Das, North 24 Parganas 232
Prodyot Ghosh, Maldah 64, 129, 341
Purnima Bagchi, South 24 Parganas 69, 138
Rabindra Bhavan, Viswa Bharati, Santiniketan 38
Regional Design And Technical Development Centre, Kolkata 51, 122, 135, 244-45, 329, 335

Sarabhai Foundation, Calico Museum of Textiles, Ahmedabad 2-4, 21, 27, 112, 214, 253, 255-56, 258-59, 261, 327, 350
Sayyada R. Ghuznavi, Dhaka 314-15, 337
Shafiul Alam, Burdwan 128
Shreyas Foundation, Shreyas Folk Museum, Ahmedabad 113
Sila Basak, Kolkata 14-6, 20, 22-4, 42-3, 46, 48, 101, 104, 115, 118, 141, 143, 154-55, 158, 161-62, 170, 173, 175, 183-93, 195-96, 198-224, 333
Somnath Ghosh, Kolkata 166
Subhra Chaudhury, Chittagong 127
Sujata Mitra, Santiniketan 136, 210
Suriya Rahaman, Dhaka 77, 120, 182, 194, 289, 292, 326, 330, 358, 359
Susoma Sarkar, Kolkata 86-7, 90
Tarapada Santra, Bagnan, Howrah 119
The University Press Limited, Dhaka – The Art of Kantha Embroidery by Niaz Zaman 1993, 152, 160, 179, 294
The Victoria and Albert Museum, London "V and A Picture Library" 7, 139, 144, 225-28,
Tofail Ahmed, Dhaka 36, 287, 318
Tripura Government Museum, Agartala 236-37, 270, 274-76, 280-84
Victoria Memorial Hall, Kolkata 47

List of Illustrations

Album

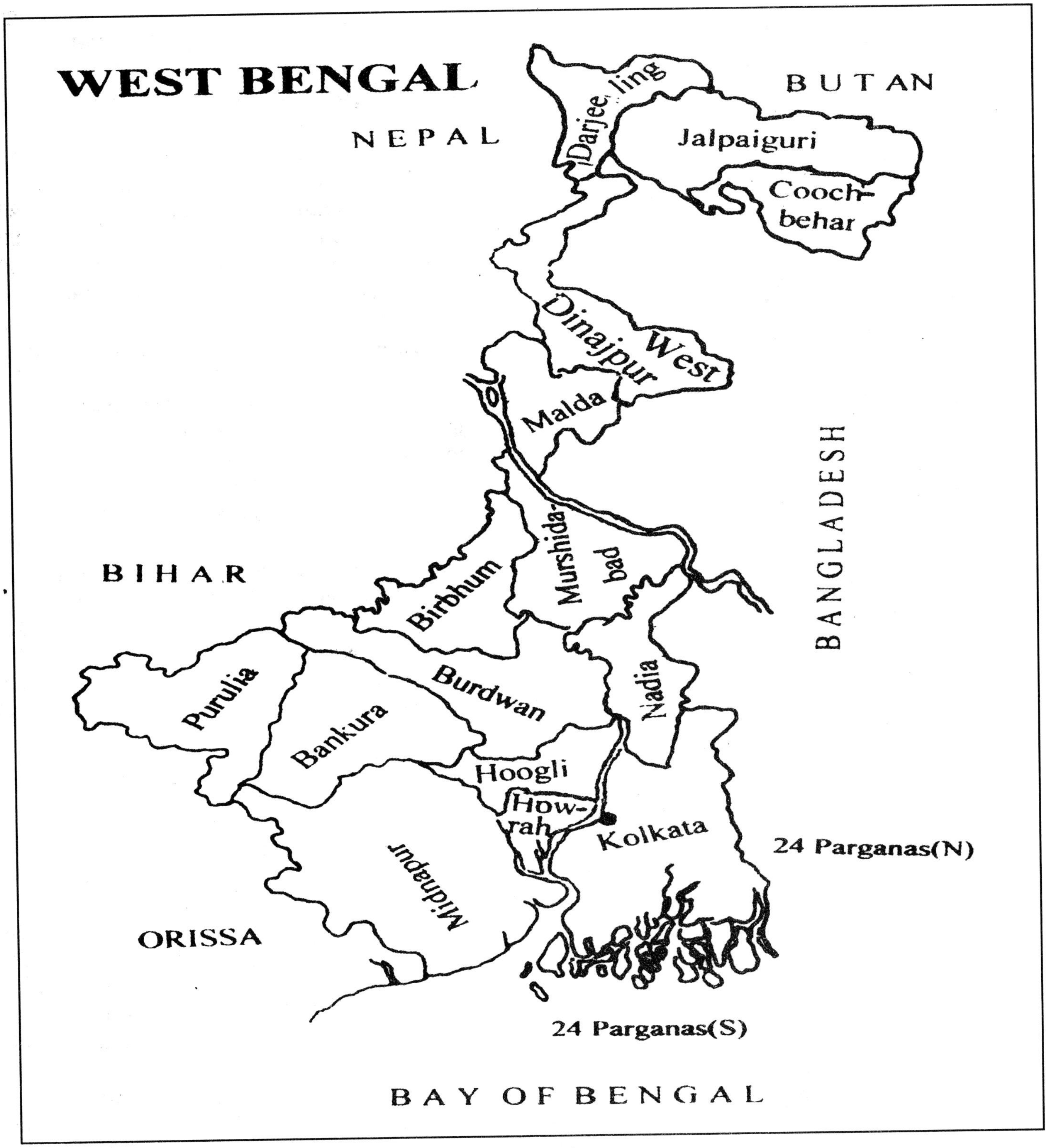

West Bengal and Bangladesh : Once known as Bengal, the remarkable treasury of kanthas was developed in this area

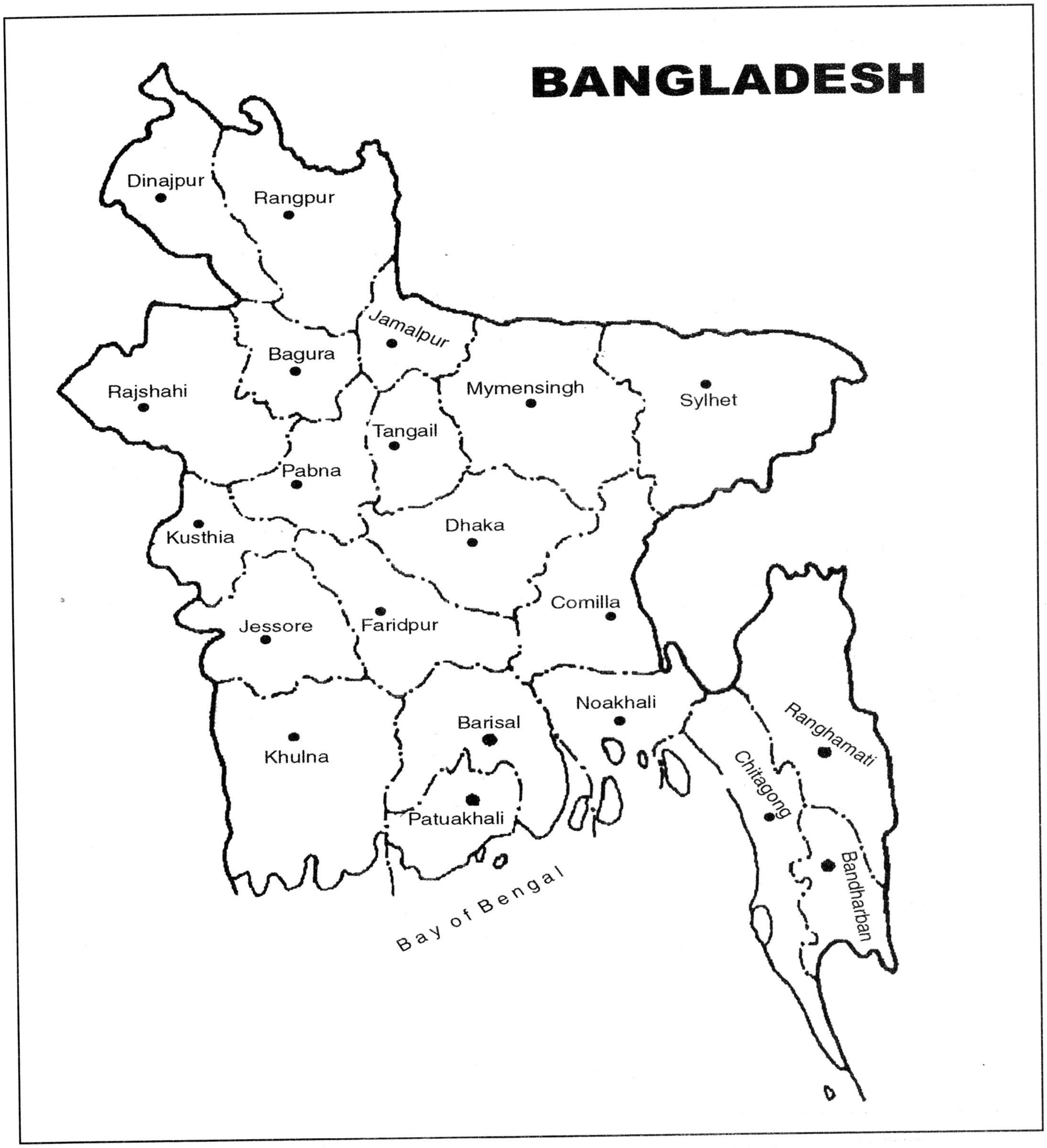
BANGLADESH
Dinajpur
Rangpur
Jamalpur
Bagura
Rajshahi
Mymensingh
Sylhet
Tangail
Pabna
Dhaka
Kusthia
Comilla
Jessore
Faridpur
Noakhali
Barisal
Khulna
Ranghamati
Chitagong
Patuakhali
Bandharban
Bay of Bengal

The Beginning

The art of designing pieces of cloth with needle and thread is as old as the hills. As ancient man settled down and built his home, he felt an urge to beautify his surroundings. First he arranged leaves and flowers to make patterns on the wall then he turned to his clothes. These, he felt, could do with a bit of designs and gradually needlework was born. The relics of ancient Egypt have shown that at first the needles were made of animal bones and then of bronze. In far away Scotland also, a bronze needle in a silver box was found in the grave of a woman dating back to the days of the Vikings. The Bible speaks of embroidered clothes and there is every reason to believe that the art was known in what is now the Middle East, three hundred years before the birth of Jesus. It was known in Thebes of yore and Byzantine.

The ancient Romans called it paintings with the needle and these spread all over their vast empire. In South America the Peruvians did not lag behind and even Eskimoes knew the art. The famed tapestry of Europe owes its origin to such needlework.

We have spoken of the bone and bronze needles but what about the cloth and thread? Mohenjo-daro has revealed the use of cotton cloth and an inscription at Babylon says cotton reached there from the Indus Valley a thousand years before the Redeemer was born at Bethlehem. The mummies in the pyramids used to be draped with cloth intricately woven and designed, the designers using thread made of cotton, silk and the hair of camels and goats. Moses was supposed to have covered God with fine silk, embroidered with threads of divine blue and red and similar were the curtains at Solomon's temple at Jerusalem. Alexander the Great was amazed at the needlework he saw in Persia. He would have seen the same in India if he had stayed longer and also China if he had gone there.

With time the designers turned more and more towards grandeur. Gold and silver threads began to be used and the cloths would be embedded with precious stones, pearls, the wings of colourful insects to make dresses fit for kings and dignitaries or canopies under which they sat. Excavations have thrown up leather bearing intricate needlework from the graves at the Altai Hills, which are remarkable specimens of the Aplique.

Such needlework like other forms of art, helps provide an insight to contemporary life. They tell us that in sixth century Persia people dressed themselves with the barks of trees and at the same time also wore ornaments. Many of the designs both in the East and the West had religious functions as subjects, the priests shown to wear clothes that matched and even surpassed that of royalty.

The ancient needlework of China deserves special mention. The Chinese designed all their clothes, whether for daily use or special occasions and no woman was considered cultured if she did not know the art. The needlework of 14th century China resembles paintings, natural and true to life. The girls of Japan were equally skilled, their kimonos bearing testimony to this.

The history of needlework suggests it owed its origin to the need to sew firm creepers or the gut of dead animals into ropes to tie up

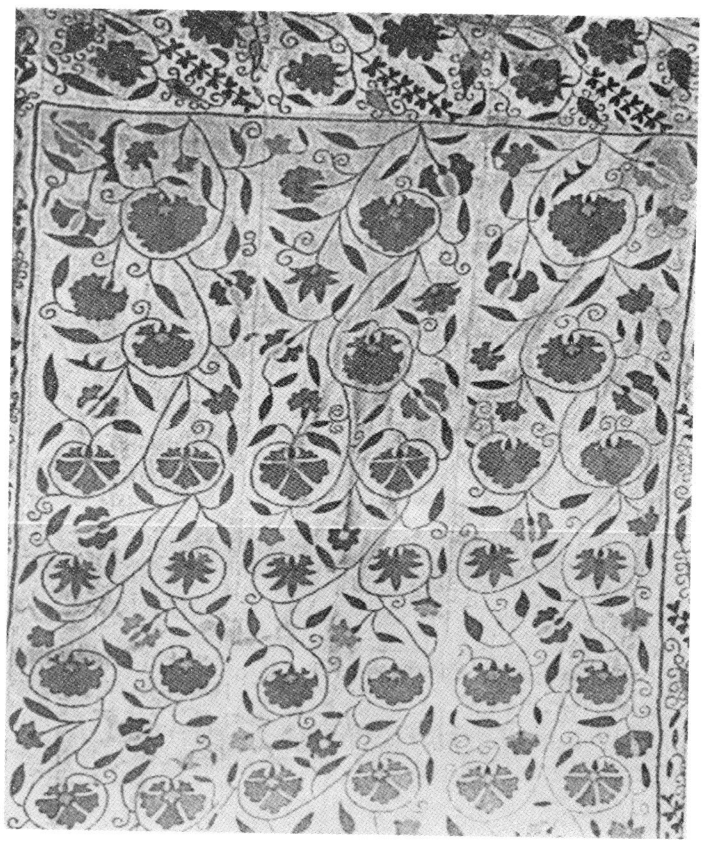

1. Sujni kantha, Peshawar, approx. 19th century.

things, using sharpened stones of bamboos as needles. By the time the Iron Age had come man had learnt to first wet and then dry fibrous materials and than join these together with thick stitches. Later they learnt the art of collecting cotton from (*simul*)and such other trees, spin these into threads and weave them into clothes. It has to be noted that primitive man had learnt of stitch and join even before he came to know the use of fire.

India enjoys a long and glorious tradition of needlework and weaving. Clothes made in this country had highly impressed the Greek historian Herodotus and later Megasthenes and Marco Polo sang to their praise. The figures excavated at Harappa and Mohanjo-daro provide evidence of the beautifully woven and embroidered clothes that used to be worn in those early days as do the sculptures at Sanchi and elsewhere.

The art of weaving is traced back to the time of the Ṛg Veda. The earliest mention of Kantha is found in Pali literature and the works of Panini, though of course Chandrabati's Ramayana also mentions Kantha stitching as one of the skills in which Sita excelled. The Mahabharata also speaks of woven clothes with their borders decorted with pearls. Designed Indian clothes were very much in demand during the days of the Roman Empire and were also found in Eighth century Central Asia. The art reached great heights during the days of the Mughals who were great patrons of needlework.

Needlework has always been an essential part of the art of weaving in this country. Evidence of this can be had all over, from Gujarat to Chamba to Lucknow to Bengal. If the designers of North India created magic with their needles and threads of gold and silver on silk, so did the folk art of Kantha stitching and designing in Bengal.

Gujarat occupies an important place in the history of the art of weaving in India. An account of 1518 speaks of the wonderful embroidery on quilts and bedcovers which were taken by the Portuguese to Europe and gained immense popularity there. This made the British East

2. Detailed design–Jaipur needlework, 18th century.

3. Bengal Kantha, 19th century.

4. Designs with mixed stitches.

5. Paar Kantha, Jessore, end 19th century

6. Bengal Kantha.

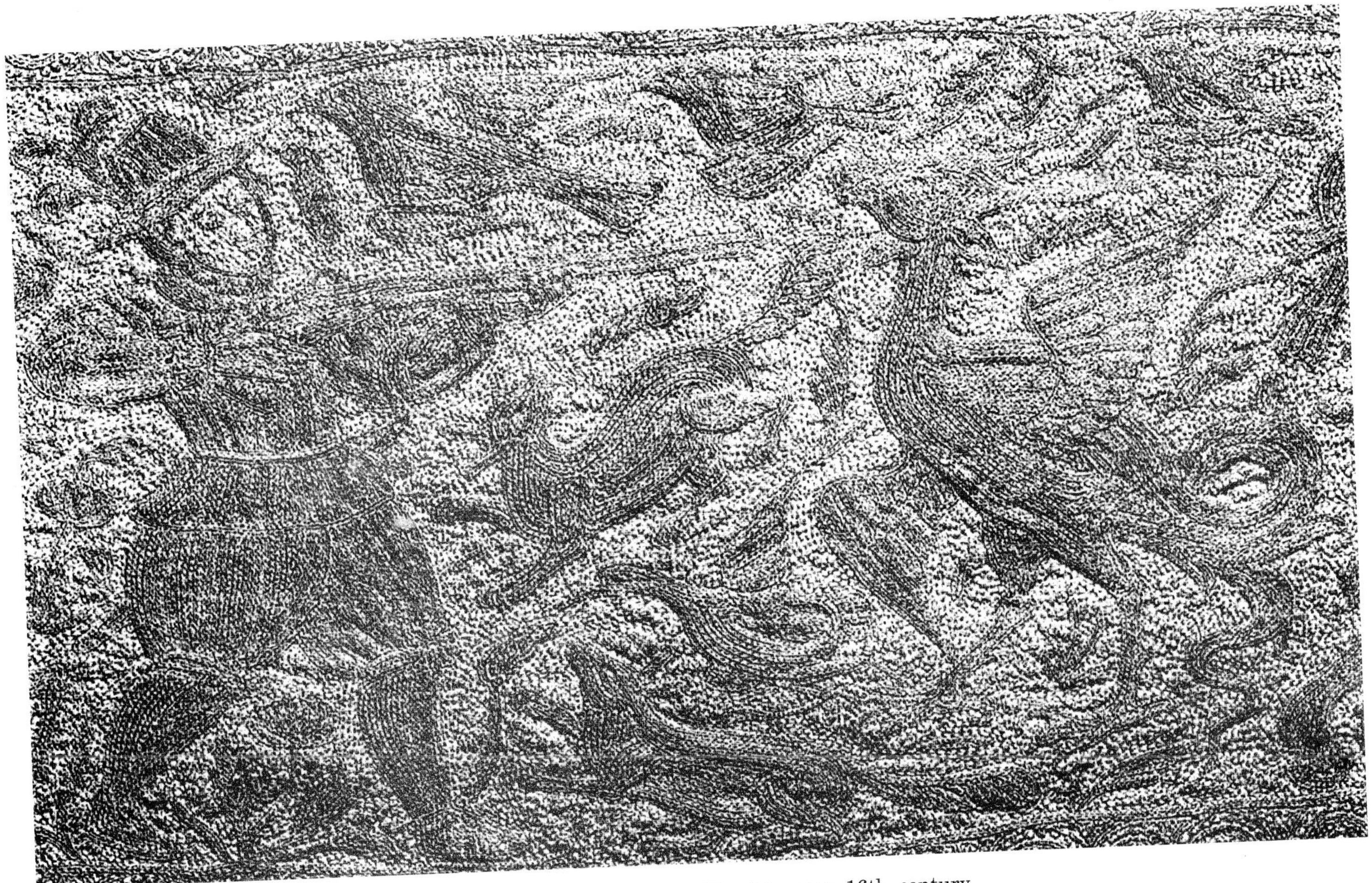

7. Needlework of Satgaon–Hooghly area–16th century.

India Company turn its eyes to these and received permission from King Charles I to export to England. Writing in 1629 the Portuguese missionary Sebastian Manrick said among the things that his countrymen used to secure large quantities of quilts, bedcovers, awnings and other such items which bore marks of Bengal's excellent needlework. The products of folk art were stated to be particularly in demand in foreign shores.

Satgaon (Saptagram) used to be the main centre for commerce in Bengal till the middle of the sixteenth century when the Portuguese built their port at Hooghly. Satgaon is mentioned in Chaitanya Bhagabata of Brindaban Das, Manasa Vijaya of Bipradas Piplai as also in the writings of Ibn Batuta. John Irwain and Margaret Hall have spoken of the kanthas of Satgaon and Hooghly which they called, 'Satgaon Quilts'.

Writing of the textiles of Bengal, Veronica Murphy said in 1979:

'The most interesting legacy from this phase is a group of embroideries made in the Satgaon-Hooghly district. They are worked in yellow tasar or muga silk (wild silk of East Bengal/Assam) on a ground of cotton or jute. The most spectacular are large coverlets to fit European beds of the period, quilted in running stitch or back stitch and embroidered in chain stitch. Coverlets and hangings had been exported regularly from Bengal before the advent of the Portuguese, but surviving examples date from about 1570-1650. When Portuguese influence was strongest, and this is reflected in the subject matter of the quilts. Designs are a wild medley of assorted elements, closely worked all over the ground and divided into a system of borders and geometrical shapes... 'Bengalla' or 'Sutgonge' quilts were

8. Indo—Portuguese embroidery, Satgaon—Hooghly, 17th century.

highly prized in England as well as in Portugal and consignments were auctioned in London when the English East India Company (est. 1600) began to trade in Bengal in the early 17th century.[1]

As Murphy has said the quilts provided a fine example of Indian and Portugese art. Structurally these quilts were very close to the *Nakshi Kantha* of Bengal. In 1620 an English factory owner at Patna reported: "I shall here provide some quilts of Sutgonge (Satgaon, the old mercantile capital of Bengal, 23 miles north of modern Calcutta) wrought with yellow silk at reasonable rates; and have already half a score in possession, and am promised more daily as they come to town". (*Journal of Indian Textile History*, No. III, 1957, 2nd edition, Ahmedabad, 1996, p. 63).

Reference

1. Textiles, Veronica Murphy, Arts of Bengal, Exhibition organized by Whitechapel Art Gallery in Collaboration with Victoria and Albert Museums, London, 1979.

Characteristics of Kantha

The Nakshi Kanta is a unique creation in the folk art of Bengalis. It is meant to keep out the cold of the early winter in rural areas. The name has various regional variations such as Kentha, Ketha, Kyantha, Kyata, Kyantha etc. It is an essentially women's art, the women giving expressions to their desires and dreams through the designs they create with needle and thread. As Amiya Kumar Bandopadhyay has said: the art created by rural women with a few ordinary ingredients is unparalleled even in the rich artistic traditions of Bengal (Bangalakshmir Jhampi prasanga Nakshi Kantha).

The word 'nakshi' derives its origin in the word 'naksha' or design. In Bangladesh the Nakshi Kantha is known variously as, Nakshi Kheta, Phulkanta Ketha, Sajer Kantha, Rakshi Ketha, In Rangpur the kantha is known as dagla and 'chyalar khyata' in Kalaberia village of Jessore. In West Bengal tribals of Bankura make a kind of wrapper with twigs and leaves to cover their bodies which is known as 'ghong'. It is not a kantha but is mentioned here as it serves the same purpose.

To make a Nakshi Kantha the woman needs one whole and one half old sari or dhoti. The whole is folded four times and the other twice. The ends are then pinned. The cloth is then smoothened so that there are no wrinkles. Then the ends of the cloth are stitched with big 'muri' stitches and the pins taken off. The cloth used must be white in colour.

The threads used for making designs are also secured from the borders of old saris. After the ends are secured, charcoal, or these days pencils, are used to draw the outlines of designs. Then begins the work of embroidering. At the centre is created a lotus, chariot wheel or some alpana design. The various motifs are created around the centre piece and the borders designed after which the remaining vacant areas are stitched with "guri run". While the designs do not apparently have any links with each other, care is taken to ensure that symmetry is not disturbed. Talking of the artistic quality of the kantha, Kamaladevi Chattopa-dhyaya has said:

Kanta is an example of a strange contra-diction, for here is an object created in an endeavour at thrift by transforming worn out textile that would normally be thrown away, into objects of rare beauty and which have in course of time become legendary. (Kamaladevi Chatto-padhyay : Indian Embroi-dery, New Delhi, 1977).

The lotus at the certre of the kantha may have petals ranging from eight to hundred to thousand. The space around this is crowded with things that are needed in daily lives or even which are not needed. Finding their places in this crowd are soldiers, sahib and memsahib, Shiva and Parvati, temple and mosque, fishmonger, milkmaid, indeed everything that came to the minds of the women as on still afternoon they stitched their kanthas. And of course ther are the ordinary household items such as crockeries, the husking pedal, combs, and of course animals and birds that are a part of daily experience. (Arati Dutta, Kantha Shilper Kram Vikase).

It is an art not taught in any school but passed on from one generation to another. The motifs are varied, ranging from mythological tales to contemporary events, the love of Krishna and Radha to battles fought not too long ago. The women also drew heavily from the life they saw around them, thus reflecting a social consciousness not always associated with what is considered the back of beyond. As Stella Kramrisch observed:

"The design of the kanthas provides wide margins for showing the contents of a woman's mind. Their figures and symbols are freely associated and rhythmically assembled".[1]

Some differences are noticed in the kanthas made by Hindu and Muslim women. In the works of the latter, the moon, stars, geometric and floral patterns dominate and are decorated with a greater use of colour. Hindu women on the other hand depended mainly on figures, tales of Ramayana and Mahabharata, temples and idols as their motif. At the same time many kanthas from the past also reflect a blending of ideas. Most extraordinary is the fact that no two kanthas are the same, each shines bright in its own distinction. Obviously the village women did not believe in copying one another, they remained happy in the joy of their own creation. Again in the words of Kamaladevi Chattopadhyaya:

"Though every kantha is functional and founded on thrift, it is imbued with so much romance, sentiment and philosophy that it transcends the orbit of a mere craft as does a painting or sculpture".[2]

The world of the kantha was essentially feminine, men played no part in it. From selecting the cloth, cleaning it, deciding the types of thread to be used, outlining the designs with juice from the barks of trees, charcoal and later pencil, and then the stitching, everything was done by women themselves. As Dinesh Chandra Sen observed:

"The kanthas, the pillow covers and small cloth bags for holding their *paan* (betel leaf) all served to turn their rooms into miniature art galleries".[3]

Kantha stitching was traditionally a seasonal occupation and for good reason. During the monsoon on rain swept afternoons, when after the morning's work it was not possible to visit neighbours for exchanging gossips, the women sat down to make kanthas. If there were extra hands in the house then they came forward to help in various ways and the afternoon would be spent in work and chatting.

The work was by no means easy. Famous poet and folk art researcher Jasimuddin has pointed out that in many cases a kantha begun by a woman would be completed by her mother's death. The work naturally took long as women had a thousand other chores to perform in the house and also because the designs planned were often too elaborate to be completed in a life time. How elaborate the work at times was can be understood from a kantha which Abanindranath Tagore had seen in Sylhet in which the woman had narrated with needle and thread various incidents of her life, starting with her marriage.

9. Dorokha Kantha—Tamluk.

10. Name and address on Kantha.

11. Dorokha kantha made by Bamasundari Dasya, Price Rs. 3/-

12. Marriage scene embroidered on Sujni Kantha.

13. East Bengal Kantha collected by Dinesh Chandra Sen.

14. Sujni Kantha, Burdwan.

15. Sujni Kantha, South 24 Parganas.

The practice of using cloth about to be discarded for kanthas dates back to the hoary past. Gautam Buddha and his disciples had such kanthas draped round their shoulders, commenting on which Stella Kramrisch said, "the patched robe of the Buddha or of a saint belongs to him in his nature of Saviour. The rags are gives a new wholeness. They clothe holiness". Kramrisch has pointed out that "Lord Chaitanya (1485-1533), the apostle and visionary, draped in a kantha the ecstasies which overwhelmed his body. The colourful patchwork of robes of saints forms part of miniature paintings of the Mughal period". Bharatchandra in his *Annadamangal Kavya* has shown Shiva as dressed in a kantha (and tiger skin) obviously drawing from the dresses of the roving mendicants who were so common in the countryside. The snake charmer. The *baul*,[4] they all invariably had satchels mode of kantha from their shoulders. It formed an essential part of the common man's possession.

16. Snake charmer with satchel of Kantha.

Here special mention needs to be made of the *Dorokha* kantha. Such kanthas have the same design on both sides so it is difficult to make out which is the right side up. A close look, however, makes it clear on which the side the design was originally made and the side where it was repeated. A peculiar feature of these kanthas is the preponderance of animals in the designs. The *Dorokha* kantha is seen mostly in the districts of Jessore, Khulna, Rajsahi in Bangladesh and Nadia, Birbhum and Bankura in West Bengal.

The kantha we have seen is made of old and about to be discarded cloth, like old saris and dhotis. This in itself is significant as it is a pointer to life in rural areas, both in the past and to a large extent even today. Hard pressed to make both ends meet, the women ensured that as far as possible nothing should go waste. If a piece of clothing had become too old to be worn, it had to be put to some use. Behind the artistry and beauty of the Nakshi kantha lies this determination to save, to practice thrift. It must also be noticed that the threads are generally red, blue or yellow in colour, being the symbols of the three natural qualities of *svatta, rajva,* and *tama*, virtunou-sness, activeness and ignorance.

Speaking of the designs, Kalyankumar Gangopadhyaya has said, "these follow a definite system". Because of these designs which acquire the quality of symbols, the art of kantha stitching stands at a higher level than other needlework. These designs have served to acquaint future generations with the social and economic conditions of the time when these were made as it is such conditions that fashion the imagination.

The kantha frequently was an item of gift, often conveying messages of intimate nature. The message could be a fervent appeal to "forget me not" or a reminder that "Kashi, Gaya and Vrindaban have no meaning for a woman, to her the husband means everything". Generally the women knitted their names on the kanthas, sometimes going so far as to write even to add the names of their fathers and villages.

Were kanthas articles of commerce? Not as a rule but there were cases of kanthas being sold. Kala Bhavan at Santiniketan has a Dorokha kantha by 'Shrimati Bamasundari Dasya' which carries the words, 'price rupees three' in her own hand, making it clear that it was sold. There is also evidence of Portuguese traders buying kantha in bulk in the sixteenth century for selling these abroad. Essentially, however, the kantha was a gift name and even today it is presented when a child is born. Sometimes girls get kanthas when getting married and though a practice in Muslims families today, in the past Hindus were also known to have followed it.

Such a practice often resulted in essentially local peculiarities in style getting carried across to other regions. During my field survey I came across a kantha at Mahidapur village in Birbhum which did not resemble the usual Birbhum kantha, Inquiries revealed that its owner Julekha Khatun was from Burdwan district and the Kantha had been gifted to her at the time of her marriage. Similarly in a 24-Parganas village I saw a kantha designed in the Jessore style as that was where its owner lived before marriage and learnt the art. There are many other such instances and in the process the art itself has prospered. The massive influx since the partition of Bengal in 1947 has enriched life in the present day West Bengal in other ways also.

Being a folk art, kantha designing has always been guided by local customs and beliefs. No woman will work on her kantha at night as this, it is traditionally believed, will bring poverty to the family. Muslim women always began working on kanthas on Fridays which is held to be auspicious and their Hindu counterparts avoided Saturdays, so as not to come under the spell of the evil star Saturn. A woman will not stitch a kantha during her pregnancy lest the new born child died at birth and if kanthas are gifted to holy places then they must carry other gifts also, five white threads and three bead necklaces in the case of Hindus and a cover for the kantha, candles, prayer beads and a bottle of rose water for Muslims. No unmarried girl should design a kantha and if a pregnant woman dreams doing so then she will give birth to a girl child. Finally no kantha will be completed if while working on it the woman eats fried food.

17. Baul with Kantha Bag.

The exact age of kantha designing cannot be deter-mined with any degree of precision. Probhas Sen says:

'The tradition of kantha embroidery is very old. It is mentioned in the definitive Sanskrit grammar written by Panini around the sixth century B.C. and also in the epic Ramayana written by Valmiki about two centuries later. The earliest mention of kantha in Bengali literature is found in the Charyapadas—the earliest known verses in an old form of Bengali that prevailed from the 8th to 11th centuries A.D.'[5]

References

1. Kamaladevi Chattopadhya *Indian Embroidery*, New Delhi, 1977.
2. Unknown India: Exploring India's Sacred Art (Selected Writings of Stella Kramrinch), Ed. by Barbara Stoler Miller, New Delhi, 1994.
3. Dinesh Ch. Sen, *Brihat Banga*, Part I.
4. Hindu Stoical Devotee.
5. Probhas Sen, *Crafts of West Bengal*, Ahmedabad, 1994.

Ingredients and Stitches

Kanthas, we have seen, are made of old saris and dhotis. To make a kantha sufficiently thick, five to seven such pieces of clothing are needed. These are placed on top of one another, folded, smoothened and then the four ends fastened with thorns of trees like the date palm or these days with pins. Then the sides are stitched all around so that the clothes become a single piece and the thorns or pins taken out.

The village women of the olden days obviously did not have mangles at their disposal. So they depended on heavy metal vessels with flat bottoms to do the job of smoothening the top of the stitched clothes. The vessels would be warmed and then pressed along the surface so that no part would be wrinkled.

For the central design and borders, they used pieces of charcoal or colour made from the barks

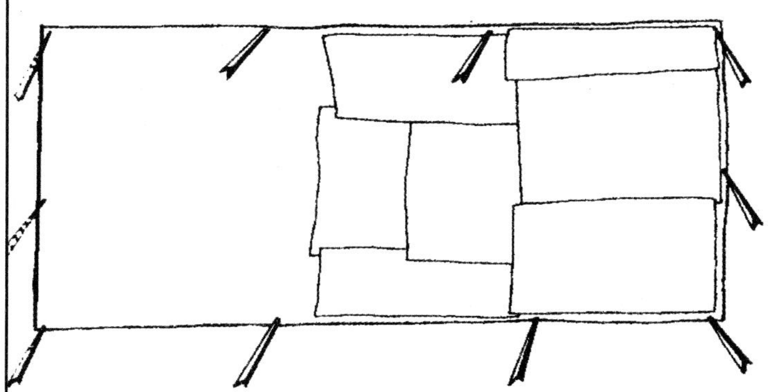

Cloth or folded cloth pinned together by a date thorn

Small bowl

Date thorn

Charcoal and Pencil

of various trees. Later pencils, when they arrived on the scene, were used to make the outlines of the designs.

Then would come the thread and needle. The thread would be got from the borders of the saris and dhotis used, thus avoiding the expense of buying these, the practice again indicating the quality of thrift in the women. The thread thus collected would be kept round a wooden reel or around the woman's own fingers. Then with the needle the thread would be used to bring to life the outlined designs in various colours. The base of kantha would always be white to heighten the designs, though on completion the whiteness would often be fully covered by the many colours of the intricate designs.

The most important part of a kantha are the stitches. Not only do these have to be firm enough to hold together the various layers, these had to be good enough to make the designs attractive to the eye. There are many kinds of stitches but the ones commonly used for kantha making are running stitch, double running stitch, darning stitch, bending stitch, back stitch, cross stitch, button hole stitch, stem stitch, chain stitch, herring-bone stitch, leak stitch and the dorokha stitch. Then there is the Holbein stitch which is found more outside Bengal, in quilts. In Bengal the stitch is used only in the case of geometric patterns, not a very common motif in this region.

It is the running stitch which is favoured most by Bengali women on both sides of the border. Often there are local variations of the names. In Muktagachha of Mymensingh district (Bangladesh) the stitches are known as *Chari Baitta, Machhi Baitta and Jinjir Baitta*. Baitta means the thread used for making kantha. In Jessore's Kaliganj the cross stitch is known as

Thread and Needle

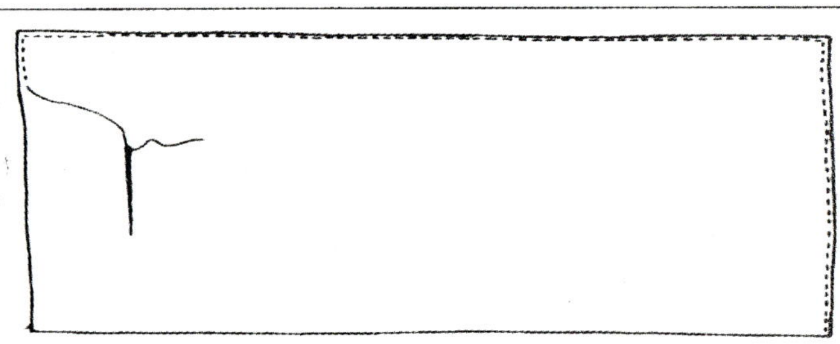

Kantha Stiching begins

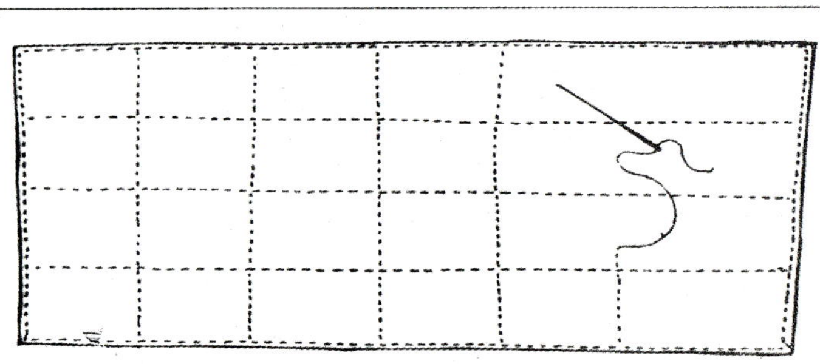

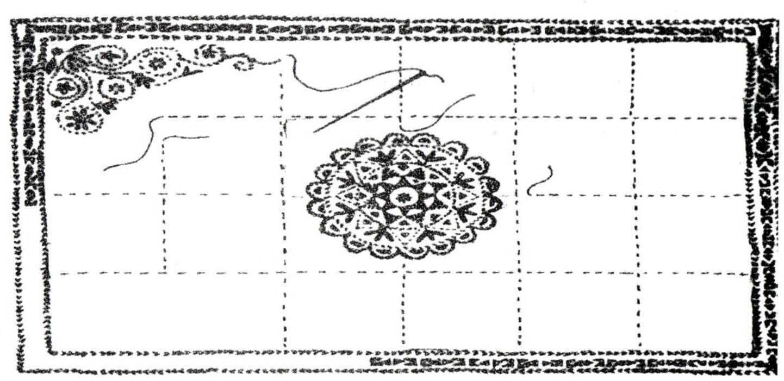

18. Complete Kantha.

tara phonr which is Shailakupa of the same district is called '*saada*' or '*kunchi*'.

The kanthas of Nababganj in Rajṣahi district (Bangladesh) deserve particular mention in the context of regional variations. Known as *lahari, leak, sujni* and *carpet*, these are made on a red cotton fabric known as '*shalu*' and the stitches are uniform throughout without any intermingling.

Let us take a broad look at the various methods of stitching:

Running Stitch: Most commonly used by kantha makers, here the needle follows the same straight line both top and bottom. The stitches are either small, following each other in close succession, crosswise, round or triangular depending on the design. The **Double Running Stitch** fills up the gap between two running stitches to give the kantha a compact look, pleasing to the eye.

Darning Stitch: As the name suggests, the method is the same as when mending clothes, the darning stitches filling the gaps between the running ones. After the outlines of a motif are drawn, the darning stitch helps to cover the enclosed space.

Bending Stitch: Also known as (*Benki*) stitch, it is a variation of the running stitch with large stitches lying parallel to small ones. The stitch is used for design of leaves, ears of corn, wheel etc. This stitch is also known as *chatai* after the date or palm leaf mat the look of which it helps create.

Back Stitch: Known as the *Bakheya*, its purpose is to strengthen the stitches as it repeats the process in every line.

Cross Stitch: Standard stitch all over the world, it is to be found in dresses from Syria and Palestine to the Balkans. The stitching is done at two diagonally opposite ends, the lines crossing at the centre. The stitch is generally

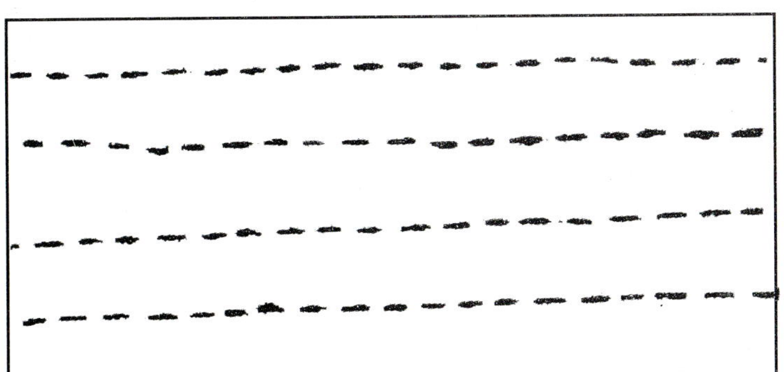

Running Stitch

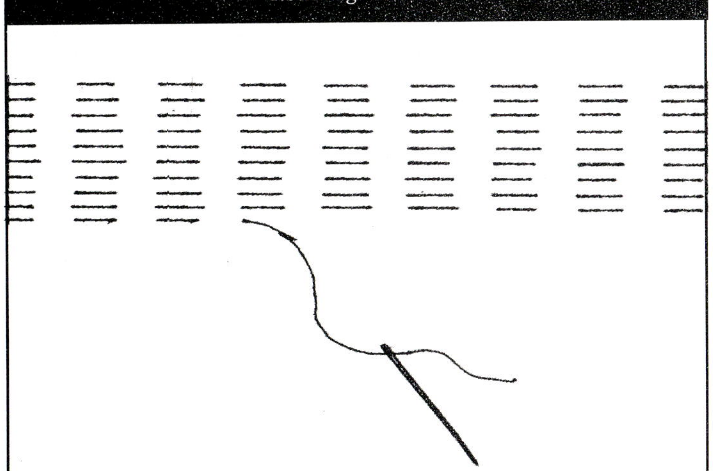

Double Running Stitch

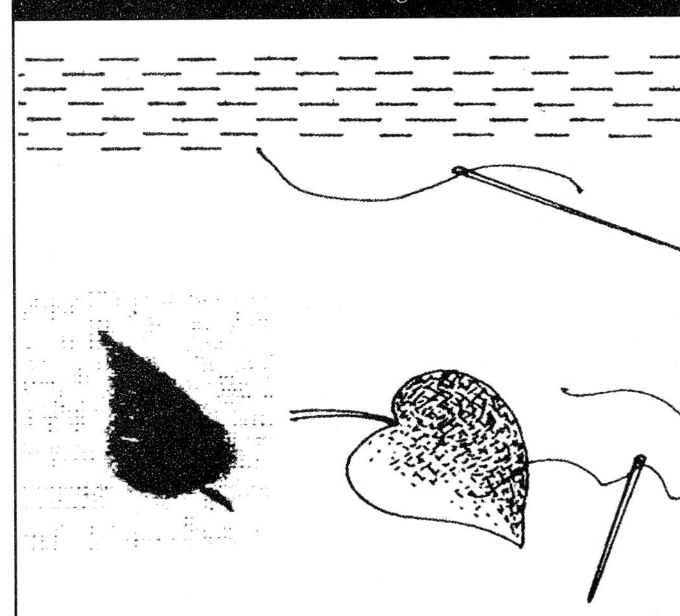

Darning Stitch

not used for kanthas except in Rajsahi where it is called *carpet design*. Like the Cross, the *Button-Hole Stitch* is also not popular with the kantha makers, who at times resort to it while designing the borders or for particular motifs.

Chain Stitch: One of the oldest forms of stitching, it is found in silk garments of China dating back to the pre-Christian era. The stitch resembles a chain and in kanthas is used for motifs of flowers and leaves.

Holbein Stitch: Used in kanthas and quilts outside Bengal for geometric patterns and at times it is seen to accompany cross stitches.

Satin Stitch: Used very commonly in China and also in India, Middle East, North Africa, Latin America and Europe, it fills up the enclosed space or a design.

Herring-bone or Shadework Stitch: It resembled the bending stitch and variations are noticed in different countries.

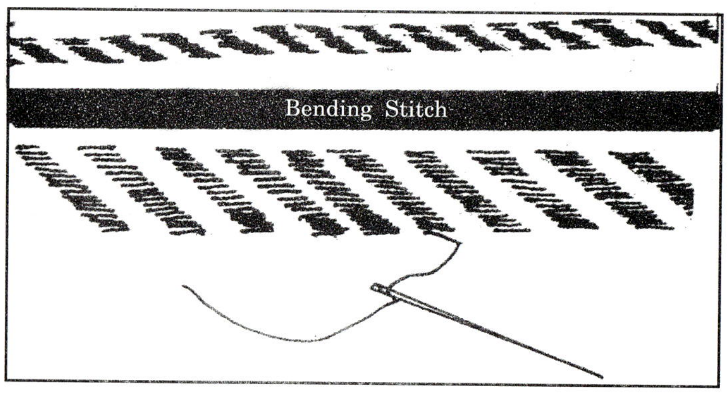

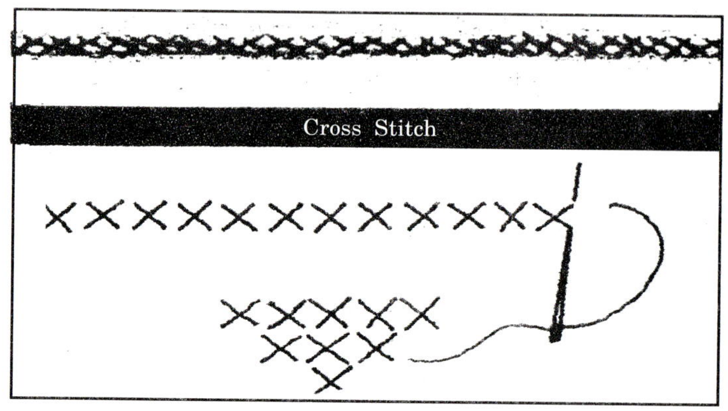

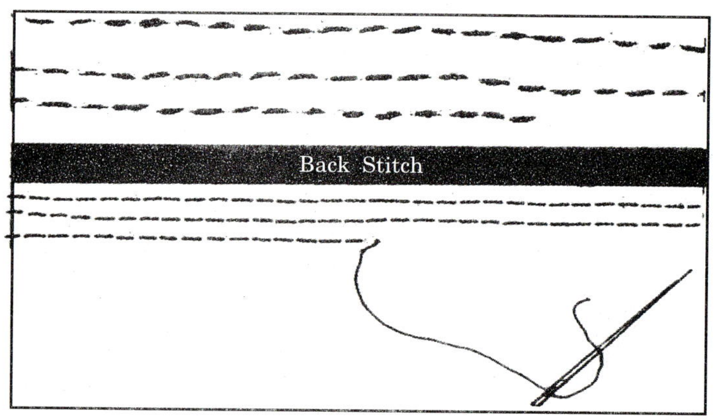

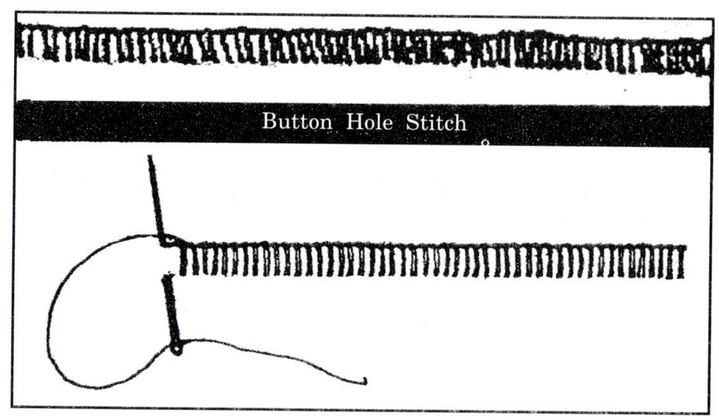

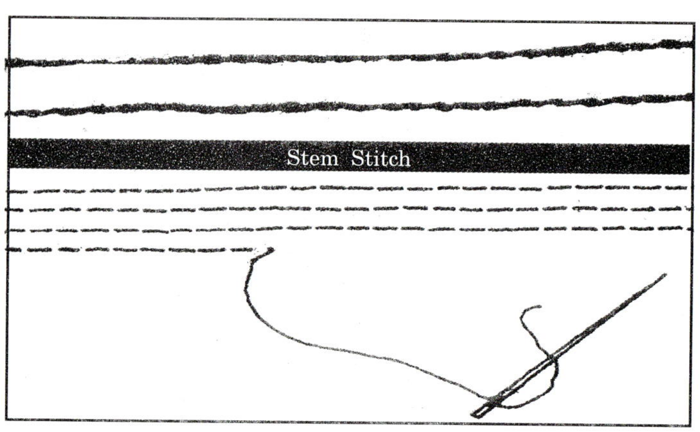

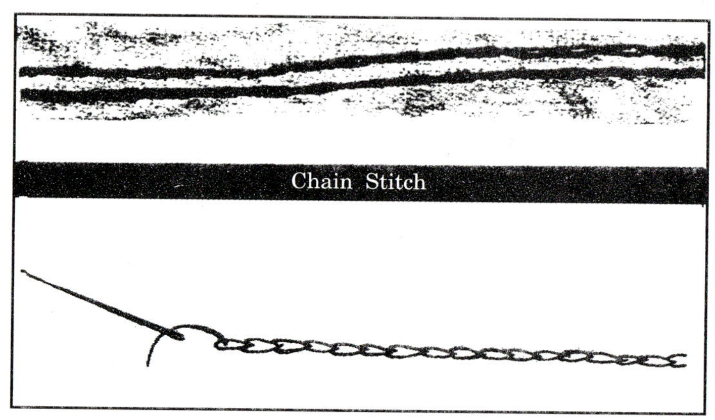

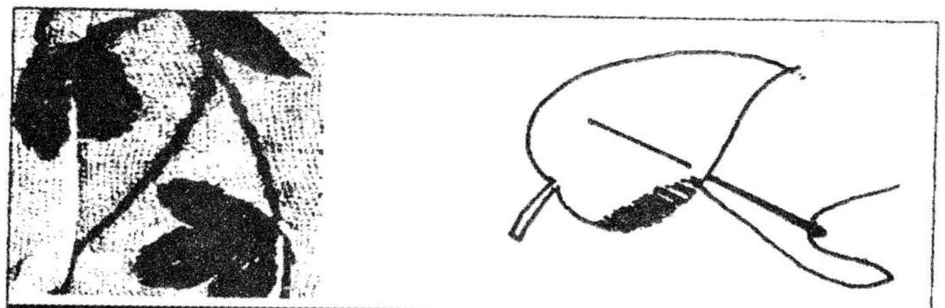

Filling Stitch

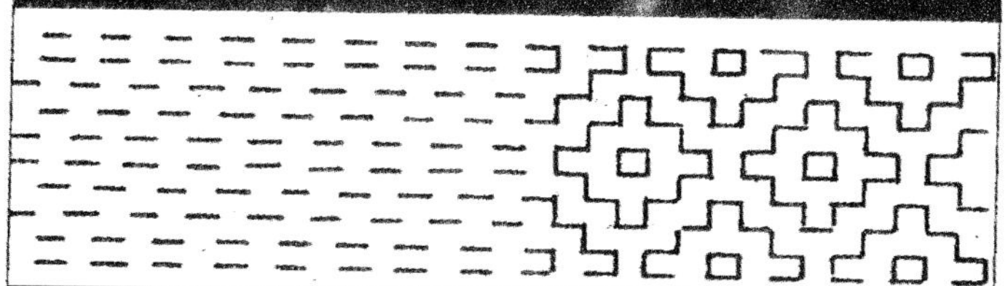

Holbein Stitch

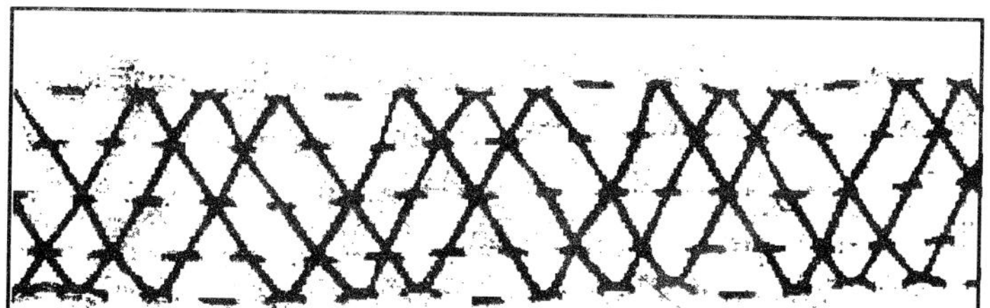

Herring-Bone Stitch
or
Shadework Stitch

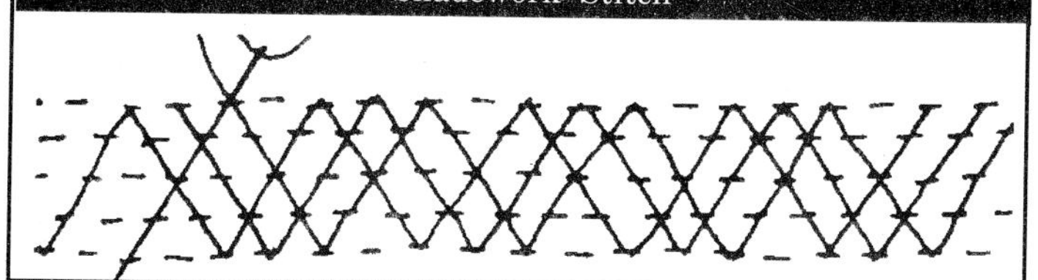

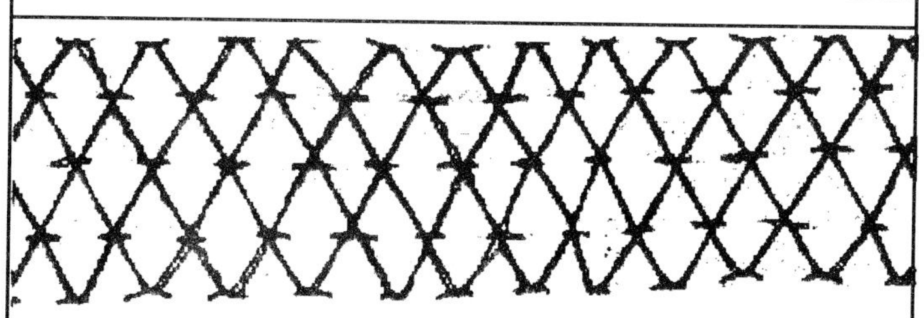

Double Harring-Bone Stitch

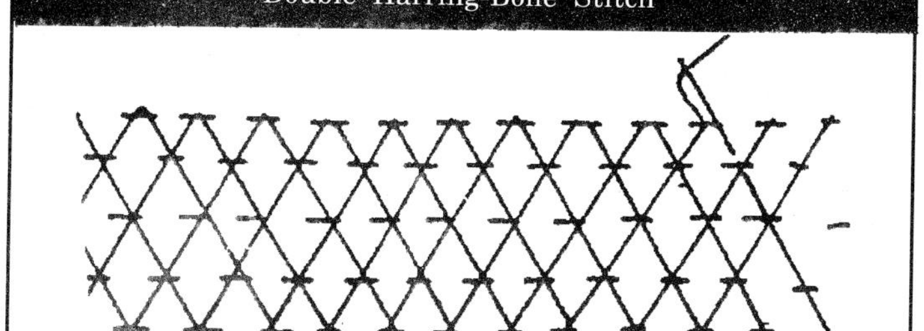

Satin Stitch

Leak Stitch

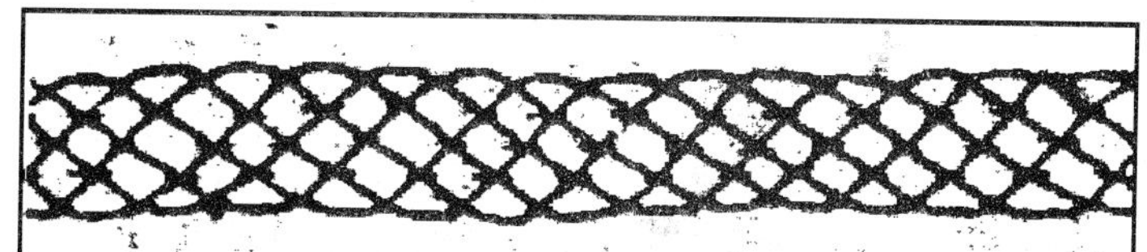

Jali Stitch

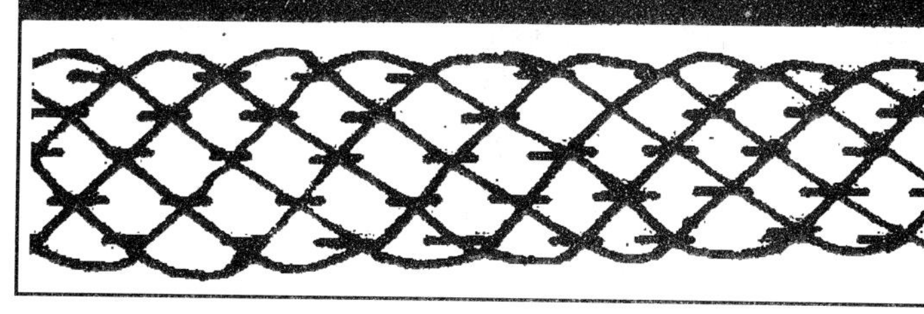

Dorokha Stitch

Chatai or Pati Stitch

19. Arsilata, Lower Bengal

Borders

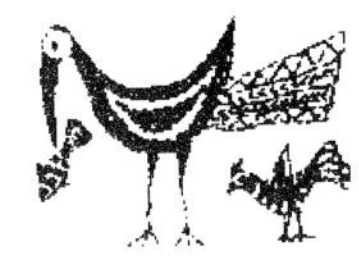

The art of needlework, reaches new heights in the borders of kanthas. The borders may be thin strips with single line designs or may be broad with several lines of design, each different from the other. In some kantha it is the same border that goes round the four sides, while in others there are two similar lengthwise borders and two others along the breadth of the cloth. In local dialects the border is also known as *taga*.

The designs here are very often symbolic. Different types of creepers occur regularly to form the central motif, the creeper symbolising that which keeps the family tied together. Stability is suggested by the *pimpra* design which shows rows of ants and *lahari* or waves are meant to indicate expansion. Similarly the *chokh* or eye in design is meant to protect from evil looks and *bichha* or scorpion to keep away that deadly insect.

The designs owe their origins to various sources. The *paan* or betel-leaf has come from the Khasi Hills adjoining Sylhet district of the present Bangladesh where this leaf is grown in abundance, and occupies a prominent place in tribal lore. The banyan leaf motif is believed to be associated with Buddhist religious ceremonies, while the broad leaves of the *kachu*, an edible root, may be reminder of the way the Goddess Durga was hidden from the demon. Taken together, such symbols also indicate the influence of various cultures, Hindu, Buddhist, tribal, on the social life of rural Bengal. A clear idea of that life helps in the understanding of the kantha art in its totality.

In the matter of borders, a slight difference can be seen in the kanthas of West and East Bengal, the latter now Bangladesh. In West Bengal the borders of other saris are very often cut and stitched on to the kantha to become its border. This is never to be found in the villages of Bangladesh, not even in pre-independence days when Bengal was one.

While designing the borders the women did not always go in for symbols or draw from mythologies. Domestic items are very often made to appear in these, like ribbons, playing cards, cycles, etc. So do vegetables like the *ucche*, bitter gourd, the *patal*, pulbul, fruits like the *anaras*, pineapple, and of course fish and fish-scales. Taken together these suggest that as the women considered motifs, they did not look beyond their immediate surroundings. For instance the *palki* (palanquin), a common mode of transport for women in the olden days, is to be found quite frequently in designs favoured in various districts.

The designs of the borders are a little more varied in Bangladesh and a comprehensive account can be had in Tofail Ahmed's *Lokshilper Bhubaney* (1994— In the World of folk art) and *Lok Aitihyér Das Diganta* (1999—Ten Horizons

Lahar Chokh Paar
Kali Taga
Cokh Taga
Lahar Paar
Chain or Mala Taga
Bunat Paar
Chain Taga
Pati Beti Paar
Maach Taga
Maku Paar
Blade Taga
Taku Paar
Star Taga
Gaach Paar
Paati Taga
Chand-Tara Paar
Kaitur Khupi Taga
Benki Paar
Ekhara Anaj Taga

Hirak Dana Paar

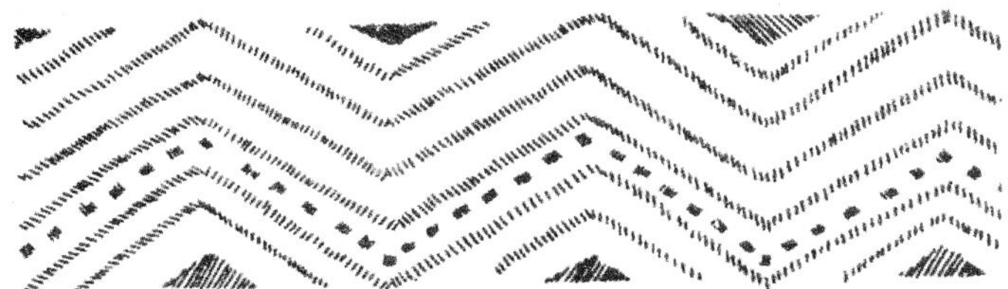
Benki Paar

Lahar Paar

Dheu Paar

Lahar Paar

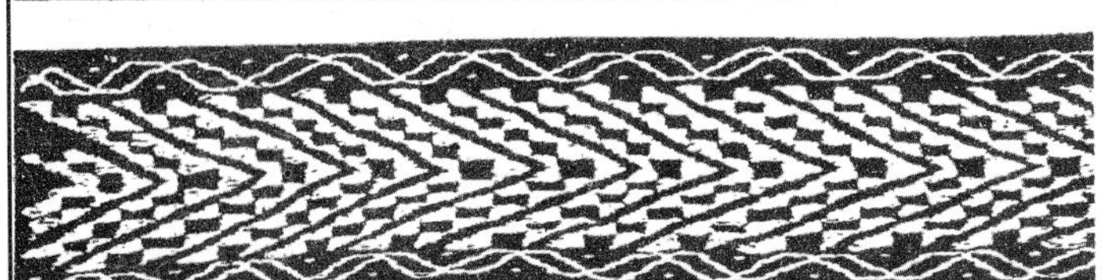
Khejur Kanta Paar

Simlata Paar

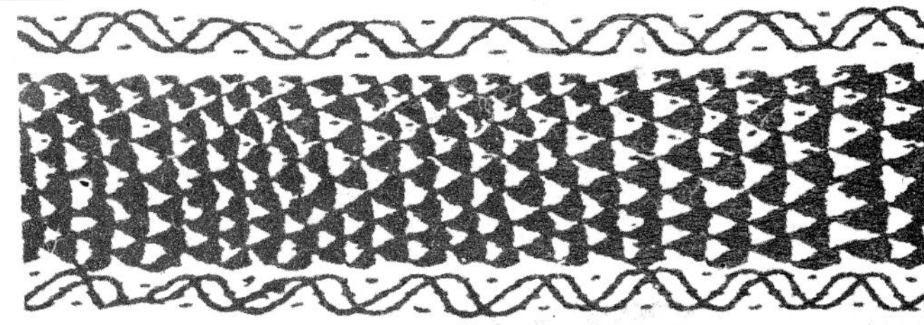
Khejur Kanta Paar

Jhalat Paar

Chokh, Dhan Taga

Chatibeti Paar

Chakphool Paar

Chain, Lahar, Taraphool, Machhi Taga Paar

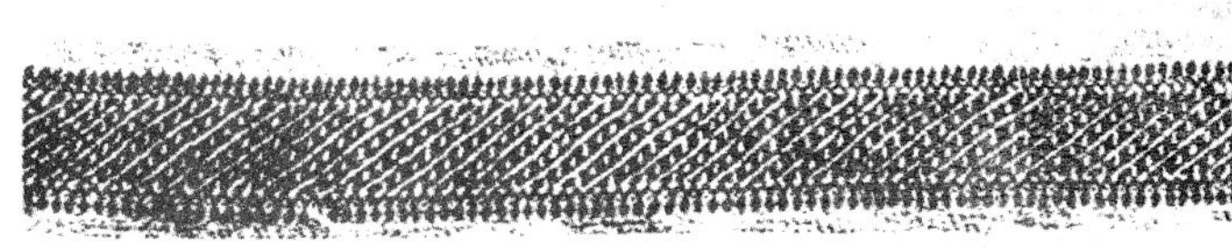
Techri, Nuluk Paar

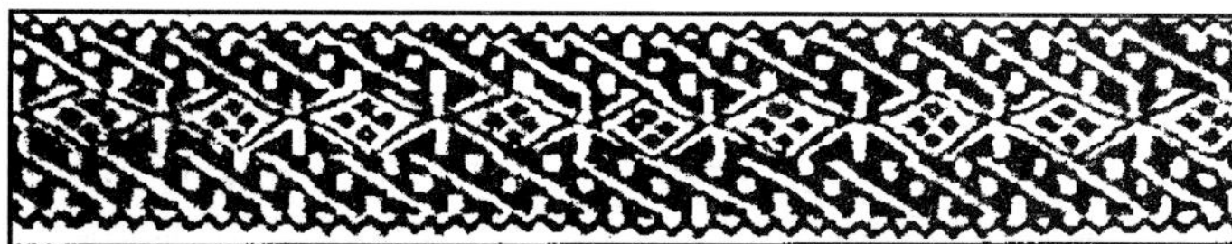

Barfi Taga

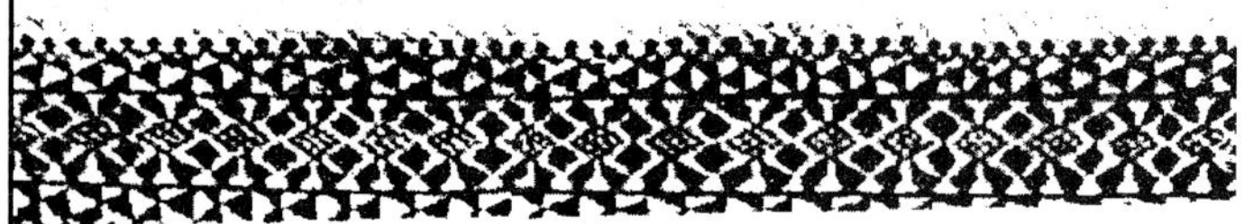

Kunti Phool

Kati Barfi and Naluk Paar

Sankhalata, Pata, Phoolkali and Kachurlati Paar

Anaj Taga

Chati Beti, Kabaj, Chati paar,

Chati Beti, Bilai, Achri, Khejur Kanta Paar

Chokh, Kata Barfi, Chataibeti Paar

Gaach Paar

Taraphool Muchra Paar

Kunitphool, Kalka Paar

of Folk Tradition). Some of these are worth looking at:

The fly (*machi*), the champa flower, cat's eye (*bilaier chokh*), mosque, rows of large ants (*daiar sangir*) are to be found in the borders of kanthas made at Maildi village of Manikganj. Various types of creepers like *kalmilata*, *chaltalata*, ears of corn (*dhanchhari*) are to be found at Savar near Dhaka. The *Kalmilata* is the creeper round the common acquatic plant *kalmi* and *chaltalata* is associated with the fruit *chalta* used for making sour dishes.

Kumarkandi village at Faridpur is known as the home of the Nakshi Kantha. The borders here have, among other motifs, cat's eyes, teeth, betel-leaf, *chelle* (resembling the zigzag movement of the scorpion) and waves of the sea. At Baidyadanga, also in Faridpur, the borders have spiders (*makarsha*) and marigold known in Bengal as *ganda phool*. Women of Jhikargachha in Jessore district design the kanthas with borders known as *narikel phali* (slices of coconut), *pimprar saar* (rows of ants) and *nauka bilas* (boat rides).

The borders are not peculiar to any district. Thus the mosque and the spider are also to be found at Atrai and the fish-scale is popular with women cutting across district borders.

The kanthas of Pabna are made with slightly thicker threads. The common varieties are *bochka*, *baton* and *sujni*. At Pirganj the kantha is used as pillow covers and *tokrai* or snails dominate the border.

Interesting are the 'I V' borders of Jamalpur where the two alphabets are found woven side by side. Similarly there is the 'W' border. Perhaps women chose these alphabets for the design they made when placed side by side.

The kanthas of Sherpur enjoy a wide range of borders, the motifs include the *shapla* (a kind of water plant), *videshi chokh* (foreigners' eyes—the village belle must have been intrigued by these—), *shankha* (conch shell), *paisa* (coin) and *maacher kanta* or fishbone. The *jalpai* (olive) though not very common in rural Bengal finds place in the borders at Singra, as do lace and necklace. The *barfi* named after the sweet is also

Surya Kanta Barfi Paar

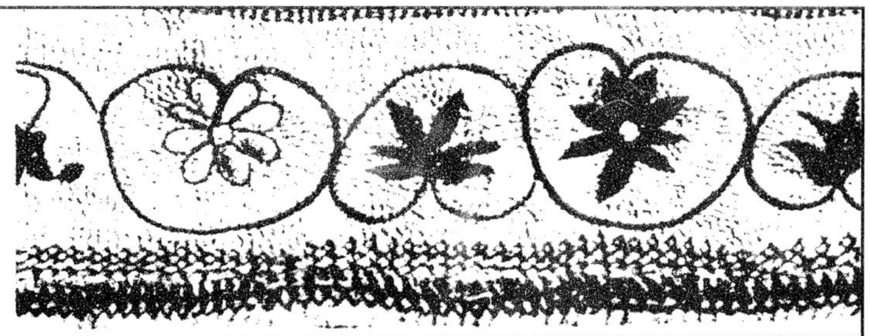

Betphool Paar

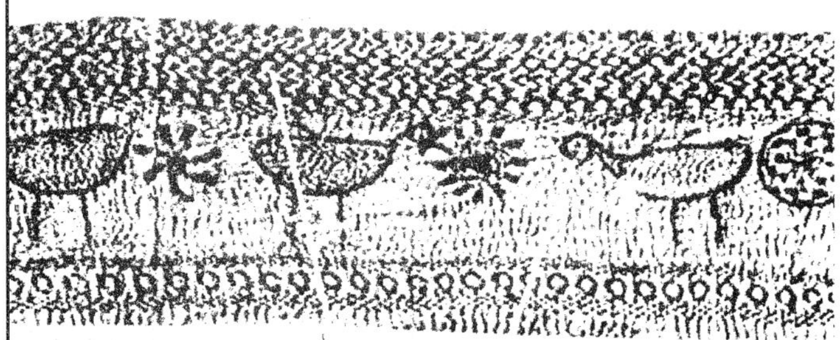

Chataibeti, Pakhi Paar

Kalka, Chokh, Chatibeti Kabaj, Khejur Kanta

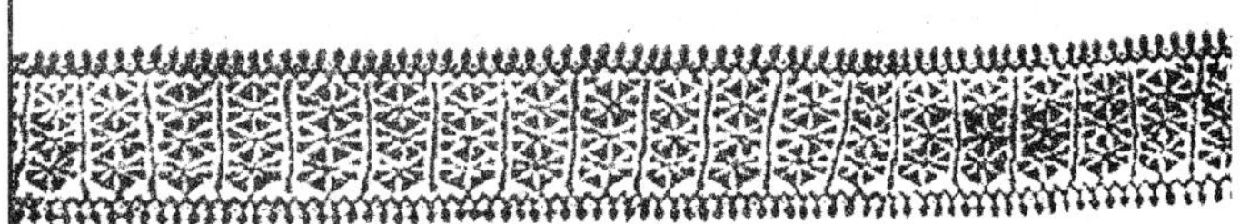

Kanta Barfi Paar

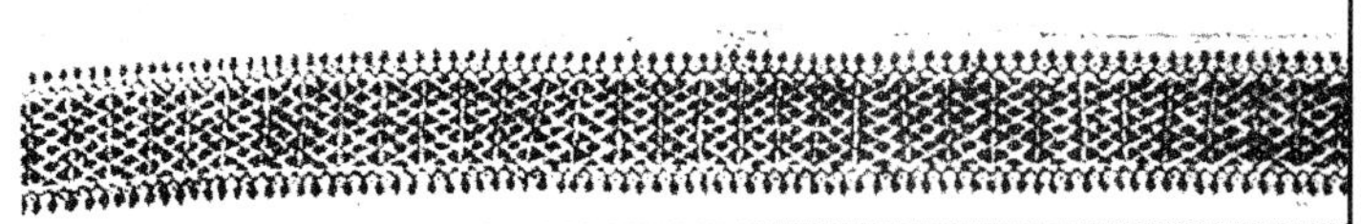

Barfi Paar

Chalk Phool, Kalmilata, Kalka Paar

Chokh Taga

Ganga-Jamuna Paar

Mayur Paar, Kalka Paar, Chokh Paar

Barfi Taga

Jap Taga

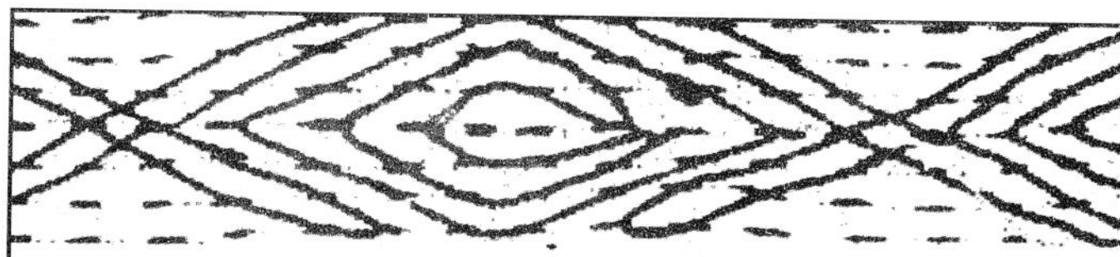
Pat Taga

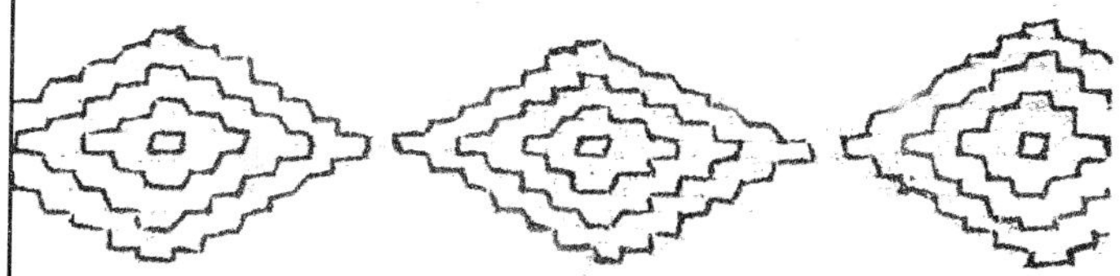
Group Taga Naksha

Nalak Taga

Dui Shir Taga

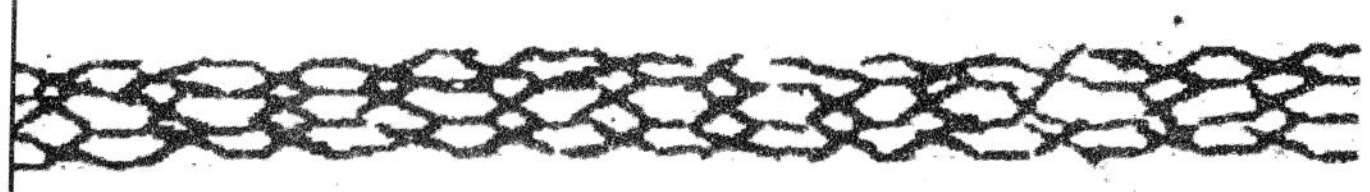
Jora Mala Taga

Shop Taga

Jinjir or Dhan Sis Taga

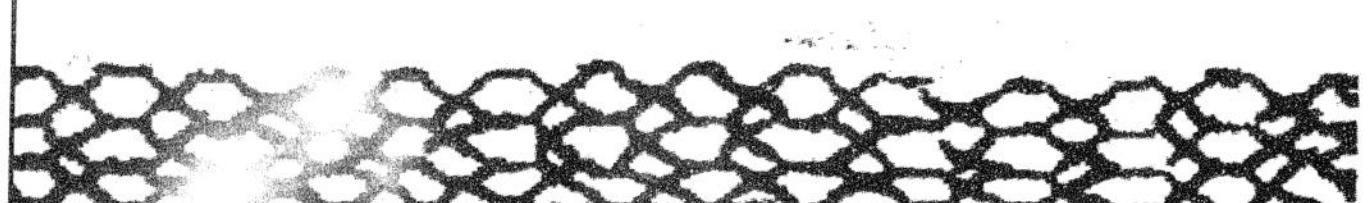
Jinjin Naksha

Shir Pata Naksha

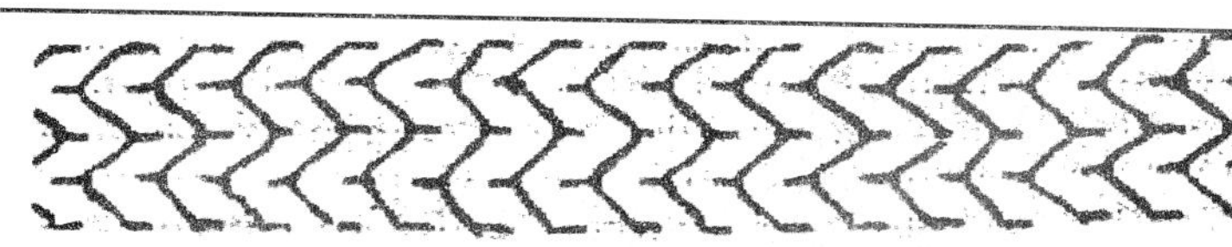
W Taga

I. V. Taga

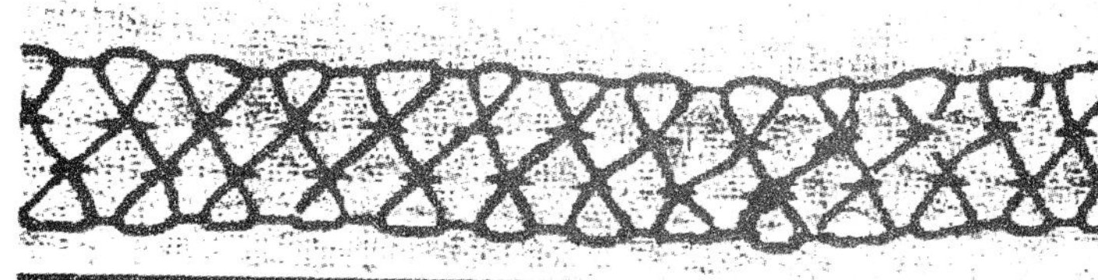
Moda Taga

Tribhuj Taga

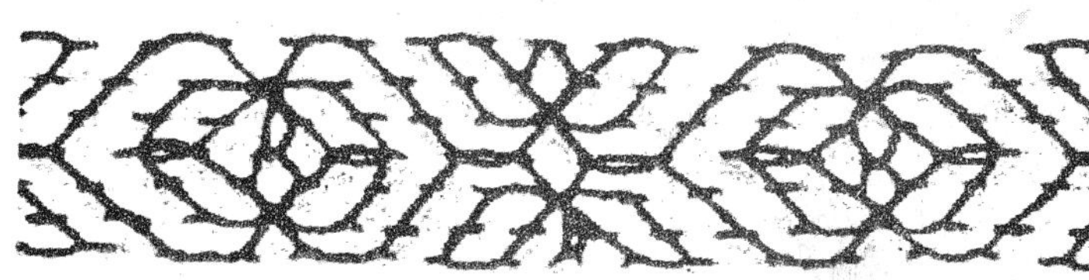
Joda Shapla

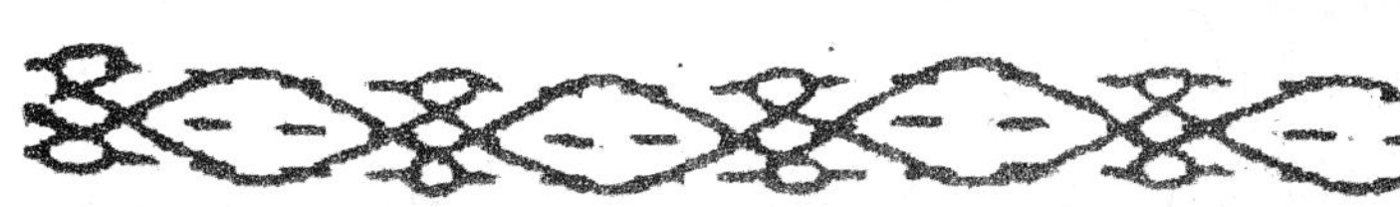
Videshi Chokh Taga

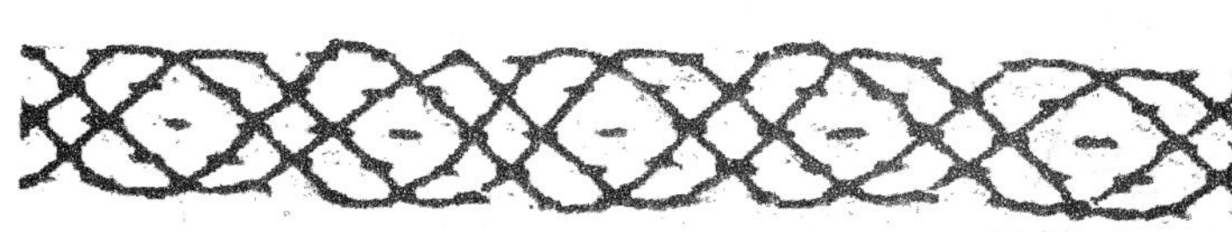
Joda Taga

Panch Angul

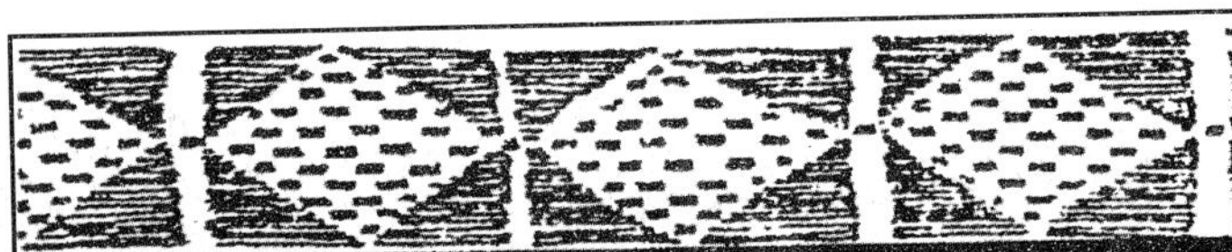
Barfi Phool Paar

Lahar, Barfi Taga

Chatai Paar

Chatibeti, Ganga-Jamuna Paar

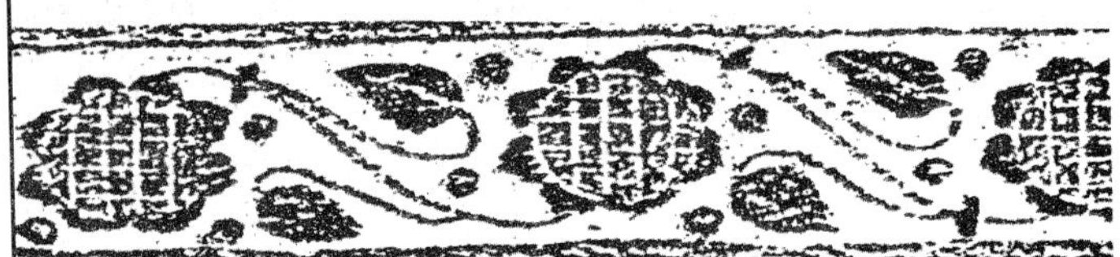
Pankha Phool

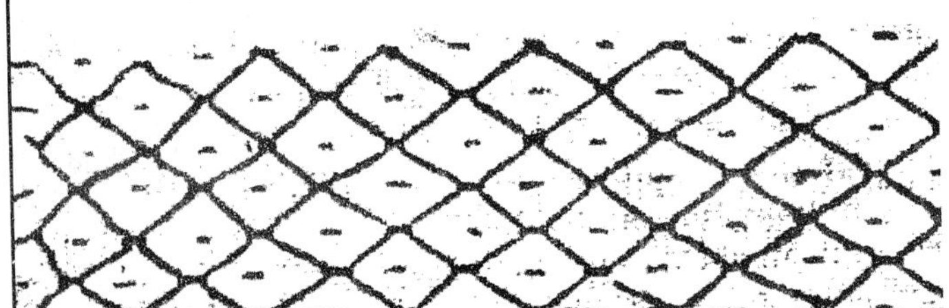
Joda Chokh

Prajapati

Kalmilata

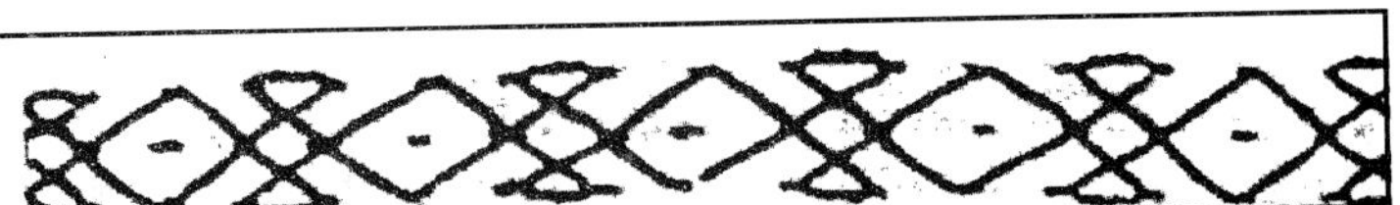
Karala Bichi Paar

Shamuk Taga

Shapla Taga

Cycle Taga

Chik Taga

S Taga

Chari Taga

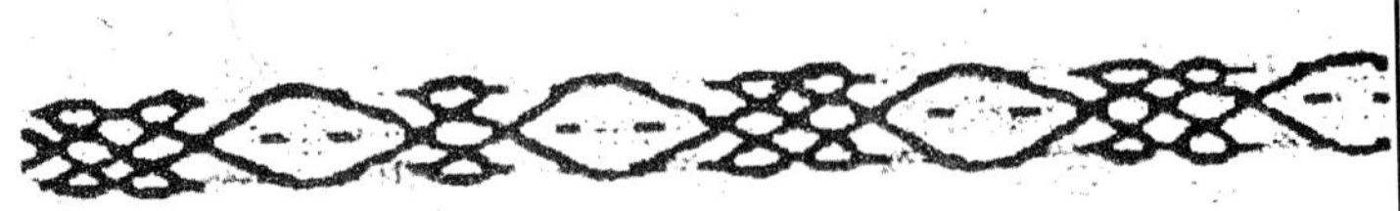
Baju Taga

Macher Kanta Taga

Saṅkha Taga

20. Designs with mixed stitches.

21. Dhakna Kantha–Different stitches.

22. Paar Kantha, 24–Parganas

23. Paar Kantha, Birbhum.

24. Paar Kantha, Jessore.

25. Sujni Kantha, Rajsahi.

26. Paar Kantha.

27. Lep Kantha.

28. Waar Kantha, Jamalpur
Pillow covers etc.

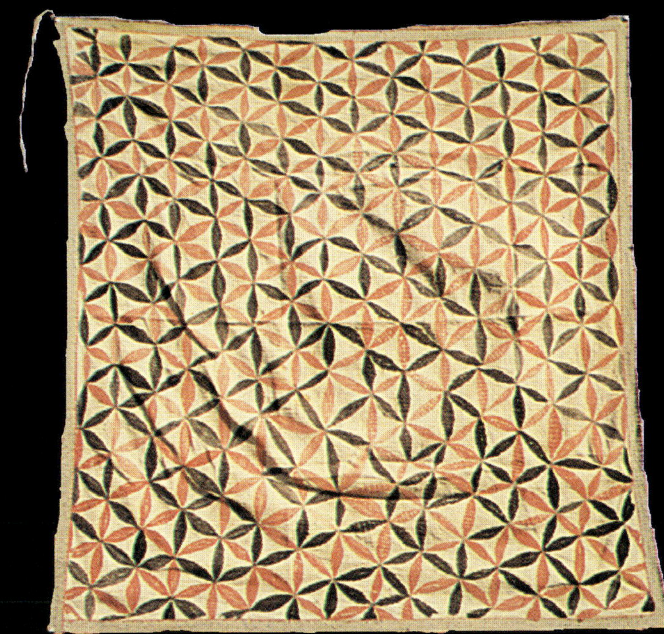

29. Bochka Kantha, Khulna.

30. Anchal Bunani Kantha, Barisal.

31. Betan Kantha, Jessore.

32. Nakshi bag, Jessore.

33. Baby's Kantha, Howrah.

34. Bartan Dhakna Kantha, Kishoreganj.

35. Paan Pachani (For keeping betel-leaves) Sherpur.

36. Khicha, Chalanbil.

37. Dastarkhan, Sherpur.

38. Kantha used by Rabindranath Tagore at Silaidaha (now Bangladesh)

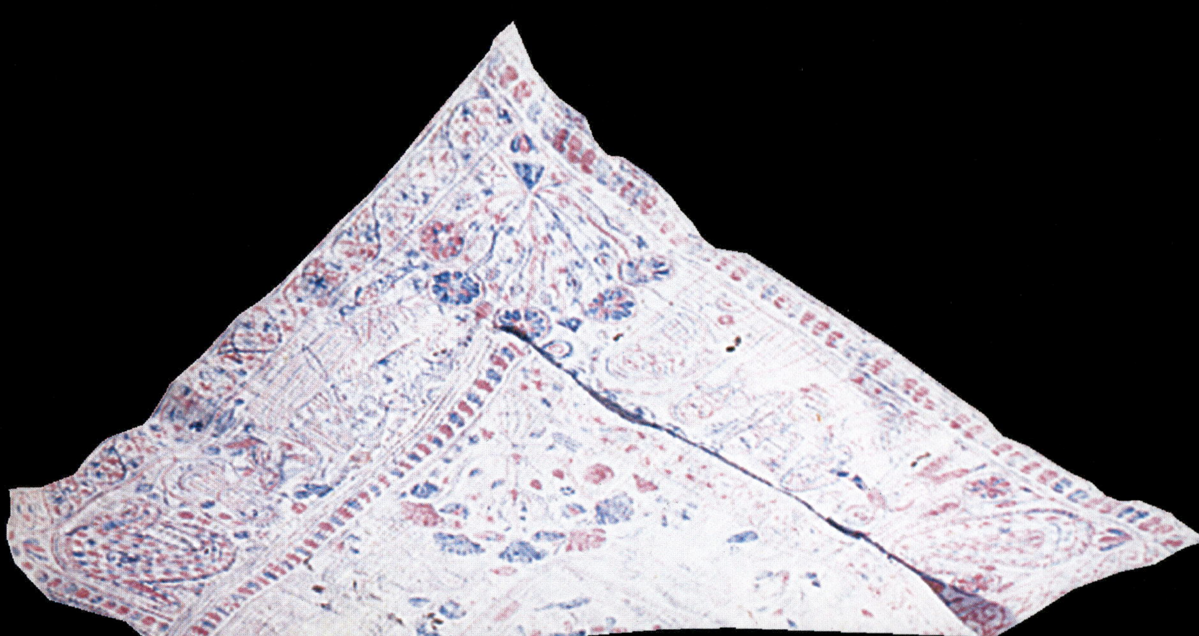

39. Dorokha Betan Kantha, Nadia.

a popular motif in Faridpur and elsewhere. The rhino's eyes and the honeycomb are seen in borders at Satkhira and Jessore. Ears of corn, hilsa fish and the biscuits are found in Chittagong, Bagura and Rajsahi. Of geometric designs mention should be made of the *tribhuj* (triangle) borders of Kusthia.

Apart from these, a wide range of other motifs also adorn the borders. Some of these are, the chain, the *swastika* (not the Nazi symbol but symbolising welfare, from the Sanskrit *Svasti*), bat's nails and of course a variety of creepers.

In the kanthas of West Bengal also the same borders are to be seen, though there appears to be a greater preference for flowers like the *siuli*, the *tagar* and cherry. If bat's nails are found in Bangladesh then it is crabs in West Bengal. Abstract designs on a four-inch thick border are to be seen in the kanthas made in the Deganga area of North 24-Parganas district.

The same border is at times known differently in different districts. For instance the *Ilshapeti* (slices of the hilsa fish) border of Bagura is known as *trisul* (trident) in Kurigram. The designs themselves also often defy convention, the moon at Pabna being shaped square and not round. Then there is the *Paar* kantha in which different types of *paar* (border) are used to design the whole lenths, laid lengthwise along the whole surface or forming rectangles on it.

The borders of the Nakshi Kantha indeed open up a vast treasure house of folk art and one can only marvel at the skill and richness of imagination of the makers, the Bengali women toiling in their little known villages. I use the word *Bengali* deliberately as that is the cultural identity shared by people of what was once one country and now divided more physically than mentally.

Some district-specific designs on kantha borders:

Mailadi village (Manikgunge) : Fly, champa flower, cat's eyes, rows of ants, mosque.

Betgari village (Bagura) : Borders are known as Mohanmala, Nadialate, Shamukmuri, Dhan-chari.

Savar, near Dhaka: Borders designed with various creepers and hence named Kalmilata, chaltalate. The 'sankha' or conch shell also features.

Muktagacha (Mymensingh) : Designs include the 'kalmi' creeper and 'cokh' or the eye.

Bera village (Pabna): The designs include the full moon, the 'barfi' sweet

Kumrakandi village (Faridpur) : Known as the home of the Nakshi Kanta, the designs on the borders are those of, cat's eyes, ribbons, tooth, waves of the sea, betel leaves and the mocha flower.

Baidyadanga village (Faridpur) : Ants, bracelet, spider, marigold, mocha, flower.

Jhikargacha village (Jessore) : The 'Sujni Kantha is here knows as Nachi Kantha. The designs are of, sliced coconut, devocot, ladder, rows ants, people enjoying boat rides etc.

Barogharia village (Rajsahi) : Waves are a recurring feature in the designs.

Kaliganj (Jessore) : Designs show playing cards, ladder, bamboo, creepers and buildings.

Goalanda: Cat's eyes.

Chuadanga: Fruits, sago plant, creepers.

Meherpur: Betal leaves, fish bones, fish scales, mocha, coconut leaves, creepers.

Gangni: Ants, flies, pineapple, tooth, frogs, cats etc.

Pirganj: The pillow cover is known here as 'tokrai' which means snail.

Pabna: The threads used are thick and the stitches are not so fine. The common kanthas are, sujni, bochka and betan. The designs are of the full moon, tooth, belt etc.

Shibganj: Hilsa sliced, pices of parwal, creepers.

Raujan: Paddy sheaves. conch shell.

Kurigram: Trident, pineapple.

Boalkhali: Sheaves of paddy, crow's nails, leaves of the 'kachu' plant.

Jamalpur: Paddy, vegetables, eyes, stars, moon and star, cycle, blade, fish bone, waves, I, V and W, and the letter S etc.

Sherpur: The water borne 'shapla', eyes, five fingers, star, conch shell, chain, paddy sheaves, fish, fish bone, the letter S, blade vegetables etc.

Singra: Lace, necklace, olives.

Faridpur: The barfi sweet.

Satkhira: Eyes of the rhinoceros, kalka design etc.

Jessore: Vegetables, snails, fizhbone, honeycomb, ants etc.

Chittagong: Paddy sheaves.

Bagura: Twenty nine types of borders are to be found. The designs are of hilsa fish, ants, eyes, waves, bamboo leaves etc.

Rangpur: Designs are of scorpion, eyes, ladder, snail, cycle etc.

Rajsahi: Betal leaves, shapla, lotus, mocha, biscuit etc.

Kusthia: Vegetables, barfi, S, shapla, ladder, traingle, waves etc.

Joda Chokh

Sankhalata Paar

Ganga-Jamuna, Chokh, Pipre Shari Paar

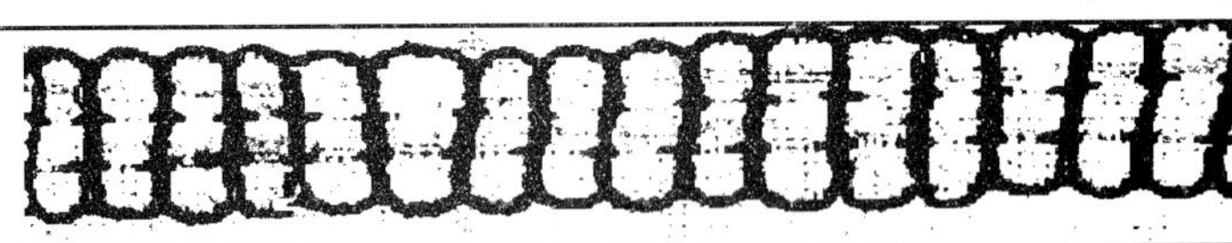

Mai Paar

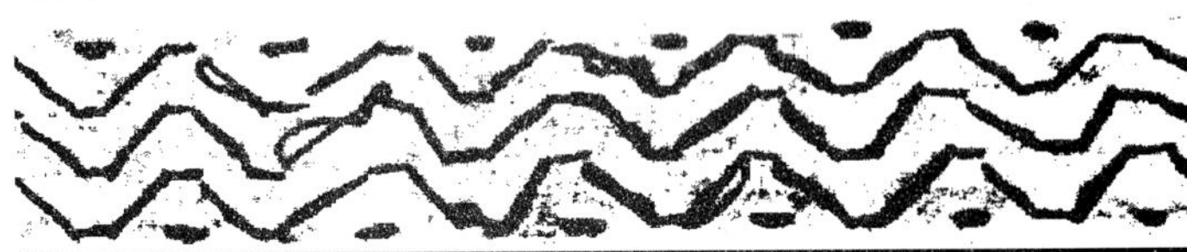

Dheu Paar

Dhanchada Taga

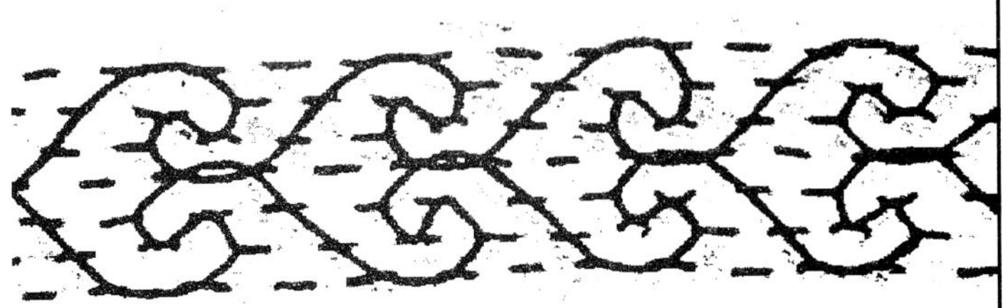

Joda Sankha Taga

Not Just Coverlets

The Nakshi kantha is an object of beauty. But it is not created just for the purpose of adorning homes, the rural families made the kanthas, and continue to do so, for specific purposes. Thus these are both art and utility object. It will be worthwhile to take a look at some of the types of kanthas.

Sujni Katha: Spread on the bed for guests to sit or lie down upon, this kantha is generally six feet long and four and half feet wide. It has a lotus motif at the centre, the borders designed with different types of flowers and plants. In places like Jessore, Kusthia and Nagaon, these are also known as *Paarér* Kantha. Tofail Ahmed says that in places like Nababganj the Sujni kantha has new red cloth as the top layer with older ones forming the other layers.

A special characteristic of this kantha is that the designs are printed with the help of wooden blocks. According to Gurusaday Dutta,"The Sujni kanthas represent the highest perfection of Bengal's ornamental needlework".[1]

The Sujni kantha can be classified into two categories. The Dorokha where the details of the design appear in identical form also on the reverse of the kantha. Then there is the *anchal bunani* where the designs resemble that at the end part of a sari. The kantha has floral designs in the Iranian style and are still spread for the bridegroom to sit on at his wedding in Bangladesh.

Lep Kantha: These are bigger in size as these are used as quilts during the winter months. At places where the winter is more severe, the kantha can be of seven layers. The lotus is again the central motif with the other designs sewn in small stitches to give the surface a wavy look which is why the kantha is also known as *lahari*, meaning waves. The lep kantha very often has geometric patterns as designs, though motifs of trees and plants can also be seen.

Betan Kantha: Smaller pieces, square in shape and measuring three feet in length and breadth. Used to wrap books and valuables, the kantha draws on animal and plant life for its designs, as also the human figure.

Baby Kantha: These act as towels for babies and designed as the others. It is customary in many families to present such kanthas when a child is born. These are small in size as are the ones used as pillow covers.

Bartan Kantha: Bartan means utensils and this kantha is used to cover plates containing food and are designed with motifs of flowers and plants.

Dastarkhan: About ten feet long and one and half feet wide, this is spread between two rows of guests as they sit down to meals and the plates carrying food placed on its circular designs. The use of the dastarkhan is restricted to Muslim homes only.

Bastani or Bochka Kantha: This is square in shape and as the two names suggest is used as a sack to carry things, the two ends tied together with a piece of thread. It may have the lotus as a single central motif or designed all over with various patterns.

Joth or Jot. A long thin kantha, it is used to keep things wrapped up in the house. Geometric patterns can be seen on it as also inter-twined motifs.

Durjani, Batua or Nakshi Tholi: Ten inches long and six inches wide, it is also used as a carry bag. Three ends are folded at the centre, the top fold a little shorter than the other two. It can be used as a purse or to carry small items like betel-leaf or nuts. The religious minded also use it to keep prayer beads. Geometric patterns or plants form the motif. In Bangladesh it is also called *khincha* and *durjani* in West Bengal.

Arshilata: Arshi means mirror and the kantha is used to keep small mirrors, combs and toiletry. It is made of a thin strip of cloth between one and two feet long and six inches wide. The dominant motifs are the peacock, the kadam tree, moon and stars etc. Asish Kumar Chakravarti says: "Rural women did not see their faces in the mirror at night for fear of falling victims to ghosts and evil spirits. To keep the mirror hidden they devised this kantha. At the same time they must also have felt the need to keep combs and other toilet items hidden.[2]

Paan Pañchani : Like the nakshi tholi, to keep *paan* and betelnuts rolled, hence *pañchani*. Designs are of betel-leaf and various creepers. In size about 16 inches long and eight inches wide.

Rumal Kantha: Made of four square pieces of cloth and measuring a foot both ways, it is

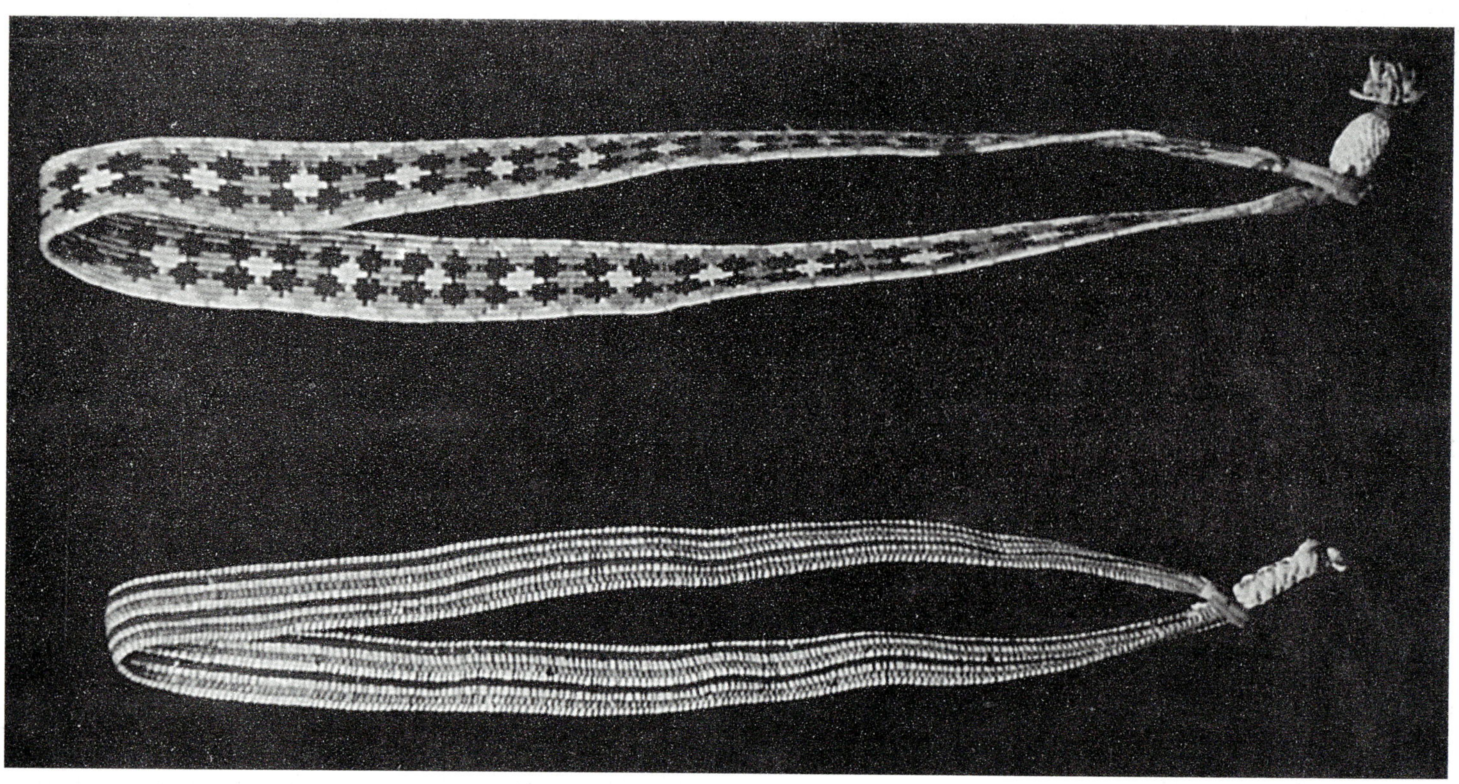

40. Joth Kantha, Faridpur.

41. Rumal Kantha, Jessore

42. Burial Kantha, Birbhum.

43. Majar (grave) cover Kantha.

44. Dhakna Kantha, Kishoreganj.

45 Gilaf, Jessore.

46. Sarinda or Abarani, Birbhum.

47. Sujni made by Bamasundari Dasya, Magura.

48. Gelap, Jamalpur.

49. Wall hanging Dhaka.

50. Parda (curtain) Kantha.

51. Kantha used in a Satyajit Ray film.

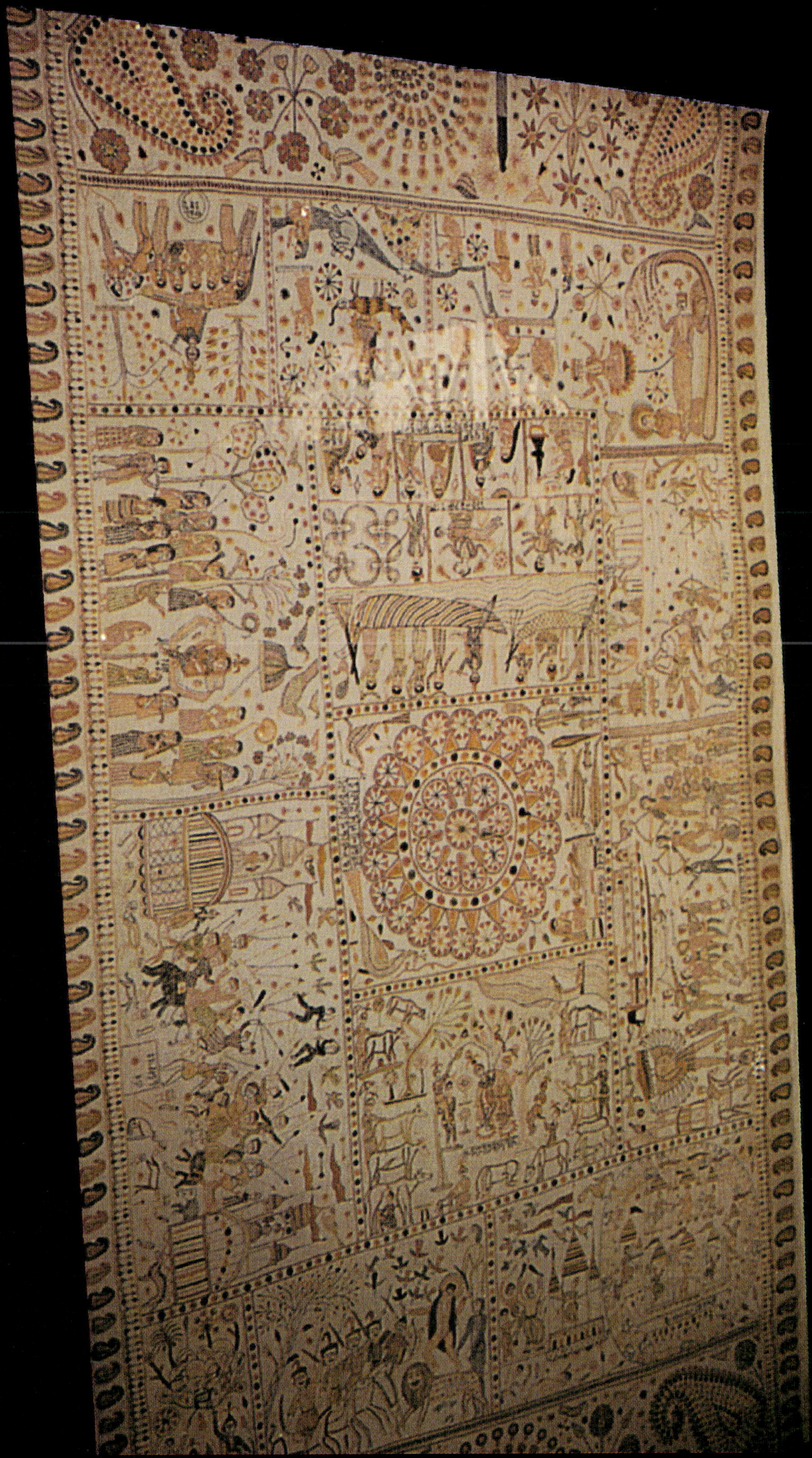

52. Dorokha Sujni made by Sonamani Dasya, Jessore
Collected by Abaniandranath Tagore.

53. Dorokha Sujni made by Manadasundari Dasya.

54. Asan Kantha, Narail.

55. Temple and Mosque on Asan Kantha, Faridpur.

56. Rakshasi (She demon) in Kantha

57. Chess board and seats for players designed in Kantha.

58. Sakuntala at Dushmantya's court.

59. Battle scene

60. Designs of King, Queen, and Jack, lobsters, peacock

61. Saheb, Memsaheb, sweeper– Reflection of historical and social scene.

62. Kantha with the Dakshineswar temple near Calcutta.

63. Rath Yatra (Chariot Festival) scene with the theme embroidered below chariot.

64. Geometric patterns on Kantha.

65. Fairies embroidered in kantha.

66. Market scene.

67. Sonargaon (Bangladesh) scene on Kantha.

68.Marriage scene embroidered.

69. Scene of the Arandhan (No Cooking) ritual.

70. Scene of Bauls singing.

71. The aeroplane, a popular motif.

72. Scene of a Yatra–open air rural theatre.

73. Men and women, Krishna and nautch girls.

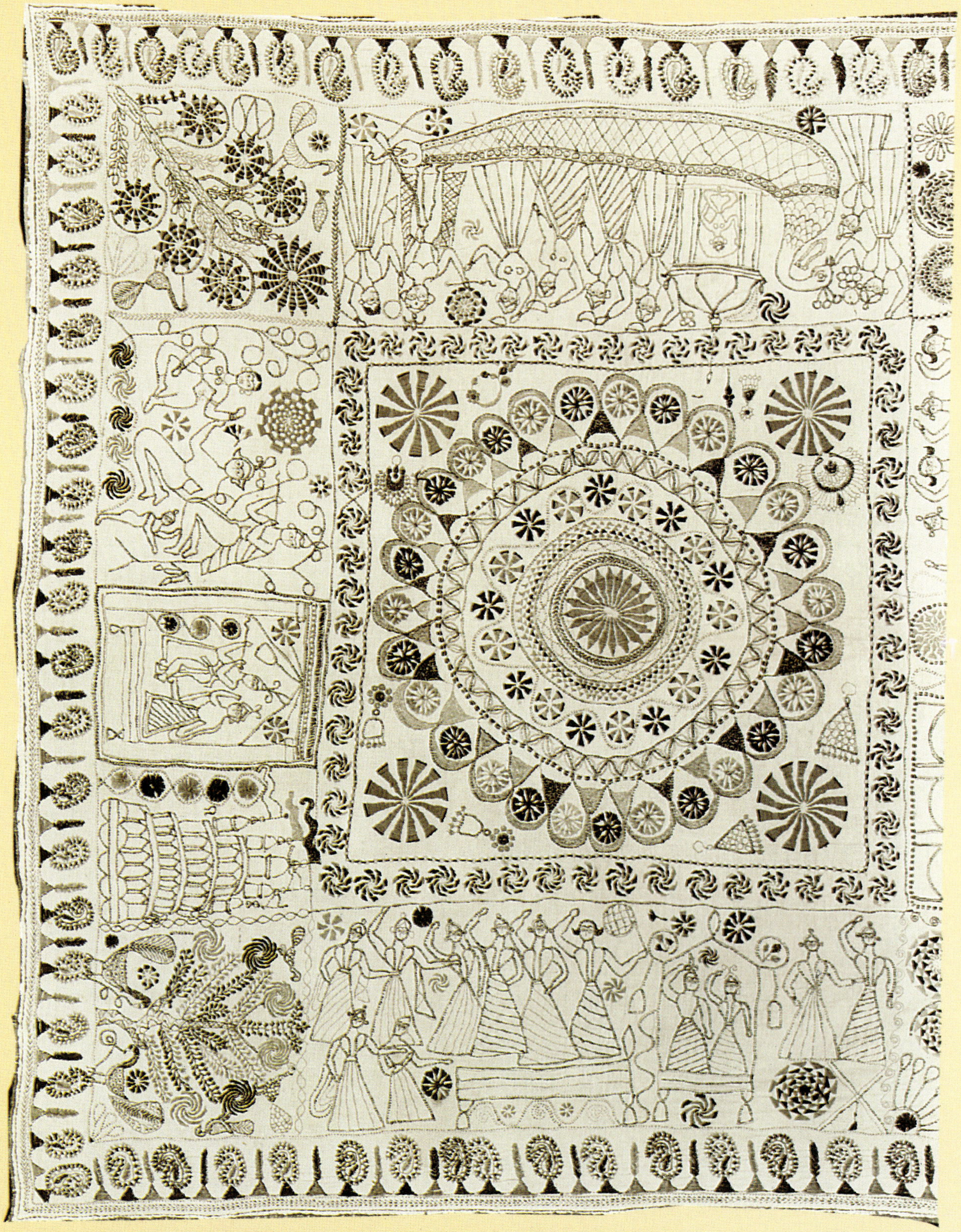

74. Scene depicting boat trip, wedding of Rama and Sita, Radha and Krishna and chariot.

used as a handkerchief or to keep crockeries covered. It is a thin kantha and is often gifted to dear ones, the artist writing her name in one corner as also that of the person to whom it is being gifted. The motifs are, butterfly, bird, lotus, rose and other varieties of flowers and creepers.

Gilaf: Used to keep religious books like the Holy Koran. Geometric patterns dominate, though plant life can also be seen.

Jainamaz: Used by Muslims at the time of offering prayers or namaz. About five feet long and two feet wide, it is on this that the person kneels while saying his prayers. The motifs have scenes of Mecca ad Medina and the pattern of a mosque is so placed that when the devotee bends his head his forehead touches it.

Asan Kantha: Used during religious functions, it is spread also for a newly wed couple and guests to sit. Also spread inside palanquins and in Bangladesh known as the *khat* or bed kantha. The motifs relate to religious and folk belief.

Burial Kantha: It is a common practice in Muslims families to cover the dead body with a kantha which is taken away at the time of burial and kept for similar use in future. Widely used in villages of West Bengal's Birbhum district, these do not have any figures adorning the surface only designs.

Dhakni Kantha: Dhaka means to cover and this kantha is used to cover furniture in the house to protect these from getting dusty. Geometric and other patterns form the motif.

Sarinda or Abarani Kantha: To keep the sarinda and other such string instruments. These act as a cover and hence the other name *abarani*.

Hanging Kantha: A decorative piece it can be of various sizes. Its beautiful designs are a testimony to the needlework of village women.

Parda Kantha: Parda means curtain and this kantha is used in palanquins, boats and bullock carts to keep the inside hidden from view. Tofail Ahmed says it is also used to spread on the top of palanquin. The motifs include butterfly and flowers.

Gelap, Chadar or Shawl Kantha: Used to wrap around the body, it is six feet long and two feet wide and has only two layers of cloth. It is dotted with design of flowers and plants at the centre and rows of decorative embroidery along the borders.

Some kantha deserve special mention:

When Rabindranath Tagore was staying at Silaidaha (now Bangladesh) he got a kantha as a present which is now at the Rabindra Bhavan museum in Santiniketan. Its off white surface has several motifs like fish, peacock, flying bird, tree of life, elephants, horses and earrings, sewn in small stitches. The thread used is light yellow.

Rabindranath Tagore who had turned towards local art traditions, found an exquisite kantha at Jessore which was with his eldest daughter-in-law Parul Devi and later his grandson Amitendranath.

It is a Dorokha kantha in muslin, seven feet, nine inches long and four feet, two and a half inches wide. It was made by Sonamani Dasya of Komarpur who used brick colour, light blue, light yellow and black threads. On the obverse is a *Jeevan Briksha* (tree of life), light blue threads used for the trunk and deeper blue for the leaves, the branches and birds sitting on these. The borders depict battle scenes, soldiers in chariots with bows and arrows, severed limbs, and dogs. The scene depict battles described in the Ramayana and the Mahabharata, different idols and tales from the mythologies, an elaborate canvas not to be seen in other kanthas.

In his film *Goopi Gyne Bagha Byne*, Satyajit Ray used a square Jessore kantha which needs to be discussed. The surface is white, with a lotus at the centre. Then there are two lines of flowers and the four ends have fish, flowers, rows of soldiers, horses in blue thread with other horses in red and yellow thread. There are elephants in leaf green and grey threads, ears of corn in yellow. The central lotus has grey in the middle and the rest done with blue, orange and part yellow, part blue threads.

Victoria Memorial has another unique Jessore creation in its Calcutta Gallery. It belongs to the Magura region and was made in 1891 by Bamasundari Dasya. It has the *barfi* design all along the borders, followed by embroidery then elephants and horses and 121 figures. Other motifs are tigers, monkeys, deer, a boy and a girl, a train, chariot and flowers, all on the right side. On the left there is a large butterfly, lions, bears, people on roof top, a man with an umbrella, aeroplane, monkeys, crocodile, coconut tree, combs and toiletry. The central motif is of the lotus with a medium size chariot on one side and a smaller one on the other. The surface is white and the threads used are red, blue, yellow green and ash coloured.

Gurusaday Museum has a fine Sujni kantha made in the 19th century in Khulna by Manadasundari Dasi. It is a Dorokha kantha, with rows of soldiers in the top and bottom and also shows a man and woman at a window, a girl dancing before a feudal lord. Other dancing girls, a woman with her head covered by her sari end, a man on an elephant, a girl in a horse carriage with a bird, lobsters, insects, kadam trees, flowers and geometric patterns. The motifs clearly bring home scenes from contemporary life. The kantha was a gift from Manadasundari to her father Baradakanta Basu and this she had sewn on it.

We have seen kanthas reflecting contemporary life in its details. The women captured with their needle and threads all events of importance and the incident involving Mohanta Madhabgiri and the woman Elokeshi in Tarakeswar in 1873 was not ignored. Playing cards was a popular pastime ever among women and cards can be seen as a popular motif. In the same way there is one kantha devoted wholly to marriage rituals and another to religious rites. It is interesting to note that the women had no problems dwelling in the past and the present at the same time and tales from mythologies co-exist on the kanthas with aeroplanes flying in the sky.

References

1. Gurusaday Dutta, Folks Arts and Crafts of Bengal, The Collected Paper, Calcutta 1990.
2. Ashish Kumar Chakravarti, Lokashilpa: Nakshi Kantha (Lokashanskriti Gabashena Patrika, Vaishak — Asadh, 1406. Mahbub Alam, Dhaka, 1983.

The Motifs

The nakshi kantha reflects the life, aspirations and culture of the village women of Bengal. The motifs used are symbols which have given this kantha a special place in the folk art tradition. These also reflects the experience shared by Hindus and Muslims alike. Some motifs, like the sun, the moon, the lotus and water are universal. Others originated in China and Iran and got assimilated into Indian life. Thus the Tree of Life (*Jeevan Briksha*) or the (*Kalka*)

Kalka

Kalka

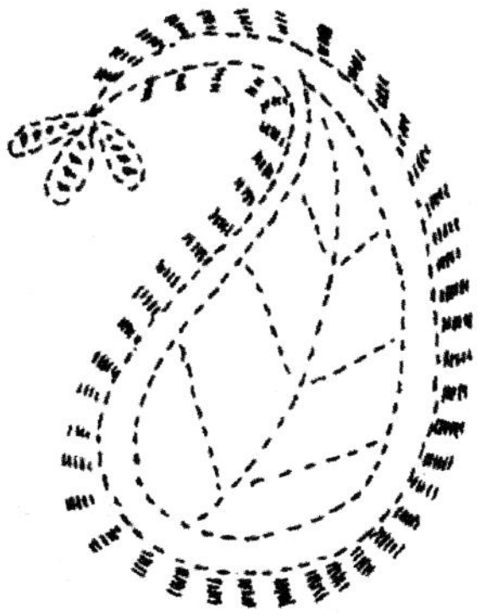

Kalka

Lotus

Kalka

Kalka

Lotus at the centre

design came from Iran. As for water, it plays a central role in every religious rite whether it be Christian, Muslims or Hindus.

Of the symbols in the motifs, Stella Kramrisch has said:

"The central, wide-open, may-petaled lotus is an ancient Indian symbol of universal manifestation and of this world in particular. The four trees are the symbols of four directions; their meaning steps from Mesopotamia".[1]

We have seen that motifs range from human figures and animals to plant life and household items. Tofail Ahmed has pointed out that folk art in this country was a product or the rites of different religions and sects, the recorded illustrations and the symbols used therein.

Let us take a look at the different motifs and what they symbolise:

Sun: Symbol of Power. Seen used in the oldest available evidence of needlework. The solar motif is seen in the chakra with the cross.

Moon-Star: Generally used as motif by Muslims. The moon is related to the tides and hence human life. The star comes as a natural companion.

Kalka: This embroidered design is a popular motif and is believed to have originated in Iran. Found its place even on shawls during the rule of the Sultans and Mughals. Enjoy affinity with the Chinese Yin and Yang, symbols of man and woman.

Lotus: The original symbol of creation, it symbolises well being and beauty. The villagers

Lotus at the Centre

Tree of Life

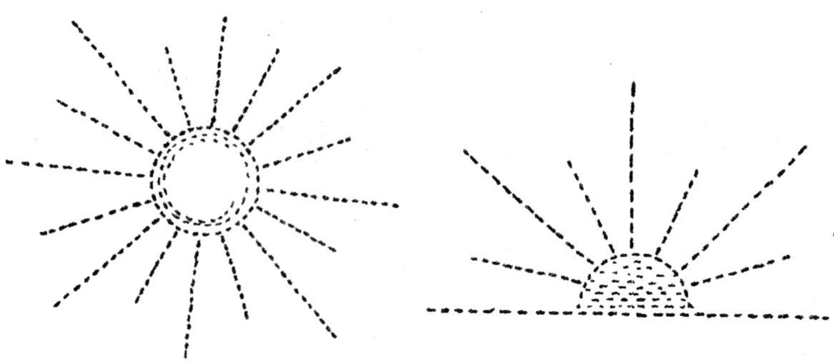

Sun

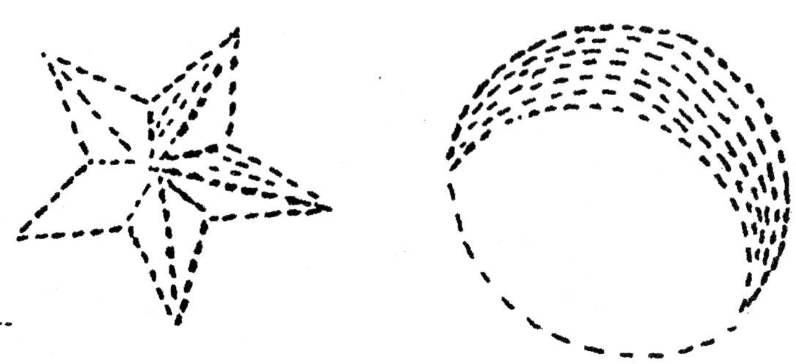

Star, Moon

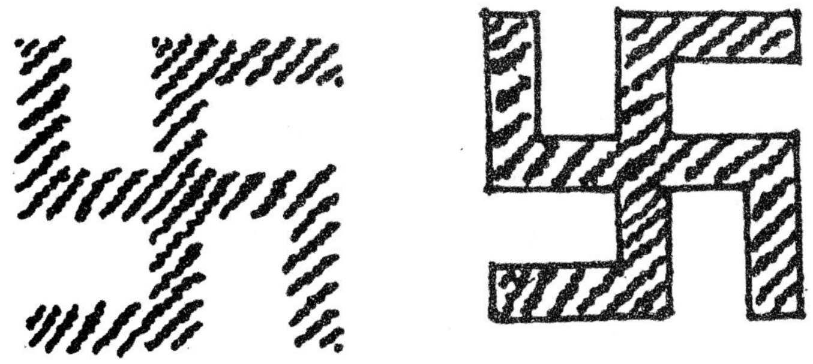

Swastika

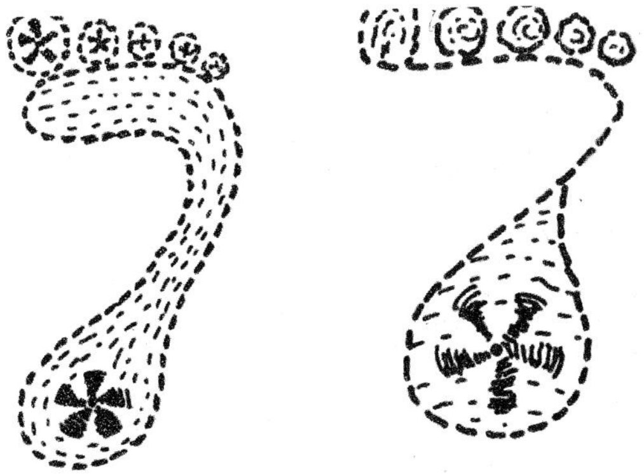

Foot prints

Fish

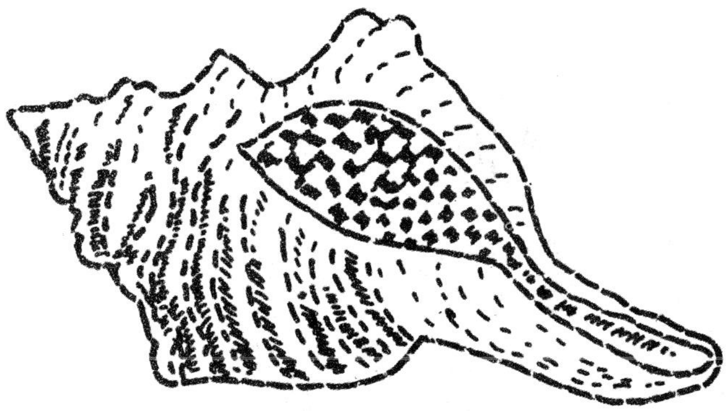

Conch Shell

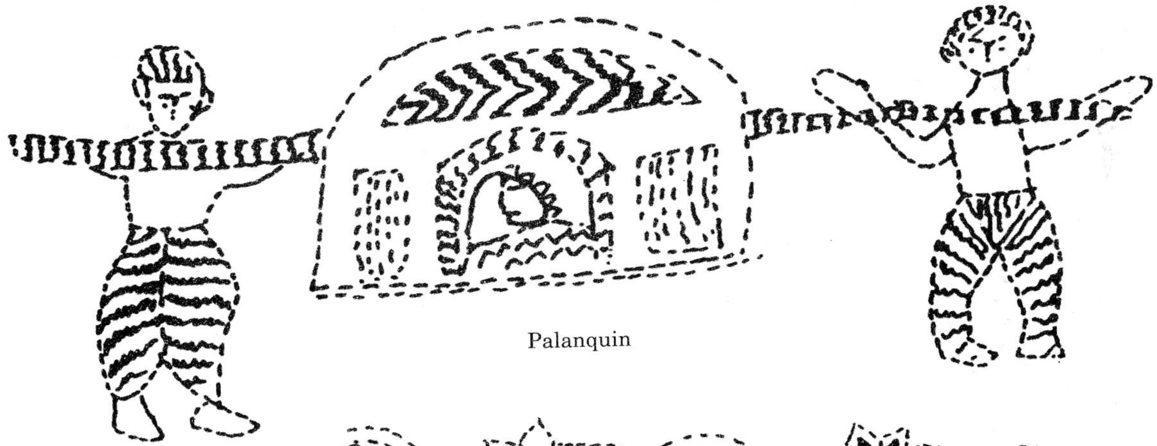

Palanquin

Creeper

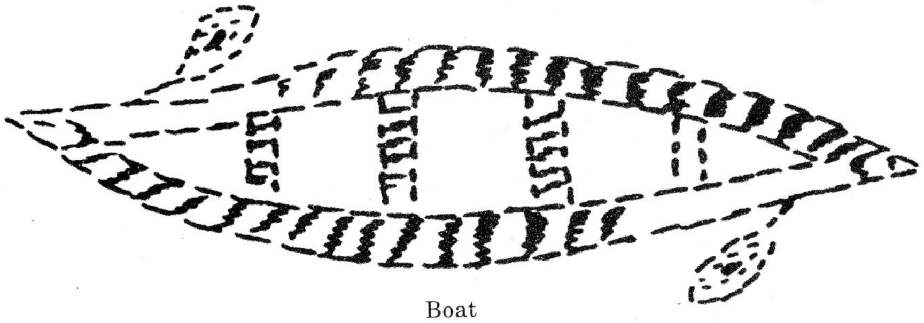

Boat

Oar

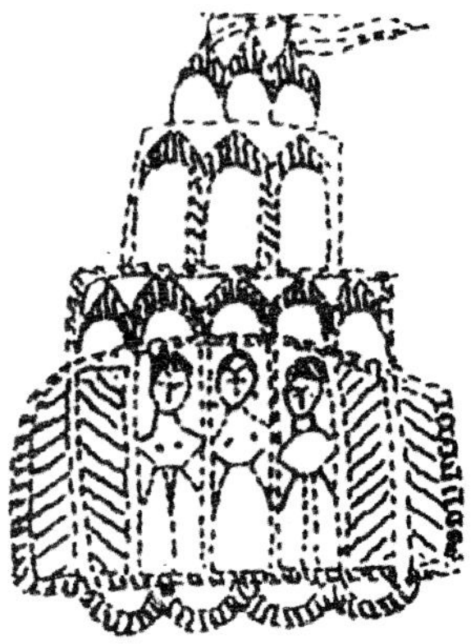

Chariot

Dugdugi-Small Musical instrument

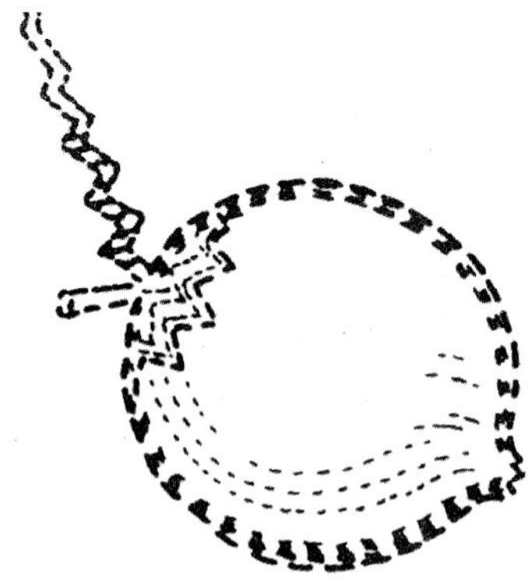

Green Coconut

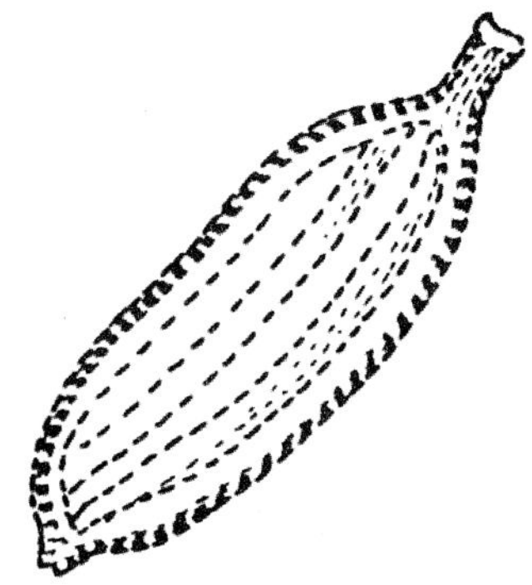

Banana

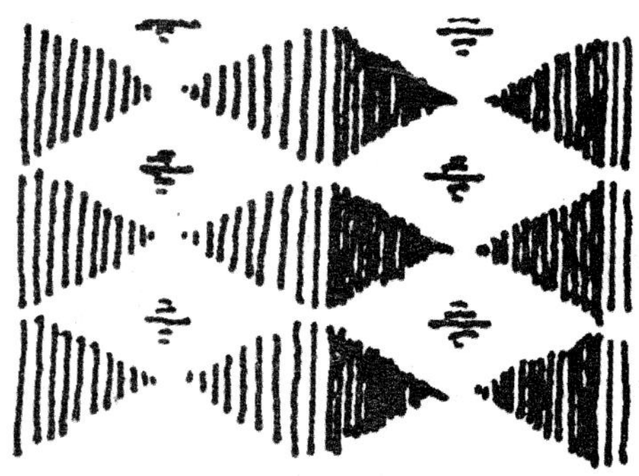

Geometric Pattern

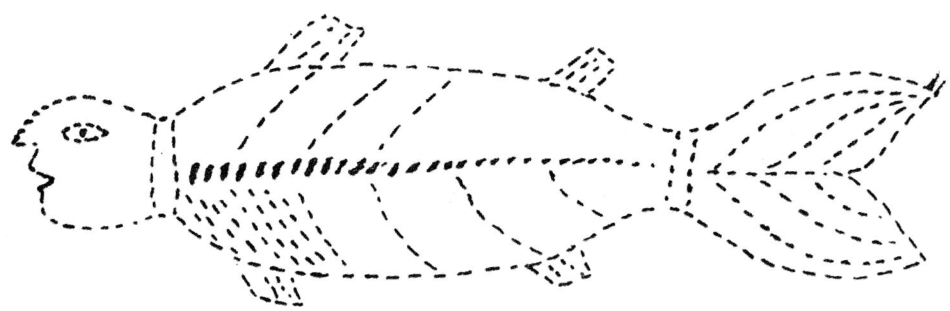

Makar-Bearer of Ganga

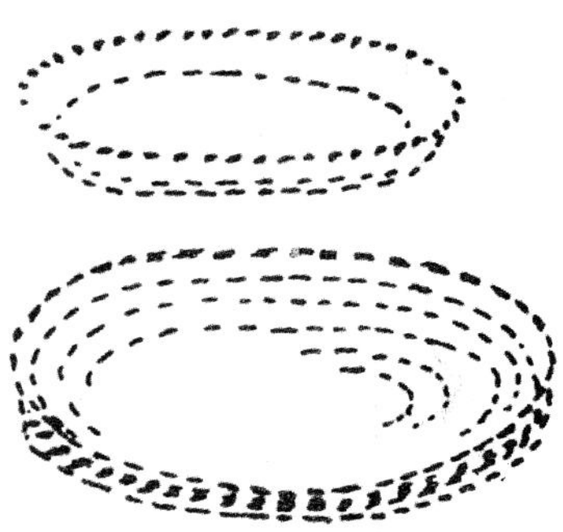

Metal Plate

Glass

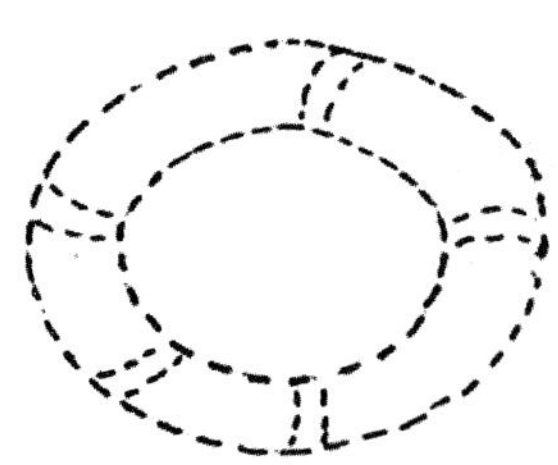

Pitcher rest

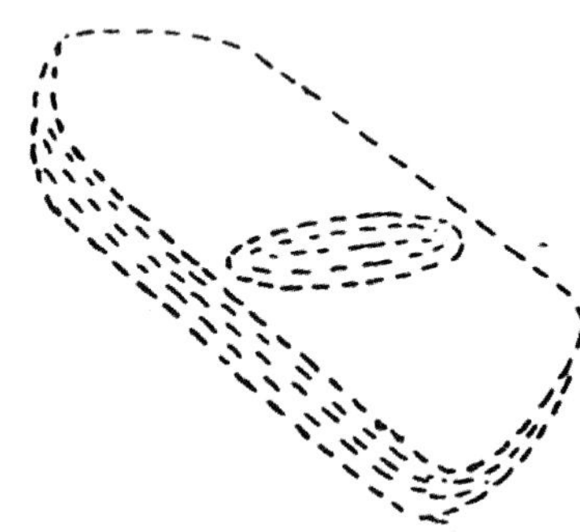

Grinding Stone

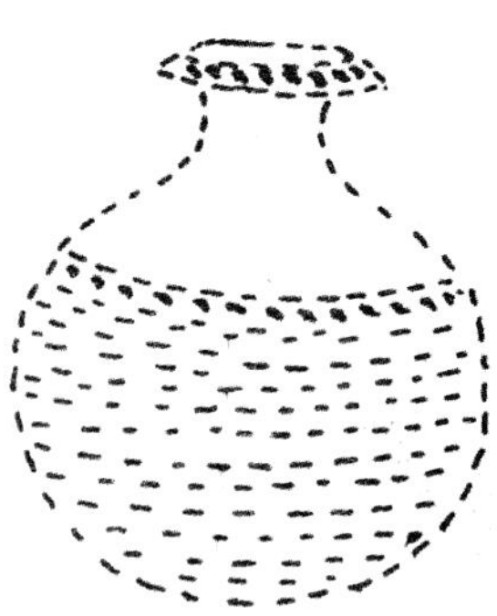

Pitcher

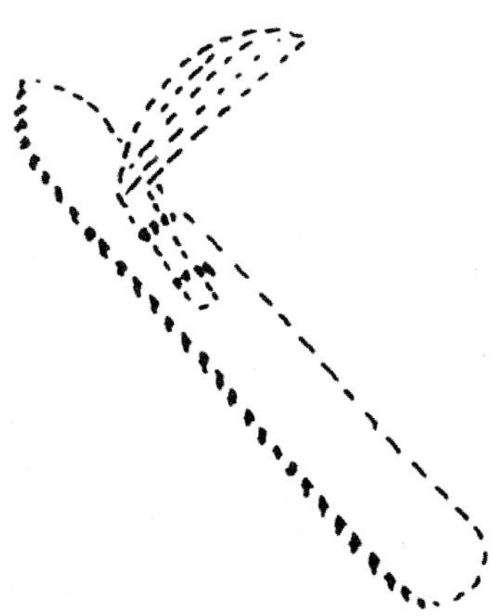

Knife Fixed on wood

Kalka

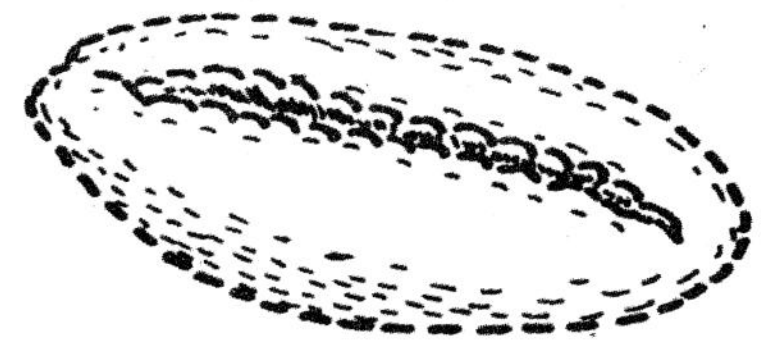

Cowrie

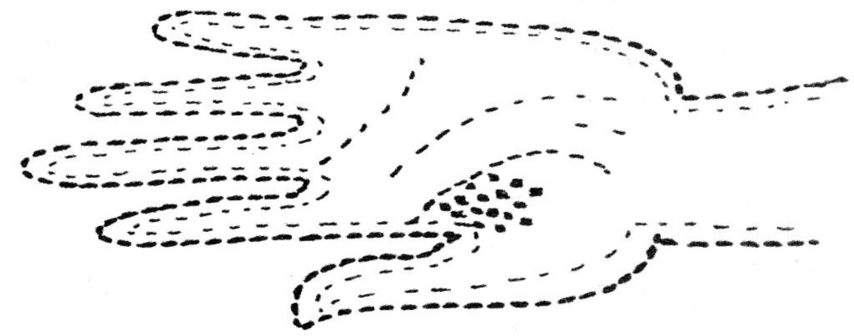

Palm and Five Fingers

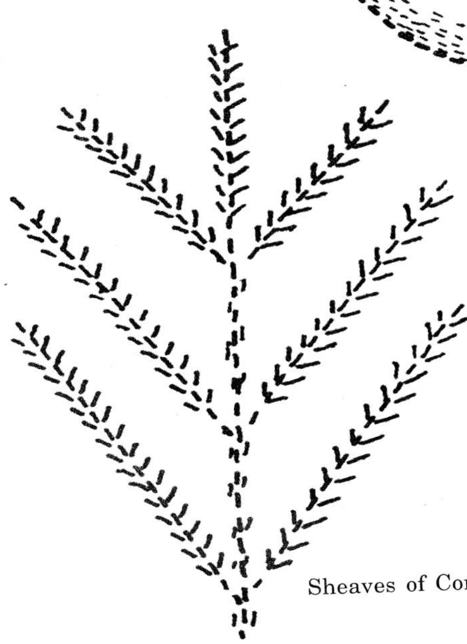

Sheaves of Corn

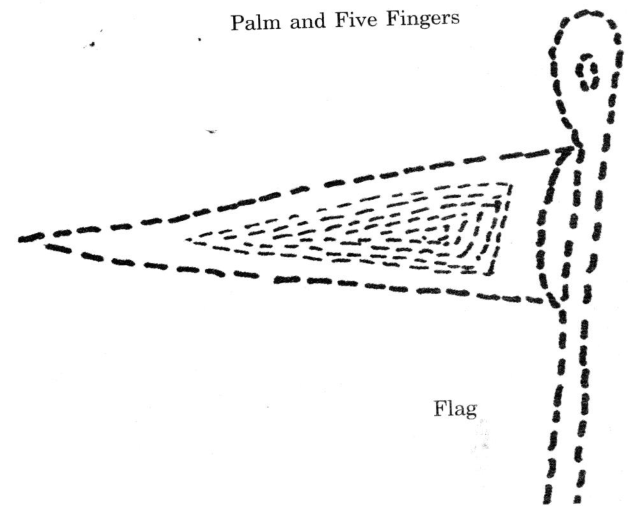

Flag

Fairy

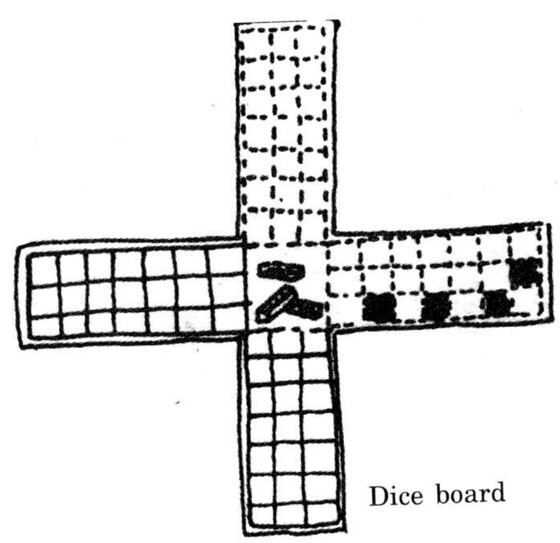

Dice board

Demon

Monkey

Dancing

Durga her carries and family

had noticed that the lotus blossoms after sunset and sunlight makes it wilt and used the motifs keeping this in mind. The lotus has its root in the ground, floats on water and looks up towards the sky, bringing to mind the state when the Cosmos floated on Chaos. The lotus symbolises creation and therefore also women.

Jeevan Briksha: A common motif in needlework. The tree symbolises life—birth, flowering, death and rebirth. The Buddhists hold the Bodhi tree in reverence and the Muslims believe there exists a tree in Heaven and whenever a leaf grows on it a child is born. So it is Jeevan Briksha, the Tree of Life. The tree motif is seen in Persina, Syrian, Korean and Czechoslovakian art also. In Bengal the motif is used as the symbol of a Goddess.

Chakra: The Wheel, symbolises Universe and Time. Vishnu holds the Chakra and the motif is also seen in the Sun temple at Konark.

Swastik: Used as a symbol of good fortune. Acknowledged as the symbol of sun in both Hindu and Egyptian mythologies.

Padachinha: Foot mark, that of Lakshmi the Goddess of Wealth. Also a symbol of good fortune and prosperity.

Fish: Symbol of fertility and is used as motif in kanthas given to women at the time of wedding. The fish also symbolises life and good fortune.

Sankha: Conch shell which symbolises the same things as the fish.

Palki: The palanquin, which was a common mode or transport when roads were largely absent in rural areas. The palanquin also symbolises marriage as girls were taken in these to their in-laws' place.

Nauka: Boat, a natural motif in riverine Bengal.

Ratha: Chariot, an integral part of Hindu religious consciousness.

Masjid-Minar-Gambuj-Tajia: Mosque, turret, cupola, all associated with Islam, the motifs found mostly on Jainamaz or prayer kanthas.

Geometric Patterns: Circles, squares, triangles, found mostly in kanthas made in Muslim families.

Palm with Five Fingers or Panja: Symbolising the Holy Five of the Shia Muslims.

Makar: Bearer of the Goddess Ganga with the body like that of a fish.

Pataka: Flag or banner, used as motif since the Buddhist period.

Lakshmir Jhampi: Basket of Goddess Lakshmi, bearing wealth.

Sheaves of Corn: Symbol of prosperity and also fertility.

Train

Lion

Amulet

Camel

Waves

Bull

Palm Tree

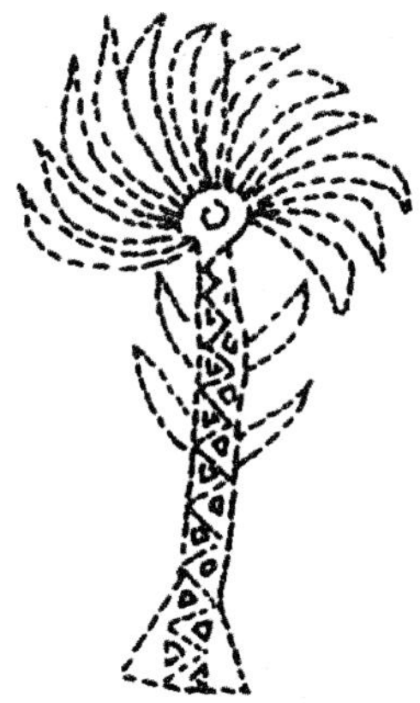

Coconut Tree

Owl

Crow

Sparrow

Cat

Tiger

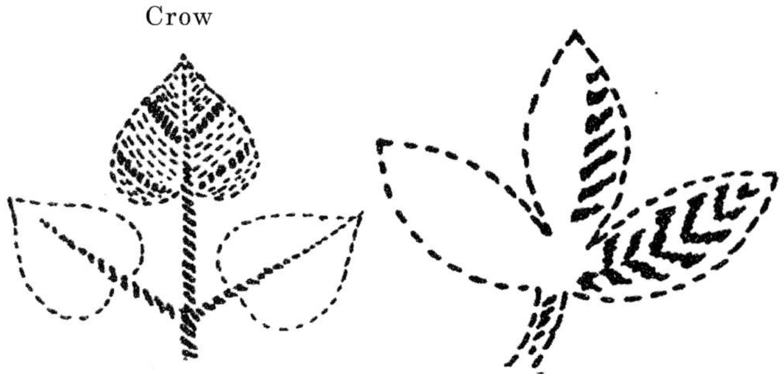

Three leaves

Running Horse

Deer

Betel leaf and Betel

Peacock

Peacock eating snake

Winnow

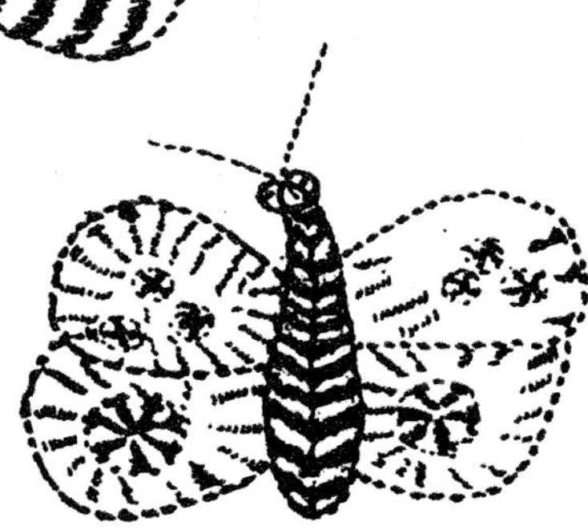

Butterfly

Gallinul

Peacock

Sahib, Memsahib: Influenced by the English rulers.

Horse Rider: Symbol of speed. The Aryans had come on horseback.

Marriage of Rama and Sita, Battle of Rama with Ravana: From the epic Ramayana.

Marriage of Shiva and Parvati: From Hindu mythology.

Raslila: Symbol of the love between Krishna and Radha.

Shiva: Symbolises power and destruction.

Kali: Same.

Indra: God of Rain, associated with cultivation.

Durga: Ends misfortune.

Saraswati, Kartik, Ganesh: Symbols of learning, valour and wealth.

Dushmanta-Sakuntala: Characters from Hindu mythology.

Pari, Rakshasa, Daitya: Fairies, demons and giants from fables.

Dancing Girls: Symbol of life among feudal lords.

Kneeling Girl: Symbol of prayer.

Mukhosh: Mask, symbol of different deities.

Baitha: The oar, symbol of crossing the river.

Bull: Symbol of farming.

Camel: Associated with Islamic culture.

Lion: Carrier of Goddess Durga.

Monkeys: Influenced by the Ramayana. A reminder of the problems they create for villagers.

Elephant

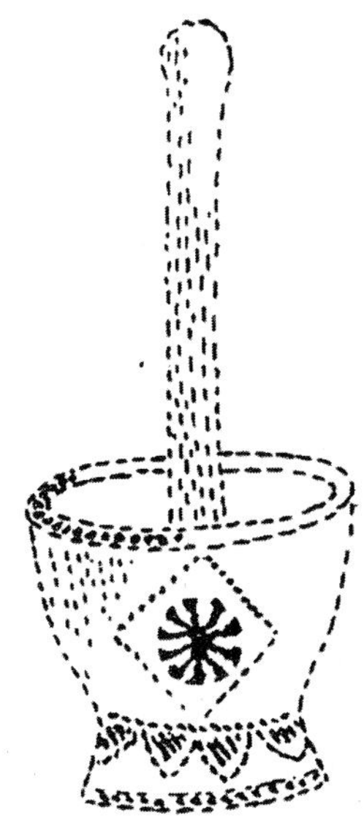

Gail-kind of ginder

Girl with head cover

Frog

Beetle

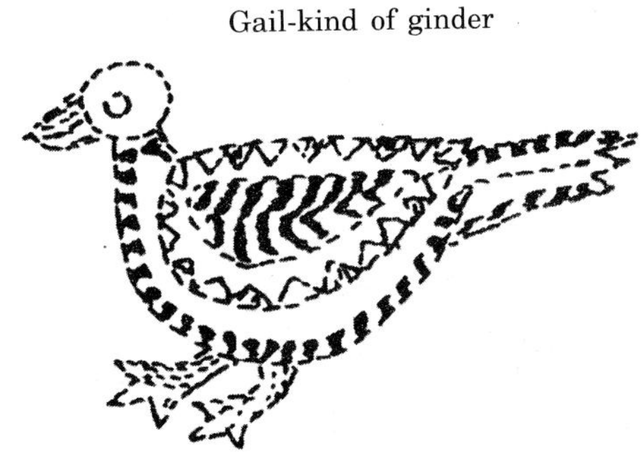

Pigeon

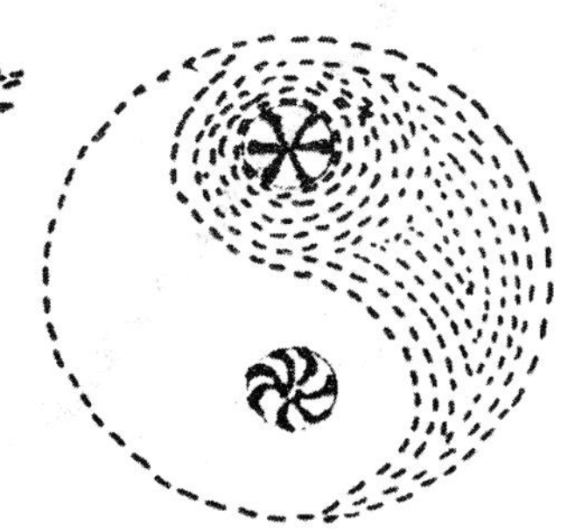

Chinese Symbol yin and yang

Barfi: A sweet. Its use shows Muslim influence.

Flying Chariot: From mythological tales.

Yogi: Influenced by the Nath sect.

Coconut three: Symbol of long life.

Bala: Wristlet, symbol of happiness.

Sea: Symbol of vastness.

Kulo: Winnow, symbol of wealth.

House: Symbol of stability.

Banana: Symbol of fertility as they grow in a bunch.

Green Coconut: Same.

Tabij: Amulet to ward off evil influence.

Swan: Carrier of Saraswati and thus associate with learning.

Crocodile: Symbol of fear.

Butterfly: Symbol of happy union, marriage.

Crow: Symbol of death.

Birds: Seen as bringing God's messages to earth. Of all birds the women preferred cocks, pigeons and sparrows because of their ability to give birth to many chicks.

Horse: Symbol of speed as well as strength.

Hunting: A common motif in the kanthas. Seen in needlework elsewhere also.

Cats: Carrier of Goddess Sasthi, the deity with whose blessing children are conceived. The symbol is obvious.

Tiger: The motif is in keeping with the practice in the Sunderbans or worshipping the tiger to keep it happy.

Peacock: Carrier of the handsome deity Kartick. Girls dream of having husbands like Kartick and hence the peacock motif.

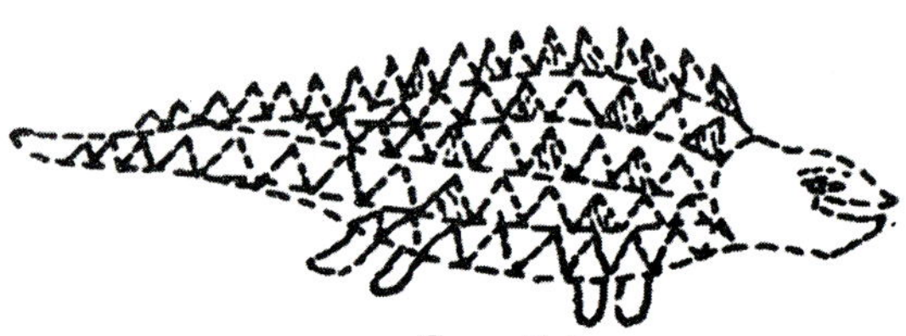
Crocodial

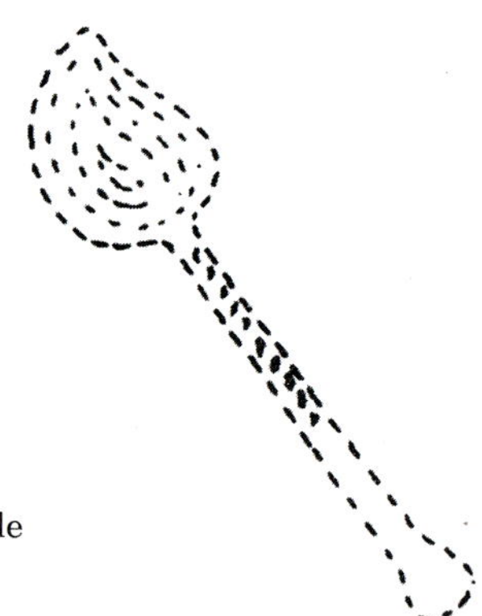
Ladle

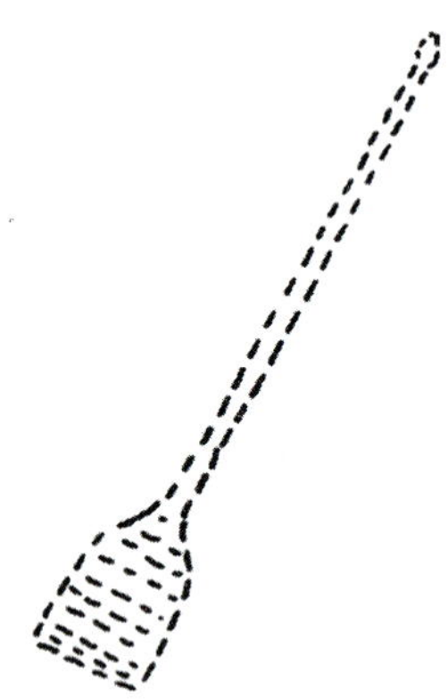
Cooking spud

Spoon

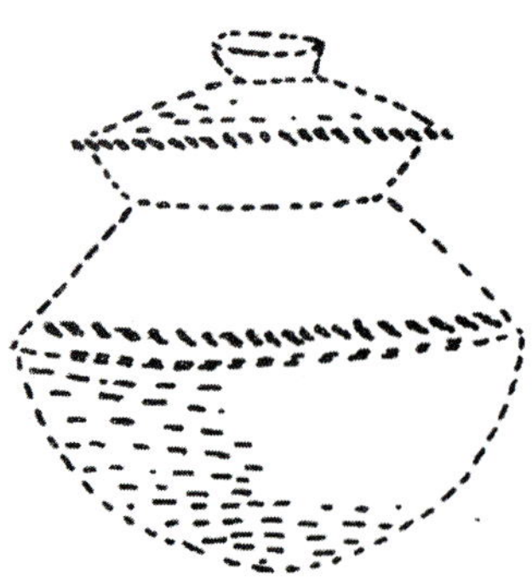
Cooking pot

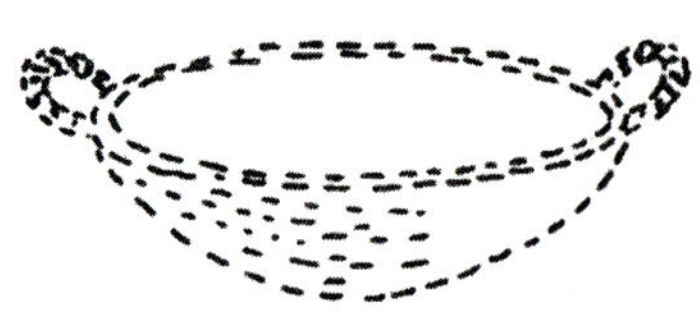
Small Metal bowl for cooking

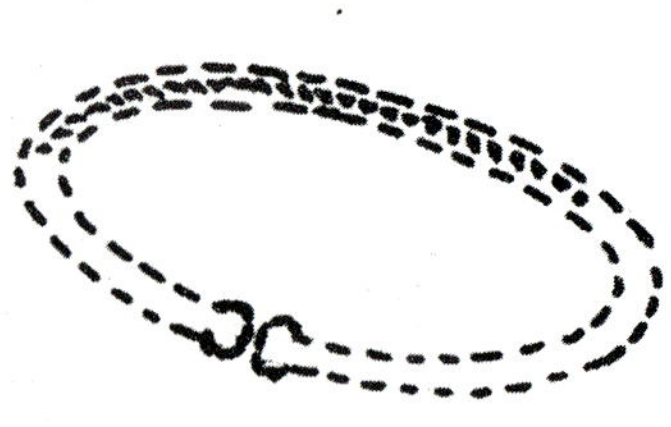
Bangle

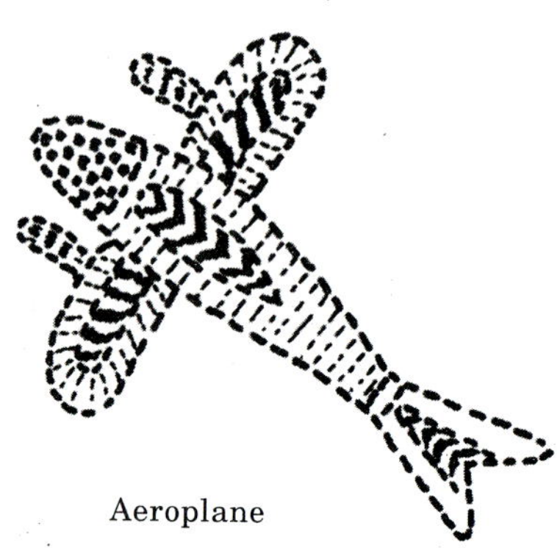
Aeroplane

Small pot

Flower tree

75. Goddess Kali, Radha-Krishna and courting peacocks.

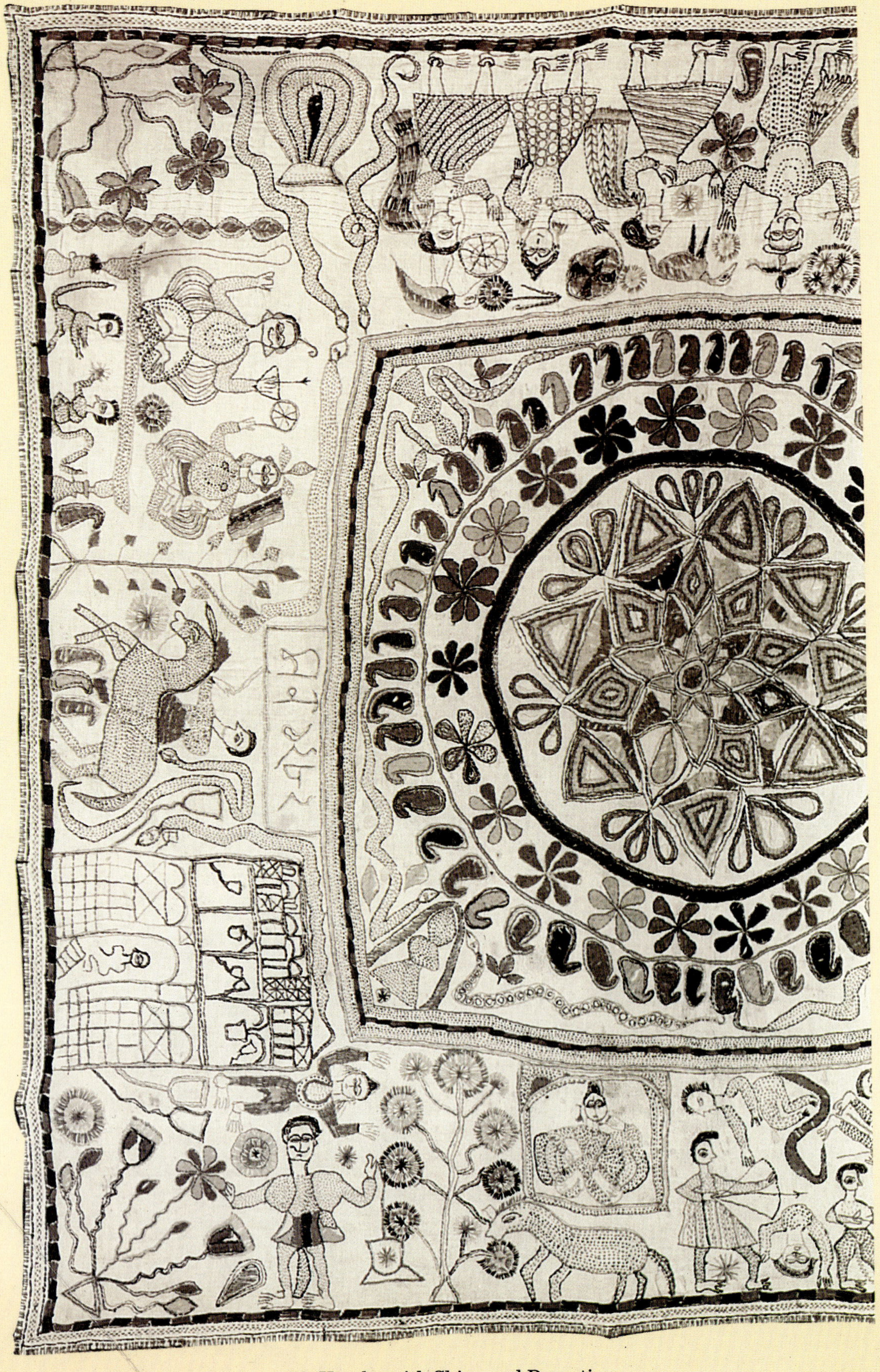

76. Kantha with Shiva and Parvati.

77. Golden village

78. Scene of paddy being thrashed.

79. The Kalka motif.

80. The Kalka motif.

81. The Kalka motif.

82. The Kalka motif.

Acolyte: Animals which are symbols of fertility. Man on horseback is a common motif in kanthas.

Elephant: Associated with royalty and richness. The women who chose this motif perhaps wished that those who would use the kantha would also acquire riches and travel on elephants.

Betal-leaf and betel-nut: Considered auspicious at all religious and other occasions like marriage etc. Associated with Khasi folklore in which a poor man and his wife committed suicide as they had nothing with which to feed the man's rich friend who on finding this out also did the same. On the place where the poor man and his wife were buried grew a betel-leaf and betel-nut tree and so these are given to all guests, rich and poor alike.

The motifs are many and varied. What is particularly noticable is the use of many coloured threads to bring variations and make these attractive. There is generally one principal motif, surrounded by other motifs, the first one done in some deep colour like red. When designing, the women never reined in their imagination and hence the motifs are so varied in nature. Everything they heard, read about or saw found expression as motifs when they sat down in the afternoon to make the kanthas.

Reference

1. *Exploring India's Sacred Art* (Selected writings of Stella Kramrisch), Ed. by Barbara Stoler Meller, New Delhi, 1994

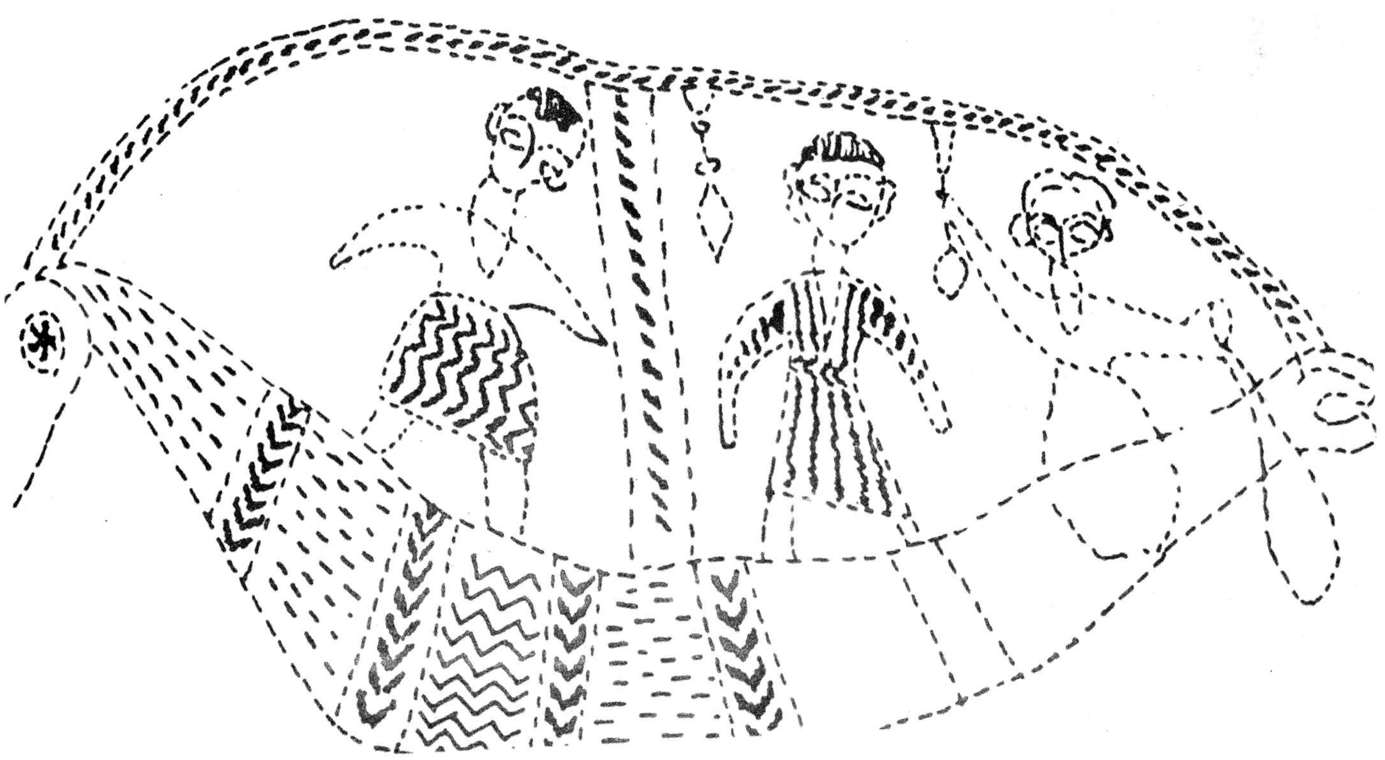

Peacock shaped boat

83. Woman's prayers to God

The Alpana

The needlework is one of the oldest forms of artistic expression, so is the *alpana*, the designs created on the floor with rice-paste. The excavations at Mohenjo-daro have shown that such paste was used to make designs around altars and later Buddhist monks were also known for the designs that they created with either a similar paste of broken rice or a preparation of gum, charcoal and leaves.

84. Design of the decorated seat used at weddings.

The word *alpana* is derived from the Sanskrit *Alimpan*. It is an ancient practice among the women to decorate the floors of their homes, the wells, the wooden seats or *piṅri* and other household items with designs made from rice-paste, or with crushed colour in which case the *alpana* would be dry. Such decorations were made both in a normal course or on special occasions. As Wakil Ahmed has said:

"At weddings or social occasions, the *alpanas* contained such motifs as would evoke pure and happy thoughts. The streets are decorated with alpana even during occasions of national celebration like on February 21, in which geometric patterns dominate the designs".[1]

The *alpana* decoration is done in a particular way. Broken rice is mixed with water to make the paste. Then with a piece of the cloth this paste is used to make the drawings. Generally an *alpana* is white but sometimes other colours are also used to make these more attractive. For red, sindoor or vermilion is used as well as crushed pieces of bricks, for black charcoal dust, for yellow tamarind or the marigold flower, for orange the stem of the siuli flower and for green the juice extracted from crushed leaves.

Different motifs can be seen in the *alpana*. Ajit Mookerjee says:

"Some of the form and motifs found in alpana drawings are hieroglyphic in character. These forms and motifs can be traced to pictographic representations of ancient times..... From the study of different kinds of alpana drawings it is evident that repetition and uniformity of motif are fundamental. The symmetrical character of the alpana designs predisposes us to suspect that there is a definite survival of forms derived, no doubt, from earlier motifs".[2]

The motifs bring out not only the sense of beauty of the woman but also her wishes and desires. The alpana drawing is to be found mostly among the Hindus and the practice can be found in almost every state, albeit under different names. In Bihar it is known as *Aripan*, in Orissa *Jhunti*, in Gujarat *Sathia* in Madhya Pradesh *Mandan*, in Rajasthan *Mandana*. The term commonly used in Maharashtra and Uttar Pradesh is *Rangoli*, though in the eastern parts of Uttar Pradesh it is *Sonha Rakhna* and *Sanjhi* in some other parts. In Himachal Pradesh and Haryana such designs are known as *Lithnua*, in Andhra Pradesh *Mungli*, *Kolam* in Tamil Nadu and Kerala and *Rangoli* in Karnataka. Like in Orissa, the alpana is called *Jhunti* also in western Midnapore district of West Bengal because of the geographic proximity of the two regions.

In Orissa the women use different types of coloured dust for the alpana and call this *Murja*. In Maharashtra and South India, women paint alpanas outside their doors and apart from broken rice also use crushed coconut, sand grains and chaff. The *Mandana* in Rajasthan is made of black, chocolate, blue and green colours and before painting, clean the ground with red soil and cowdung. The designs are round or square. The Malayali women use the white of coconut and chaff for their alpana and for colour use

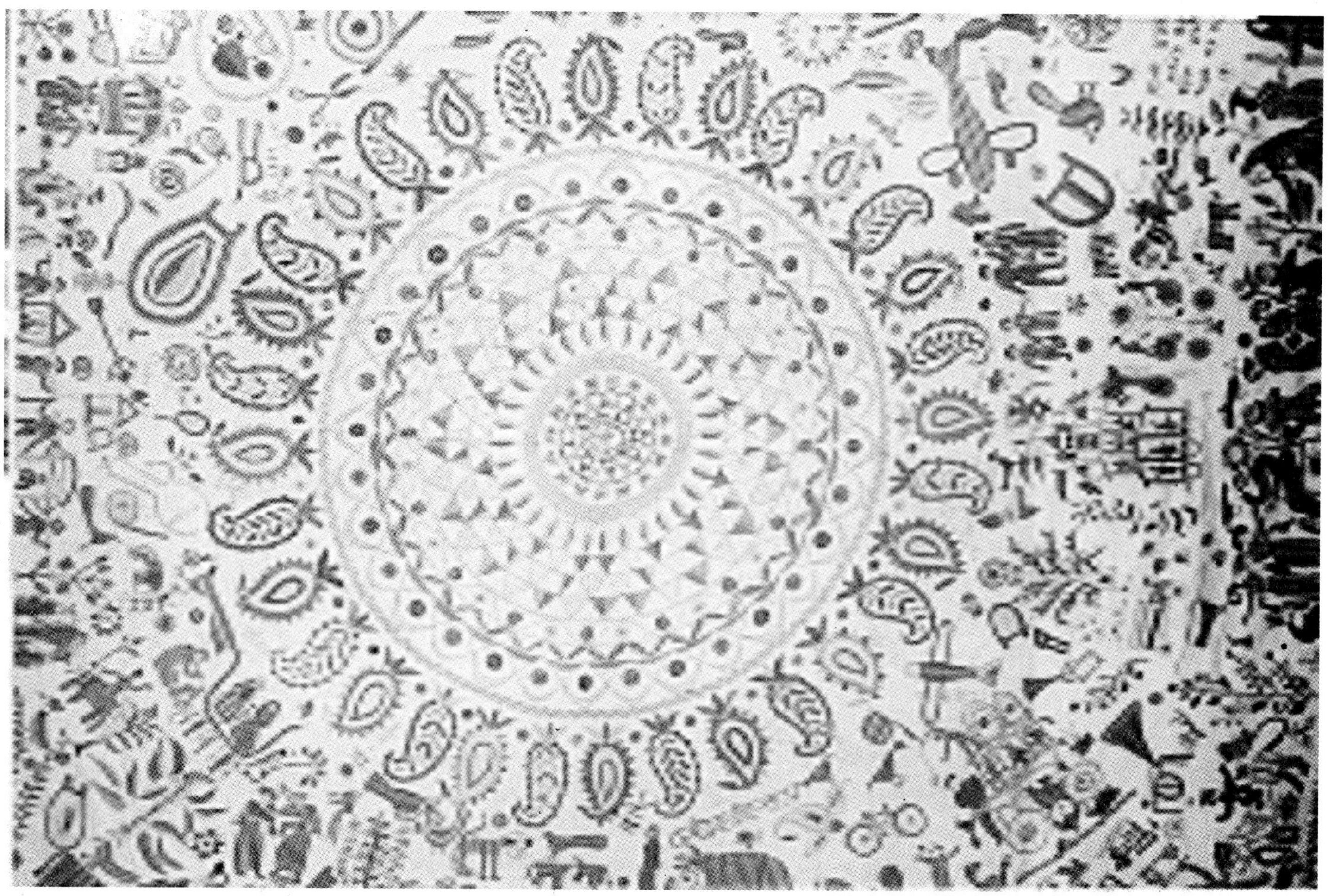

85. The Alpana Design.

86. Alpana with different creepers.

different kinds of flower. The alpana or Kolam is a must in Kerala homes at harvesting time, just as in Gujarat homes and streets are such decorated during Deepavali.

The designs are always associated with beliefs that have come down through generations. In South India, for instance, the Kolam is for Shiva on Monday, Kali on Tuesday and Lakshmi on Friday. On Wednesday the Swastika is the design. In Uttar Pradesh the scorpion in the motif symbolises sorrow and in Bihar the *Doka* alpana is painted to ward off the influence of evil spirits. In riverine areas the fish symbolises happiness.

Some similarities can be noticed between Bengal and other regions. Rafiqul Alam rightly says:

"Except in the case of some Adivasis (original inhabitants), it is the women who paint the alpana, and it is a joint effort of all women present. No professional artist is ever engaged, it is essentially the work of amateurs. The alpana is painted on special occasions, religious or social, certain symbols are always used and it is never an expensive affair even the poor can afford it. That way the alpana is truly a prople's art".[3]

The alpana is generally round, with Hindus and Muslims using different paintings. Both, however, share the practice of painting the alpana on their winnowing vessels. Muslims sometimes use turmeric paste for alpanas at their weddings. Detailed accounts of such painting can be had in Sanskrit literature in the *Mymensingh Gitika* (Songs of Mymensingh). Dinesh Chandra Sen has given a graphic account of how a girl goes about painting the alpana. First she wets fine rice, cleans it and then makes a paste out of it. Then she first draws the footmarks of her father and mother, then sheaves of corn as also the footmarks of the woman of the house. Then she draws Shiva and Durga, their heavenly abode, followed by Lakshmi, and Narayan. Other motifs mentioned in the song include the *Bana Devi* or Deity of the Forest, Rama, Lakshmana, and Sita, Kartick and Ganesh, the sea, the sun, the moon. The only picture she does not paint is of herself. After the alpana is complete she lights a lamp of ghee, clarified butter, then kneels down and touches her forehead to the ground in respect.

Abanindranath Tagore has divided the alpana into two parts. The first resemble the Egyptian hieroglyphics, like the ornaments, the houses, trees, which are not really works of art but together form a chart of human desires. On the

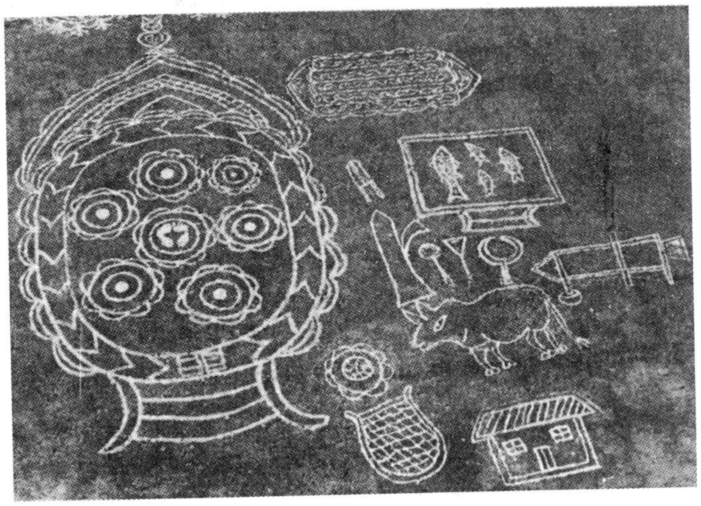

87. Alpana at the Paus Festival.

88. Alpana on *Senjuti Brata* ritual.

other hand, the different types of lotus, the various creepers, the designs painted on wooden seats, these have come from the imagination and constitute decorative art.

The alpana is an integral part of religious rites in Bengal. Various symbols are used in these paintings which perhaps have their origin in the ancient faith in magic. The ancients believed that through their paintings they would be able to bring to life the desired expressed. Thus, a hunting expedi ıon would be organized if they painted hunting scenes, the picture of a sheaf of corn would lead to a bumper crop and so on. Behind the symbols in the alpana works the same faith, it is essentially a product of emotion more than any religious faith. Together with the faith in the power of magic, the alpana designs also speak of fertility and are a continuation of ancient art and sculpture.

Various motifs can be seen in the alpana. The transition from hunting to farming led to a change of symbols and hence we have corn, plough, creepers, household items and of course the foot marks of Lakshmi which, it is believed, will usher in prosperity.

89. Designs of the Decorated Pinri in Kantha.

90. Alpana on the occassion of Annaprasana, the first day when a baby is fed rice.

Whether it be the alpana or the nakshi kantha, it is the same emotion at work and naturally the designs of the former are often seen

91. Alpana at doorstep and corner of room.

occupying the central position in the latter. Perhaps the same faith in magic is not noticed in the kantha designs and these are a little more secular. Also of course the kantha designs last far longer than the alpana which is scubbed off once the occasion passes, to be painted again on a later occasion. Even with such differences, however, the designs in both are essentially an expression of a woman's wishes.

A special occasion in Bengali homes is *Paush Sankranti*, the last day in the ninth month of Paush from mid-December to mid-January. Amiyabala Sarkar gives a detailed account of how the day was observed. She says:

"It used to be a day of rejoicing. The whole house used to be cleaned and alpana used to fill the floors. The visuals used to be many – old man and woman walking with baskets on their heads and backs, fish playing about in the pond, domestic animals like cows, dogs and cats, chariot with, banner, lotus offering itself to God, various kinds of sweets, haystacks. In the evening the alpana on the *tulsi mancha* (raised platform where the auspicious basil is grown) would be offered flowers, oil and vermilion, the conch-shell would be blown, and we would partake of the sweets which had been part of the offerings to the deity. The next day would begin with viewing the alpana, followed by the ritual holy dip and entertaining the guests who would come with sweets. Even though the country has been partitioned, this tradition continues".

Another popular ritual is *Senjuti Brata*. As women draw the alpana, they sing:

'As I draw bangles of rice paste

So may, I have bangles of gold....'

The motifs in the Senjuti Brata alpana,

92. Another alpana design in a Kantha.

cooking utensils, necklaces, bangles and earrings, are also to be seen in the kantha, making it clear what is in the women's mind.

The alpana is painted on other occasions also. The alpanas painted in Dhaka on February 21 (to remember the martyrs who fell to police bullets under the Pakistani regime as they championed the cause of the Bengali language) are similar to the nakshi kanthas, the motif being the lotus and the borders decorated with the kalka.

In South India, the alpana is to be seen mostly in Tamil Nadu. There the ninth day of the Durga Puja (*navami*) is celebrated as Saraswati Puja when alpana with geometric patterns are painted. The first day of harvesting is celebrated as Pongal and the motifs include the lotus, butterfly, flowers and leaves.

Generally associated with religious rites as these are, the alpana is also a prayer for fulfillment of wishes while the nakshi kantha isn't necessarily so as these are not made on any particular occasion. The kantha is more an expression of happiness, sorrow and imagination and hence more living than the alpana. From an artistic point of view of course, the alpana matches the kantha, as one can only marvel at what fingers can achieve with a bit of rice-paste.

Rabindranath Tagore had great love for folk art. Poet Mohitlal Mazumdar recalls that one when he had gone to see him he found some nakshi kanthas in the room and a hole lot of brown paper scrolls on which were sketched various Alpana designs "and it appeared the Poet was particularly fond of these".

References

1. Wakil Ahmed, *Banglar Lokasanskriti*, Dhaka, 1974.
2. Ajit Mookherjee, *Folk Art of Bengal*, 1946.
3. Rafiqul Alam, *Bangladesher Lokashilpi*, Alpana, Bangla Academy, Dhaka, 1400.

93. Mahasundari Devi painting the alpna at Mithila, Bihar.

94.Design of Creepers.

95. Alpana on Lakshmi Brata ritual

96. Lakshmi Brata Alpana, Orissa

97. Feet of the Goddess Lakshmi.

98. Three generation at work on a Pous festival alpana.

99. Kantha with motifs resembling a Pous festivel

100. Riual alpana motif on Kantha

101. Alpana on Dhaka street on Martys day, feb 21.

102. Alpana at a Ritual

103. Motif of the Senjuti brata ritual

104. Geometric patterns at South Indian alpana -Chennai

105. Alpana on the occasion of Pongal festival, Tamil Nadu.

106. Geometric patterns..

107. Kantha motif resembling Pongal alpana

Nakshi Kantha: Comparative Analysis

Taken as a whole the nakshi kantha is an art object and at the same time one of daily use. But these vary from place to place in terms of stitching, depending on local conditions. The kanthas of places like Murshidabad, Rajsahi and Bogura are heavier because of the more severe winter. The stitching is also not as fine as elsewhere. On the subject of stitching it will be worthwhile to take note of what Tofail Ahmed has to say:

'The kanthas of Bangladesh may be divided into two schools, the Jessore and the Rajsahi or to be precise Champainababganj (now a separate district). While the Jessore school is known for its artistry, it is style which marks the other. Five types of kanthas are made in Champainababganj, the lahari, leak, sujni, carpet and chhoptana with no intermingling of the types of stitches. A single stitch completes the entire kantha, like the cross stitch for the carpet or the *Ek Phonr* (one stitch) for the sujni'.[1]

The Champainababganj kanthas are also marked by the preponderance of drawings which cover the entire surface. These include betel-leaf,

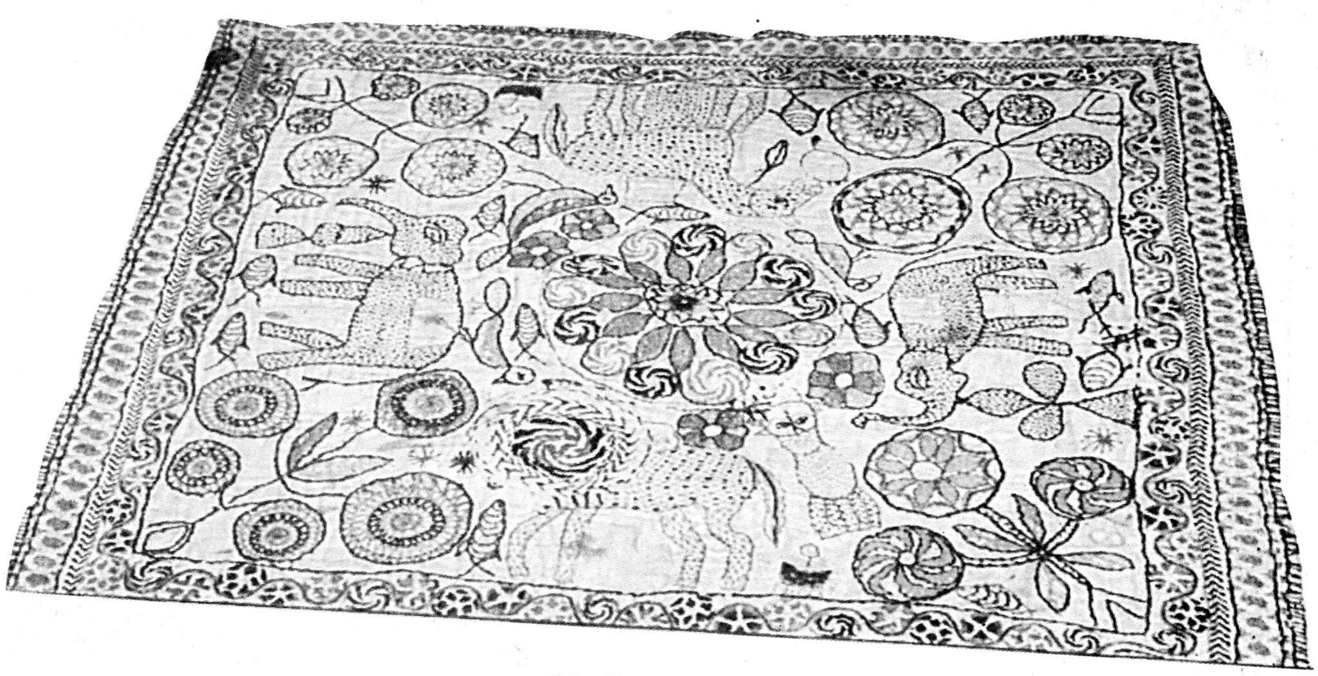

108. Sujni Kantha, Jessore.

shapla flower, rose, pomegranata etc. The motifs include, atlas, elephant, deer, peacock, parrot, nest of the weaver bird, mosque etc.

The oldest kantha of Rajsahi and Champainababganj is the *lahari* and the most famous design is the carpet design, with which various types of flowers are created. The common stitches are, single, double button-hole, and the 's' stitch. Though the kantha is made in many villages or the district, Ajaipur stands out in terms of volume.

The Jessore kantha is marked by its fine stitching. The parts between the many colourful designs and motifs are filled by small *run's*, the colour of the thread matching the surface. The many small *run's* give the kantha a wavy look and because it is less cold there, these are three-fold ones. The Jessore stitch is well-known in the world of needle-work and the stitches commonly used are the snail, the honeycomb, benki, pimpri, the motifs include various types of flowers and creepers. The dorokha is also made in Jessore.

Let us take at the kanthas in other Bangladesh districts.

Khulna: Thin with fine stitching and marked by the use of different coloured threads.

Faridpur: Neither too thick nor too thin. Not as finely stitched as those in Jessore. Beautiful, asan kantha's are made here, both for sitting in rooms or inside palanquins.

Kusthia: Thick kanthas, large but not very finely stitched. The Bending Stitch is generally used here for children's kanthas. The influence of Rajsahi is seen on the kanthas here. In matters of design there is a preference for vegetables, the eye, the barfi sweet etc.

Bagura: Very thick kanthas, mostly of the paar variety and many coloured threads are used to make rows of borders, each acting as a symbol.

Pabna: The sujni is the most commonly found kanthas here. The kanthas are closely woven and have a lesser number of motifs than those of other districts.

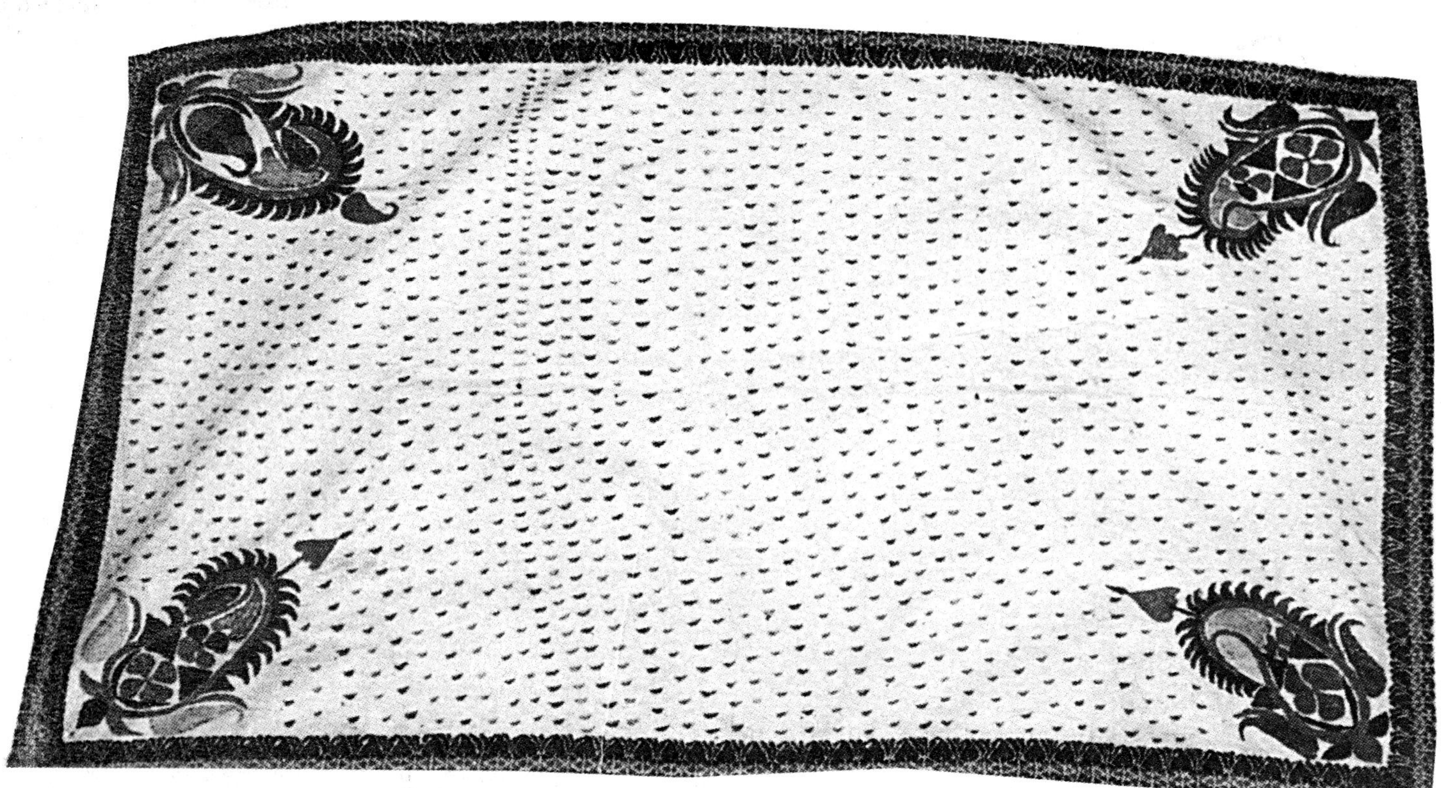

109. Sujni Kantha, Kusthia.

Mymensingh/Tangail: As colourful as the Jessore kanthas but lack the fine stitching of the latter. At Sherpur the *run* stitch is used to make dastarkhan and jaynamaz. The Jamalpur kanthas are noted for their varied designs and the *taga* stitching which means small uneven *run's*. In the matter of filling up the surface a similarity can be noticed in the kanthas made at Jamalpur, Sherpur, Jessore, Kusthia while those of Rajsahi and Manikganj are different. Here the kanthas have the centre alpana design or the lotus around which are woven other designs. Of the motifs the elephant is most common, the others being horse, fish, snake, peacock, kalka, butterfly, tiger, mosque, palanquin, boat etc. The designs and motifs are multi-coloured. (Note: Jamalpur, Sherpur, Tangail were originally parts of Mymensingh though now these have become separate districts).

Chittagong: Geometric patterns, flowers and creepers are embroidered on the kanthas. The stitches are light and the *gada* flower (kadam flower in Dhaka) is used very often in the designs. The main *run* stitch is known here as the straight stitch and in addition the chain, shade-work, cross, button-hole are also used. The sheaves of corn design is known here as *crow's nails*. In Chittagong it is the Hindus who go in more for kantha stitching and it is customary to give at least two at a girls wedding. The customs is prevalent among Muslims also. Generally the coverlet is stitched here.

Barisal: The kanthas here are completely different from the others. The designs are linear and the stitch is button-hole.

Sylhet: At one time the nakshi kantha was known here as *nanka* kantha. These are thick and enjoy an abundance of motif.

Rangpur: Comparatively lesser number of motifs. Here an even stitch is followed by an uneven one. The designs are many.

Dinajpur: The practice of stitching kantha is

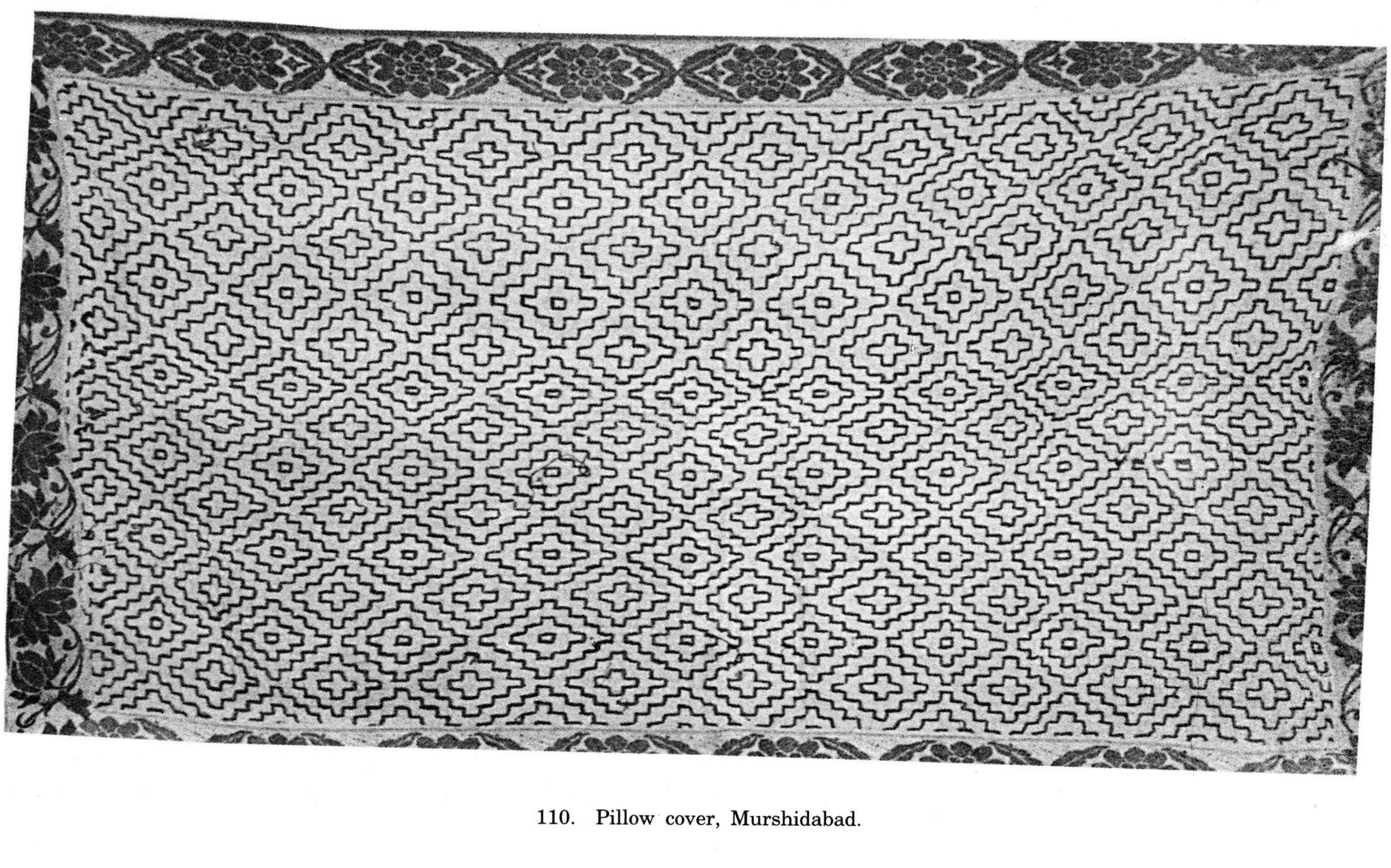

110. Pillow cover, Murshidabad.

less widespread. It is the Asan Kantha that is most often made with the designs of the *paar* kantha.

The tribal girls of Bangladesh are also experts in needlework. Their quilts and wrappers are often designed with geometric patterns and are also very colourful.

The districts of West Bengal which deserve mention in the context of nakshi kantha stitching are murshidabad, Malda, Nadia, Bankura, Midnapore, Howrah, Burdwan, Birbhum and North and South 24 Parganas. The dorokha is also made in West Bengal and here also the kanthas stand out because of their varied designs and motifs.

Murshidabad: The kanthas are thick. The *run* stitch, including the small or *guri* run, is used. The types of kanthas made are sujni, lep, asan, arsilata, pillow covers with the lotus motif in the centre and alpana and floral designs. The motifs used are flowers, creepers, elephant, peacock, owl, bird, betel-leaf etc.

Malda: Known for beautiful kanthas. The designs are *lahari* (waves) and geometric, with small runs used in the vacant spaces of the designs. The motifs seen are those of peacock with plumes spread, sun, betel-leaf, boat, mat, flowers and creepers.

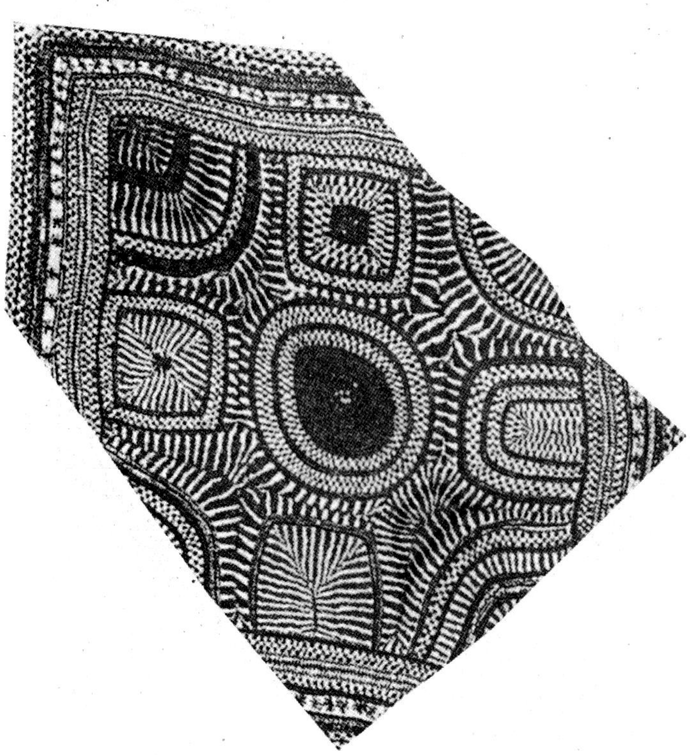

111. Nakshi bag, Rangpur.

West Dinajpur: Kanthas are quite heavy. The small *run* stitch is used and the motifs are tiger, elephant, peacock, bird, duck, horse, fish, fan, nut-cracker, flowers and creepers.

Nadia: Sujni, asan, durjani, dorokha kanthas can be seen here. The *run* stitch is mainly used as also the small or *guri* run. The lotus and alpana dominate the designs. The motifs most seen as conch-shell, peacock, elephant, fish, kalka, human figures, Tree of Life, deities, household items.

Bankura: In the southern parts of the district are found people from Orissa, who have settled there and brought with them their own traditions. Floral and other designs attract particular attention. The motifs are, Tree of Life, peacock, dog, bear, monkey, betel-leaf, kajallata or the vessel for preparing collyreum etc.

Midnapore: Practice of stitching kanthas less prevalent than in other districts. The main stitch is again the *run* and the motifs are the same as elsewhere.

Burdwan: Here the Muslims call the *guri* run the *jire* (cummin) run. Temples are designed with the 'tooth' stitch. The tradition of giving the bride kanthas at Muslim weddings is still followed.

Birbhum: The same tradition as in Burdwan is also followed here. The Muslims also cover their dead with kanthas which have no motifs of human figures as the body cannot be covered with anything that represents life. The Muslim girls also insist on the geometric pattern. Hindus of the district also make kanthas. A particular characteristic is the twisted flower in the kanthas. The most common motif is the flower, though other motifs are also to be found.

North 24 Parganas: Kantha stitching enjoys

112. Awning, Orissa.

a long tradition here, and the designs are varied. The women go in for almost every stitch, from the *run* to *Kashmiri*, *herring-bone button-hole* etc. desending on the design and the size. The designs in the borders include geometric, the abstract and of course of various creepers. The motifs are, kalka, fish, elephant, peacock, boat, conch-shell, scenes from the epics, deities, human figures etc.

South 24 Parganas: Not a widespread practice but even then some beautiful kanthas can be seen here. There is one such kantha at Sonarpur showing details of how the popular folk ritual of *Arandhan* (No Cooking) is observed. The kantha was made by Sudeshna Ghosh Dastidar and is in the possession of her mother Purnima Bagchi.

The kantha is 5½' long and 4' wide. The surface is white and the designs outlined with *run* and *double* stitch. Yellow thread had been used to bring out the colour of brass, dark brown to show the colour of the earth. The other threads used are black, white, pink, blue, purple, green, mustard and majenta colour. The name of the ritual has

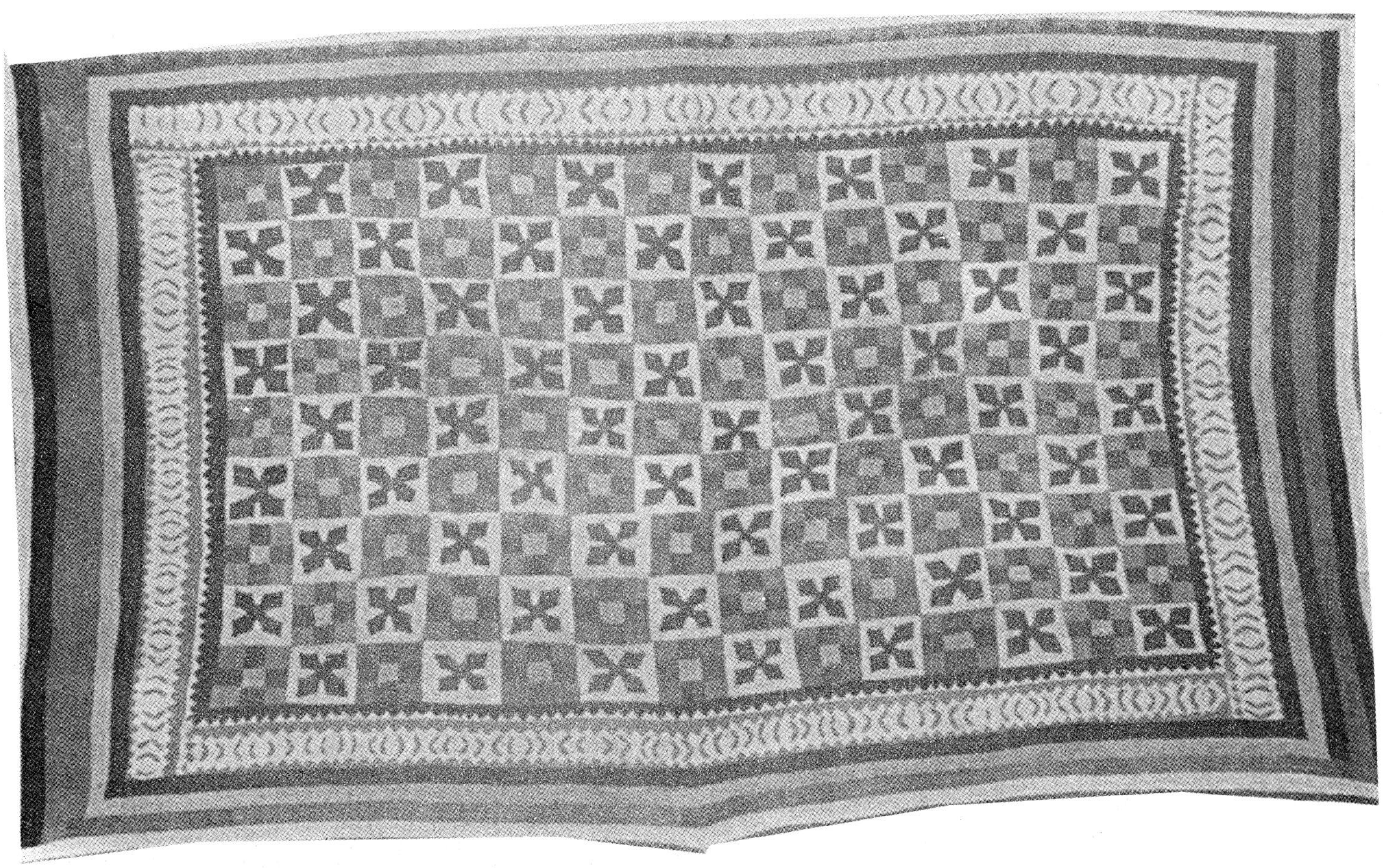

113. Lep Kantha, Gujarat.

114. Asan Kantha, Rajasthan.

been written with black thread.

There are three women. One is placing a pitcher with ingredients for the ritual, one blowing the conch-shell and the third touching the praying her respects. A couple of hilsa fish have been designed in a circle, an earthen oven is shown as also various kitchen items. Each corner has two rohu (carp family) fish and there are various flowers and birds.

Needlework in India has a tradition, colourful and varied. The excavations at Mohenjo-daro, the sculptures in the old Buddhist stupas show human figures draped in stitched clothes, as do the figures of the Kusan age. This is also seen in the paintings at Ajanta and the descriptions of clothes in the works of Kalidasa and others.

A new age came into being with the arrival of the Mughals who brought with them the Persian style which blended easily with the local tradition. This added to the beauty and during the days of Akbar, these Indo-Persian creations began to travel abroad and attract attention there. The Indian *lep* or quilt was to be seen in European markets in the sixteenth century. These used to be made of yellow coloured silk and finely stitched.

The art acquired a new dimension in India with the artistes describing religious rites along with scenes of every day life. This was particularly to be found in the coastal regions like, Bengal, Orissa, Tamil Nadu, Maharashtra and Gujarat.

The nakshi kantha of Bengal is similar to the needlework of other places in terms of motifs and the style of stitching. The sujni of Bihar, particularly Gaya, Darbhanga and Madhubani, are also made exclusively by women using old pieces of clothes and threads from the sari borders. The designs, however, are simpler though the motifs, like in Bengal, are drawn from every day life like boy flying a kite or old woman going on pilgrimage.

Orissa is known for her applique work. The designs are varied. The awnings made here are famous and have as motif the lotus in the centre made with 'run' and 'chain' stitches. As in Bengal the designs are often floral, clearly born out of Mughal art.

Needlework in Gujarat has always been while

115. Kalka in Kashmiri Shawl.

116. Dance poses.

admired. In the Bhuj area of the state, the patchwork can be seen. In Kutch the kantha designs are called the 'Kabira'. The people here use coloured thread to make beautiful motifs and designs with the chain stitch. Commenting on the needlework of Kathiawar, John Irwin has said:

"The kanthas being more sophisticated in conception and of a high standard of craftsmanship, in Kathi work the predominating qualities are exuberant imagination and rich colour".

A distinctive feature of the Rajasthan creations is the use of folk designs which can be seen in the seats made for horse and camel back or in the bedcovers. The best examples of this art in Rajasthan can be seen in Jaisalmer where together with stitching their own clothes, the woman also make seats for horses and camels, pillow covers, bedcovers, quilts, decorating these with attractive designs and motifs. The applique is also used in which small 'run' stitches can be seen.[2]

Chikan is the name for using white thread in needlework on cloth. The art originated in Dhaka and from there travelled to Lucknow and Rampur. The stitch is known as *bukhia* and also *chhaya* and *jali*. A net like effect is created on the obverse side with fish bone stitches on the reverse on which designs are created with fine stitches.

The fish-bone or herring-bone is also favoured in Madhya Pradesh.

Punjab is renowned for the Phulkari or the

'garden in full bloom', needlework. Thick clothes are used and the threads are either colour or white depending on the colour of the cloth. The designs are so stitched on the reverse as to give the effect of tapestry work. The borders are so covered as to make it difficult to distinguish between the cloth and the needlework. The motifs at times resemble those on the kanthas of Bengal.

The kalka motif has come from Iran and is found very commonly in the needlework of Kashmir where natural scenes, like lakes, snow capped mountains, the chinar tree, are designed. Motifs of birds with wings are also be to be seen. The flowery bushes remind the viewer of the needlework of China. The stitching is done so cleverly that, like the dorokha, it appears that the cloth has been worked on both sides. The stitches, like herring-bone rafugiri (local name), corsida, jalakdeji (chain stitch), batachikan, amli daal. It has to be noticed that the kalka has travelled from Kashmir to the kanthas of Bengal.

Himachal is known for its *Chamba Rumal*. These have colourful borders and the darning stitch is used on the cloth, the thread being silken. The Chamba Rumal an unique example of the art of the Himalayas, the artists drawing heavily on the mythologies for their designs. As in the kanthas of Bengal, the dorokha stitch is also to be seen here.

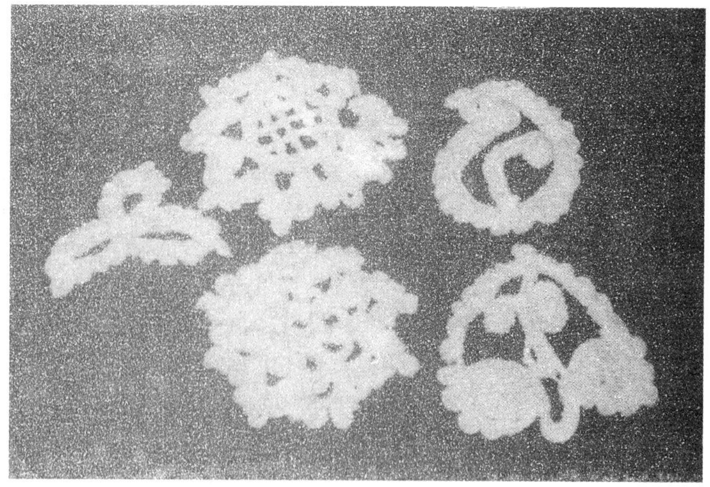

117. 'Gayna Bari', Midnapore.

Mention here needs to be made of the *kasuti* (kasida) needlework, to be found all over North

118. Women making designed pies in Kishoreganj.

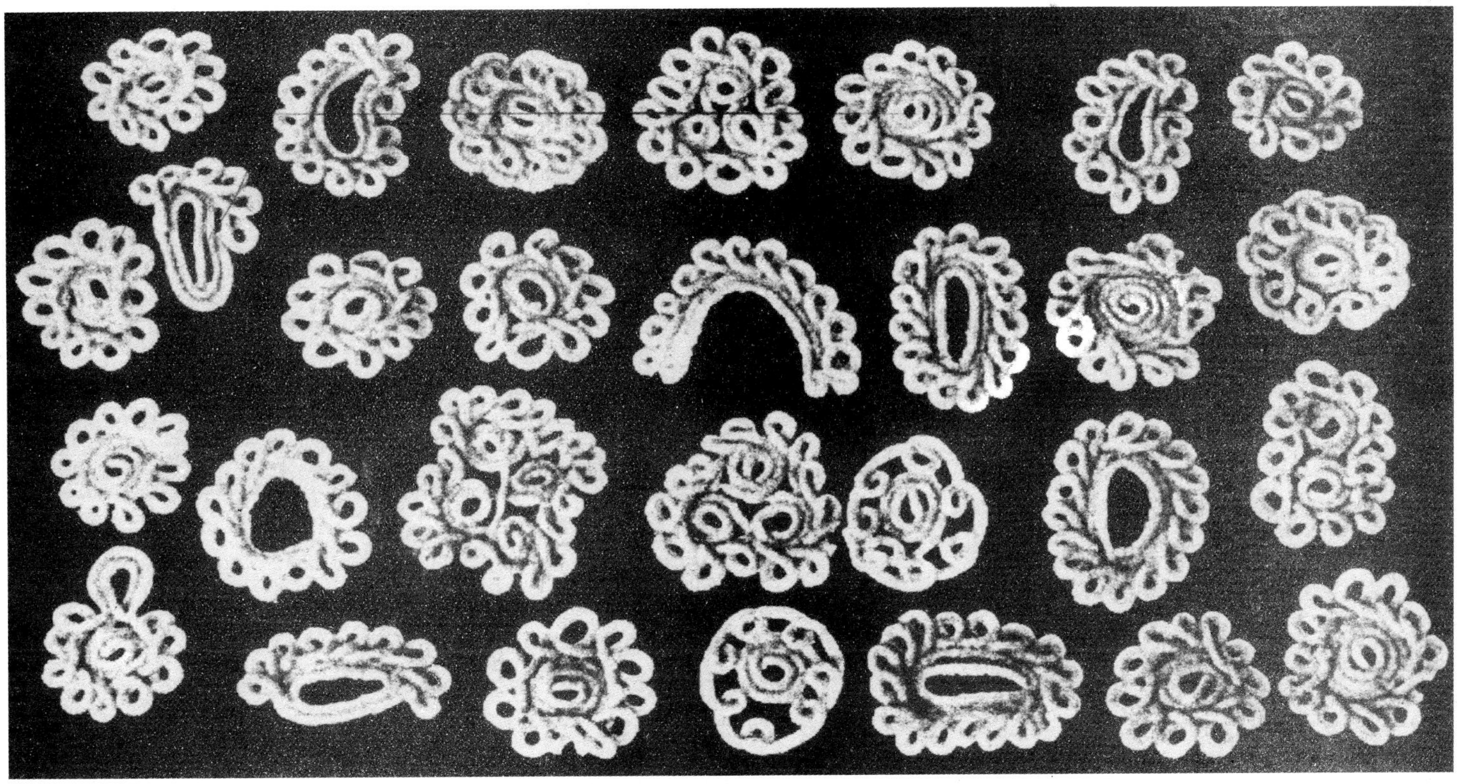

119. Women making designed pies in Kishoreganj.

India and also in Maharashtra and Mysore. Many kinds of stitches are used in the kasuti, the *run* and the *cross* to be found also in Bihar and Bengal.

The word *Pat* is derived from the Sanskrit *Patta*. These are scroll paintings which have come down through generations of rural artists. The rolled up paat is 12 to 16 feet long and about three feet wide and the square pat is one foot long and around ten inches broad. In the rolled up pat, paper is stuck on cloth and scenes of various tales painted on it. While displaying the pats, it used to be a practice with the artists (patuas) to describe the scenes through songs, the subjects drawn generally from the mythologies and folk tales based on the deities. In West Bengal beautiful pat paintings are to be seen in Midnapore, Birbhum, Bankura, Murshidabad and outside the state mostly in Gujarat where the artists are known as Chitraka this or those who narrate tales through pictures. Jyotindra Jain has said:

"In Gujarat the oral tradition has been mainly preserved by the Bhat-Charans, the Hana-Bhattas, the Bhavai performers, and the Garoda priests. All these are almost extinct but some Garodas in the Panchmahal, Sabarkantha, Kaira and Ahmedabad districts still posses their traditional knowledge".[3]

Commenting on the pat of Bengal, T. Richard Blurton has said:

"In Bengal, pats or scroll paintings on paper, made up of narrative panels one following the other, have for many centuries been used by travelling storytellers to accompany recitation – just as in many other parts of India ....Scroll paintings are still produced by villages artists in various parts of Bengal and are occasionally used for their original purpose". [4]

Some motifs used in nakshi kanthas are to be found in the Yama Pats, which reflect the ancient faith in magic. A kantha in Faridpur shows Yama standing with two attendants, one carrying a sword and the other a mace, a common scene in the Yama Pats which showed scenes of sinners being punished by Yama in various ways.

The Kalighat pat deserves special mention.

Made in the Kalighat area of Calcutta, these have always been fascinating works of art. Tofail Ahmed says:

"The patuas of Kalighat were carpenters by caste. They enjoyed a bold style of painting. First the lines would be drawn and then the colours spread. Since the paintings used to be displayed in natural light bright colours were always used, each painting, though flat or two-dimensional, acquiring grace and poetic qualities because of the boldness of strokes and variety of colours.

The paintings on the Kalighat pat are particularly distinguished by the fact that these are wholly in keeping with traditions of Indian art. Tales from the mythologies are followed by scenes from local fables, then historic events and contemporary happenings, bringing into focus the life-styles of the age. Jyotindra Jain is right when he says:

"The story of Kalighat pat is the story of transformation of a folk art form into a popular genre; of a robust encounter of rural artists who had migrated to the city of Calcutta with the forces that operated there in the nineteenth century: the new manners and customs of the British settlers that had percolated in various degrees to different social and economic strata in combination with revivalist exercises in the past practices of Mughal court culture, the new avatar of Sanskrit drama on the proscenium stage and the various products of the new technology of mechanical replication".[5]

Like the paintings on the pat, terracotta motifs can also be seen in the nakshi kantha. Numerous examples of terracotta art can be seen in West Bengal in temple walls at Hooghly (Hanseswari temple), Burdwan, Bankura-Bishnupur, Birbhum, South 24 Parganas, Howrah and Midnapore. In Bangladesh the places that deserve mention are Savar, Lalmai-Mynamati, Paharpur, Mahasthangar etc. The terracotta work on the Kantaji temple at Dinajpore also should be mentioned here. In other parts of India also terracotta work can be seen, Stephen P. Huyler observes:

"Although divided by geography, social structure, language, custom and belief, almost all of the hundreds of thousand Indian potters have a similar creation myth. They believe they are descended directly from the Lord of creativity".[6]

Some of the best examples of terracotta motifs finding their way to the kanthas can be seen in those preserved at Kala Bhavan and Gurusaday Museum. Picture of girl sitting at the window in the terracotta fashion can be seen on these kanthas.

Wall paintings have for long been in fashion for decorative purposes. They resemble the alpana but are painted with brushes instead of fingers. Painted in many colours during festivals, both religious and social, the subjects are drawn both from the mythologies as well as the world around. The paintings at Orissa and Madhubani of Bihar are marked by the use of motifs symbolising good fortune. The motifs also include flowers, creeper, different animals, idols etc. which are also to be found in the nakshi kantha. In some villages of Murshidabad district of West Bengal, the owl is painted on the walls during the Lakshmi Puja. Gurusaday Dutta has pointed out that the owl is not only the carrier of the Goddess, it also destroys rats and thus is a symbol of protection as rats eat away the farmers' crops. Santhals and other tribals in different parts of the country are particularly known for the way they paint the mud walls of their huts and use the same motifs as the others. Not only on walls, the motifs of the kanthas are also to be found in the designed clay pots of Bengal and also hand-fans.

Sweets occupy a prominent place in Bengali cuisine and in the context of designs, the *nakshi pitha* (sweet pie) of Bangladesh deserve mention, particularly those made in Kishoreganj, Netrakona,

Tangail and Narsingdi. Powdered rice is boiled and the paste is flattened and designs made on it with bamboo strips. As in the kantha, the designs are varied ranging from flowers to earrings. It is also an art that passes down through generations, and is not taught in any school. Some of the prominent nakshi pitha makers of Kishoreganj are, Anwara Khatun, Shamsun Nahar, Hajera Khatun and Shahnaz.

It is not only the sweet pie that is designed, but also the *bari*, small balls made out of the paste of pigeon-pea or pulses, dried in the sun and eaten after being fried. The designed or nakshi bari is a speciality of Midnapore where certain families make these, the designs resembling various ornaments and hence also known as *Gayna* (ornament) *bari*.

Here it will not be out of place to take a look at the needlework in other countries. China and Japan first come to mind. The two countries share a similarity in that both have a tradition of embroidering birds and flowers with golden thread on silk. The Korean *kungsu*, with its attractive colours and the use of motifs like mountains, animals etc. is also in the same tradition.

In neighbouring Pakistan the quilts made by the people of Sind deserve mention for their stitches. In the Middle East, Iran was the first country to use motifs in needlework. The Christian women of Iraq make bright shawls and dresses using the cross stitch. The cross stitch is also noticed in the work of the bedouin women of Syria and East Egypt who also favour geometric patterns in their dresses, while in Jordan it is the herring-bone stitch that can be seen. Turkey is also known for her needlework and the floral designs on items of daily use, like handkerchiefs and towels.

Needlework is, however, not just an Asian art. The quilts made in the Durham area of N-E England stand out for their many designs embroidered with coloured threads. Attractive also is the patchwork on quilts of Pennsylvania, USA, where the designs are simple and straight forward but not so the stitches which are fine and complicated.

References

1. Tofail Ahmed, *Nakshi Kantha, Shilpakatha Magazine*, Dhaka, 1992.
2. John Irwain, *Indian Embroideries*, Ahmedabad, 1973.
3. Jyotindra Jain, *The Painted Scrolls of the Garoda Picture Showmen of Gujarat*.
4. T. Richard Blurton, *The 'Murshidabad' Pats of Bengal* (Picture Snowmen, Vol. 49, No. 3 Bombay, 1998).
5. Jyotindra Jain, *Kalighat, Paintings*, Ahmedabad, 1999.
6. Stephen P. Huyler, *Gifts of Earth*, Ahmedabad, 1996.

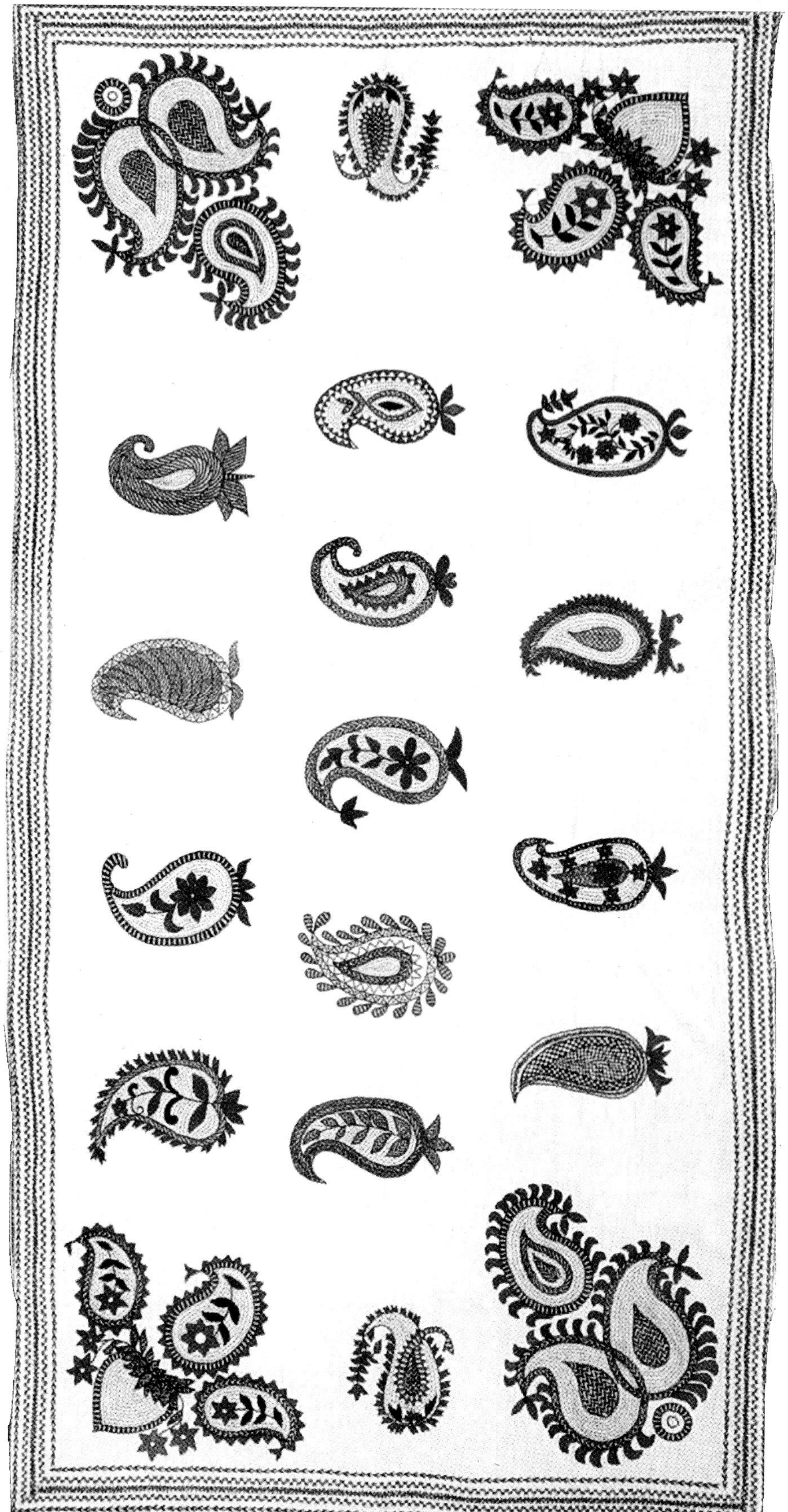

120. Kantha-different Motifs, 20th century.

121. Jaynamaz,Asan Kantha, Jamalpur.

122 .Betan Kantha, Faridpur.

123. Betan Kantha, Khulna.

124. Sujni Kantha. Pabna.

125. Asan Kantha, Mymensingh.

126. Sujni Kantha, Bogura.

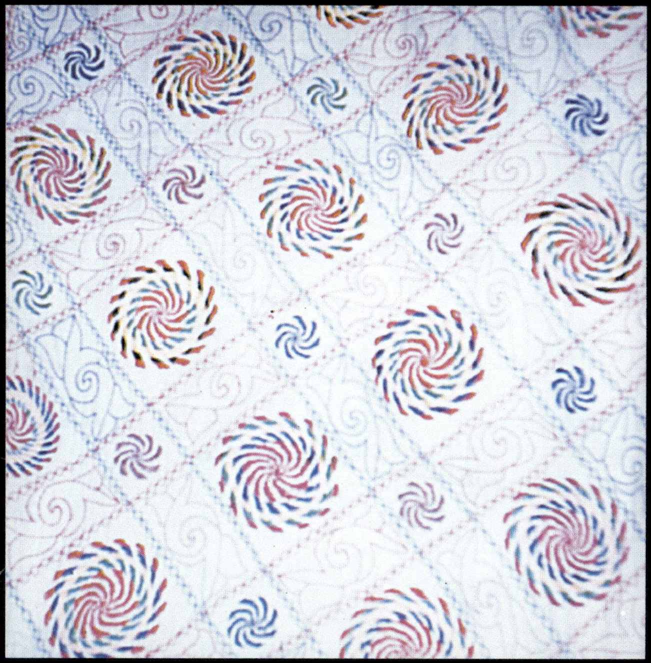

127. Sujni Kantha, Chittagong.

128. Sujni Kantha, Burdwan.

129. Sujni Kantha, Malda.

130. Arsilata, Rangpur.

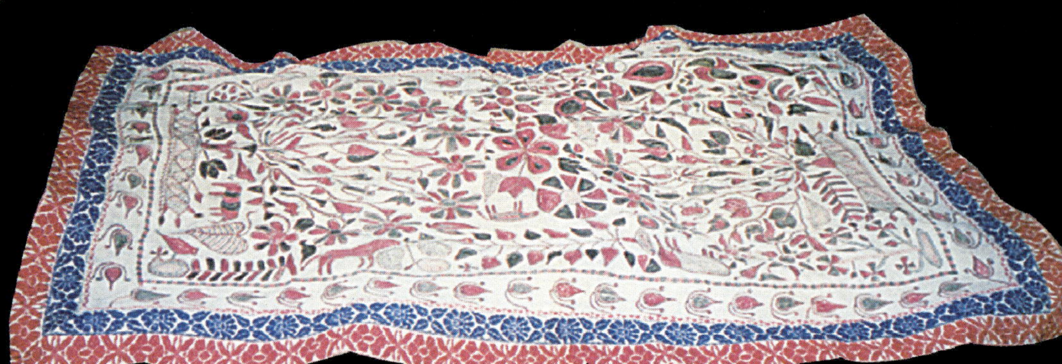

131. Dorokha Sujni Kantha, Bankura.

132. Sujni Kantha, Dinajpur, made by Oraon tribal woman.

133. Betan Kantha, Dinajpur.

134. Sujni Kantha, Nadia.

135. Sujni Kantha, Midnapore.

136 .Sujni Kantha, Birbhum.

137. Sujni Kantha, North 24 Parganas.

138. Sujni Kantha, South 24 Parganas.

139. Kantha made in Pakistan by Sindhi community.

140. Wedding scene, Madhubani, Bihar.

141. Jamdani sari border, Dhaka.

142. Jamdani sari border.

143. Phulkari, Punjab.

144 Chamba Rumal, Himachal Pradesh.

145. Turban, Kantha, Kutch, Gujarat.

146. Dance poses in pat painting.

147 Dance poses in kantha.

148. Dance poses in rolled pat.

149. Yama in pat.

150. Kantha design resembling dance motif in pat.

151. Palanquin in pat.

152 Two friends with Yama in Kantha.

153. Kantha design resembling dance motif in pat.

154. Lotus motif in terracotta.

155. Terracotta design.

156. Kantha-woman sitting at window in terracotta style.

157. Kalighat pat.

158. Lotus in terracotta.

159. Calcutta 'baboo' in pat.

160. Kantha resembling pat.

161. Painted pitchers.

162. Designed earthen bowl.

163. Designed wall. Sarpukurdanga, Bolpur.

164. V[illegible] motif in Kantha.

165. Terracotta lotus in Kantha.

166. Designed wall in tribal home, Singhbhum.

167. Designed wall at Madhubani.

168. Nakshi bamboo fence.

169. Nakshi hand fan.

170. Fish designed in nakshi sweet.

171. Nakshi mat.

172. Kantha with motifs of fancy pitcher, mat, bamboo fencing.

173. Different nakshi sweets, Kishoreganj.

174. Motifs of 'Gayna Bari' in kantha.

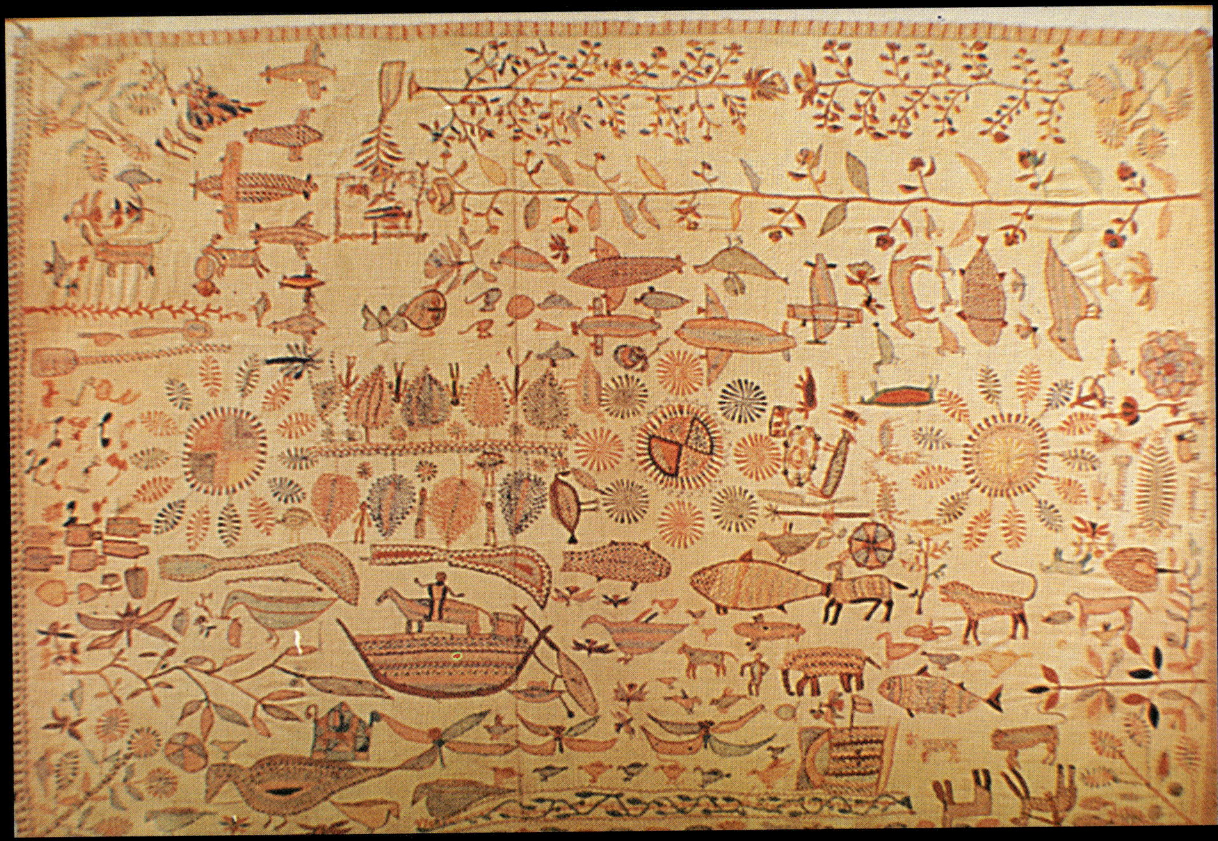

175. Motifs of 'Nakshi Pithe' (Designed Pie) in kantha.

176 Sanskrit slokas and the 'Hari' name in Bengali in Kantha

Nakshi Kantha in Literature

Just as the varied experiences of human life find expression in literature so in the case of Art. The fine needlework of the kantha artistes give expression to the beauty of life all around, creating poetry on threads, bringing out the many untold tales of love and affaction. The Nakshi Kantha has kept alive many an art form that would otherwise perhaps have got lost in time.

To what extent the Kantha was associated with Bengali lives can be understood through a perusal of Sanskrit and Bengali literature. Just as there are many mention of the Kantha in works such as Chaitanyacharitamrita, Nath Gitika, Ramayana of Chandravati, Annada Mangal and Purba Banga Gitika so have innumerable songs, riddles, rhymes been created on the Kantha. The Kantha has also given expression to Sanskrit slokas and advice on education.

Sanskrit Sloka and the Bengali Hari Nam on Kantha

A fine instance of this can be had in a shawl kantha kept at the Government Industrial and Commercial Museum in Calcutta. Made in Barisal in Bangladesh, it is estimated to be 150 years old. It has eleven kalka designs at the bottom and nine on the top. Lengthwise around the centre is written:

Ramarkrsihna hare hare ||Yathan Devabh-aven brahmano kape ahe rooshbantajya stette smanta vara thad || Ramakrishna hare hare Ramakrishna hare hare ||

Written breadathwise is, Man ekbar hari balo, balo, hari balo, balo haradhan chaitanya Charitamrita

Regarding the use of the Kantha and its value, Krishnadas Kaviraj says:

A man in Gaur has washed his kantha and out it out for drying

Comes another and says, "brother dome a favour

Take this gift and give the kantha to me".

Says the other laughing,

"Why this expensive gift for the kantha"

He sayd laugh not listen to the truth

Take the gift and give me the kanths

Saying this he took the kantha and gave the gift

Came to his preceptor with the kantha around him.

(translated from original found in Krishnadas Kaviraja Virachita Chaitanya Charitamrita, Calcutta, 1983, edited by Sukumar Sen)

Chaitanya Bhagvata

In the eighth chapter of Chaitanya Bhagvat we find:

When my poor disciples with kantha round their shoulders

Arrive at Vrindavan look after them

(Sukumar Sen edited vrindavan Das viractam Chaitanya Bhagvat, Calcutta 1991)

In Nath Gitika we find description of the king being dressed in the Song of Gopichand. There, among other things, the king has a kantha being draped around his body.

In Chandravati Ramayana is given a detailed account of the many qualities of Sita. One of these was her ability to beautifully stitch kantha,

Kā̃nthāy ākila kanyā c̃ad suraj pāhāḍ

On the kantha she painted the moon, sun and hill (Nakshi Kantha, Ashraf Siddiqui)

Annada Mangal Kavya

In his Annada Mangal Kavya, Bharatchandra Roy has Gauri referring to the Kantha, along with tiger skin, while talking about Siva's attire:

Jhuli kā̃nthā bāghchāl sāp siddhi lāddu

Shoulder bag, Kantha, tiger skin, snake, bhang and laddoo

Purba Banga Gitika

In Bheluar Baramasi of the Gitika there is:

Māgher śite bāgh dõre āmār ye ki hal

Cokher jale kā̃thā bhijāi ghatailām janjā

Tiger roar in the winter of month of Magh

Tears from my eyes made a mess of the Kantha

(Purba Banga Gitika, Third Volume, Second part, complied and edited by Dinesh Chandra Sen, Calcutta 1930)

The songs composed by the bauls or roving minstrels of Bengal abound in the mention of the Kantha. One of such songs by the famous Lalan Fakir, we find:

Lālān Sā̃ier bhāver Kathā
Tā śunle māthār byathā
Lalan sā̃ier chẽḍā kā̃thā
Gāye dile ki śit māne
The thoughts of Lalan Fakir
Hear of them and get headache
Lalan Fakir's torn kantha
Can it keep the cold away

Similar thoughts can be found in Lalan's disciple Duddushah's

śune ei ājgaibi kathā
katajane muḍie māthā
Nila gale tuli kā̃thā
Chela dharbār kāraṇ
Hearing such strange words
Many shaved their heads
Wrapped kantha round shoulders
To catch young boys

(Upendra Nath Bhattacharya, Banglar Baul O Baul Gaan, Calcutta 1388)

Mystic poet Pagla Kanai sings,

Pāo halo khoḍā
Dhuay dilām joḍā
Gāye chila ek chẽḍa kā̃thā
Leg got lame
Washed and put right
Had a torn kantha round me

(Kavi Pagla Kanai, Majharul Islam, Dhaka, 1997)

Songs of the Sahebdhani Cult

Bhek laye bairāgya halām
Muḍie māthā chẽḍā kā̃thā galāta nilām
Put on appearance of renunciation
Shaved head and put a torn kantha round the neck

(Sudhir Chakravarti, Sahebdhani Sampraday, tahader Gaan)

Similar references to the Kantha are to be had in the songs of the Balahari community also.

And then fables. To what extent the Kantha was inseparable from the daily lives of Bengalis can be judged from these tales. In Dakshina-ranjan Mitra Mazumdar's Thakurmar Jhuli we read: "Coming out of the tunnel the prince saw a kingdom in which sat only a hundred year old woman stitching a small Kantha".

The Kantha repeatedly appears in the rhymes of Bengal. One of these from Rajsahi district of Bangladesh asks,

Kyāre balad tui kyātā khās kyan

Bull why do not eat the kantha

In the rhyme the Kantha is spel kyata. Another variation of the word is 'kheta'. A rhyme from Dhaka says,

Corer mār kā̃thā pudi

Burn the kantha of thief's mother

There is also a rhyme in which the girl tells her lover that she must have a sari from Dhaka or she will lie down wrapped in her kantha...*rag kaira suia thakbo gaye dia katha.* In another a poor woman says she has been able to arrange for a *chẽḍā kā̃thā* (torn kantha) for her son-in-law to sit on.

Proverbs

An important component of folk literature is proverb. There are proverbs for almost every aspect of daily life and the kantha has not been ingnored. Thus:

Kātrā cokher ghum lechḍā kā̃thār um

Broken sleep is the wramth of a torn kantha

kā̃thā muḍi diye ghee bhāt khāoa

Kantha round the shoulder and eating ghee and rice (Poor but talking big)

Bādir beṭā moḍal halo, kā̃thār pare bāp mālo

Maidservant's son becomes headman, father died lying on kantha

Mānuṣ balle kā̃thā kāpaḍ chiḍle kā̃thā

Speak and words are made, tear cloth and kantha is made

Eta sukh yadi kapāle, kā̃thā kena bagale

If you are fortunate then why a kantha under your arms

Rājār māyer ṣājer kathā kāthāy ghunger bāje

King's mother's dress, bells in the kantha

Songs

The Kantha features in many songs also:

Áśmān joḍā fakir re bhāi

Jami joḍā kẽthā

Esab fakir marle pare

Kabar habe kothā re

Mendicant covers the sky

Kantha the earth

When such mendicants die

Where will they be buried

(Folklore of Bangaldesh, Volume Two, Edited by Shamsuzzaman Khan: Nakshi kantha: Md. Syedur, Dhaka 1952)

Among the Muslims in Bangladesh songs are sung during the marriage of girls and many of these songs are on the Kantha. No songs are, however, sung during the stitching of the Kantha or at the bridegroom's place. The songs at the bride's house speak of the girl decorating the Kantha with pictures of peacocks, horses and other birds and animals. One song says there is nothing to worry because the girl's husband has come as, "*bāir bāḍi bichāi thuichi ārśilatā kā̃tha....*"/ Spread in the front room is the Arsilata Kanth. Similarly a song in a folk theatre says there is nothing to worry as well designed Kanthas are spread at the door on which the bridegroom's party can sit.

Biharilal Chakravarti: Sadher Asan

Poet Biharilal Chakravarti had been presented a small carpet by Kadambari Devi, wife of Jyotirindranath Tagore, elder brother of Rabindranath. To mark the occasion Biharilal wrote a poem *Sādher Āsan.*

Rabindranath:

The Kantha found its place in many of Rabindranath's works. In his poem Ebar Phirao More, we find *Rājputra padiyāche chinna kā ̃nthā* meaning : Prince is wearing a tattered kantha. And in his short story Panraksha, there is Rasik who stitched a beautiful Kantha for his lover Sauravi. Tagore describes, "the kanthas stitched by women had some definite designs but Rasik's designs came from his imagination".

Najrul Islam

In the warmth of the kantha the child finds the security of its mother's lap. In one of Nazrul's poems we find.

Uṣā didi othār āge uthbo pāhāḍ chuḍe

Dekhbo nice ghumāy sahar śiter kā̃thā muḍe

Will climb the mountain top before sister sun rises

Will see below the city sleeping wrapped in kantha for warmth

Nakshi Kanthar Math

In this long poem of Jasimuddin there are three characters, Rupa, Saju and the Nakshi Kantha stitched by Saju with all her love and sorrow and which at the end emerges as the central character, On her death bed Saju tells her mother,

Ekṭu āmāre dhar dekhi mā go sũc sutā dā o hā te

śeṣ chabikhānā ẽke dekhi yadi kono sukh hay tate

Hold me up a little mother, give me thread and needle

Let me paint the last picture and see if that gives pleasure and then

Ei kā̃thākhāni bichāia dio āmār kabar pare

Bhorer śiśir kā̃diā kā̃diā eri buke yābe jhare

Spread this kantha on my grave

The morning dew will weep and drop on it

On may kanthas are to be found advices on codes of conduct. A dastarkhan, on which meals are served, in Dhaka advises against over eating and also wastage as there are many who go hungry. It is also advised to keep something in the plate for the domestic pets.

What the woman feels about her family is beautifully brought out in a message on a kantha. It reads:

Saṃśar sukher hay

ramaṇir guṇe

Family becomes happy

If the woman makes it so

And in one kantha the maker Rahima Khatun has inscribed, Do not Forget Me. An appeal that is innermost in every mind.

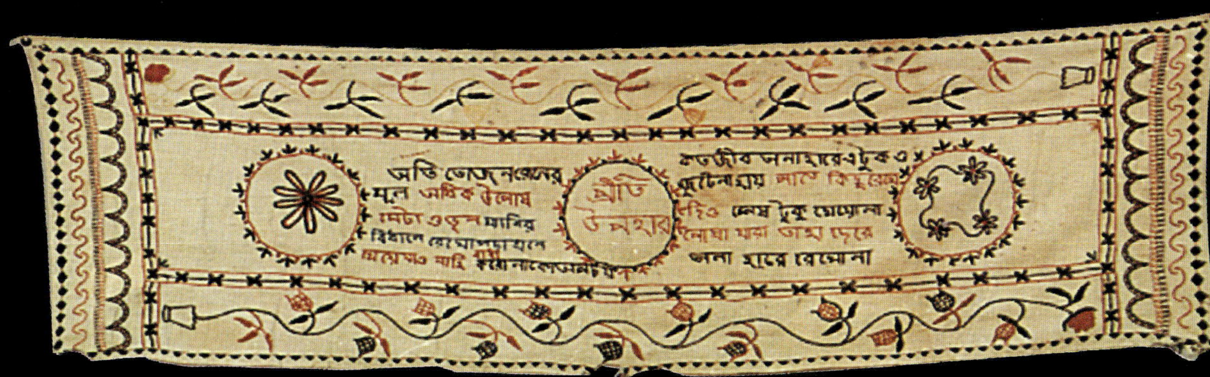

177. Moral lessons embroidered on kantha.

178. Asan K antha presented to poet Biharilal Chakravarty by Kadambari Devi wife of Jyotindra Nath tagore, elder brother of Rabindranath Tagore

179. Wife's faith in husband embroidered on Kantha.

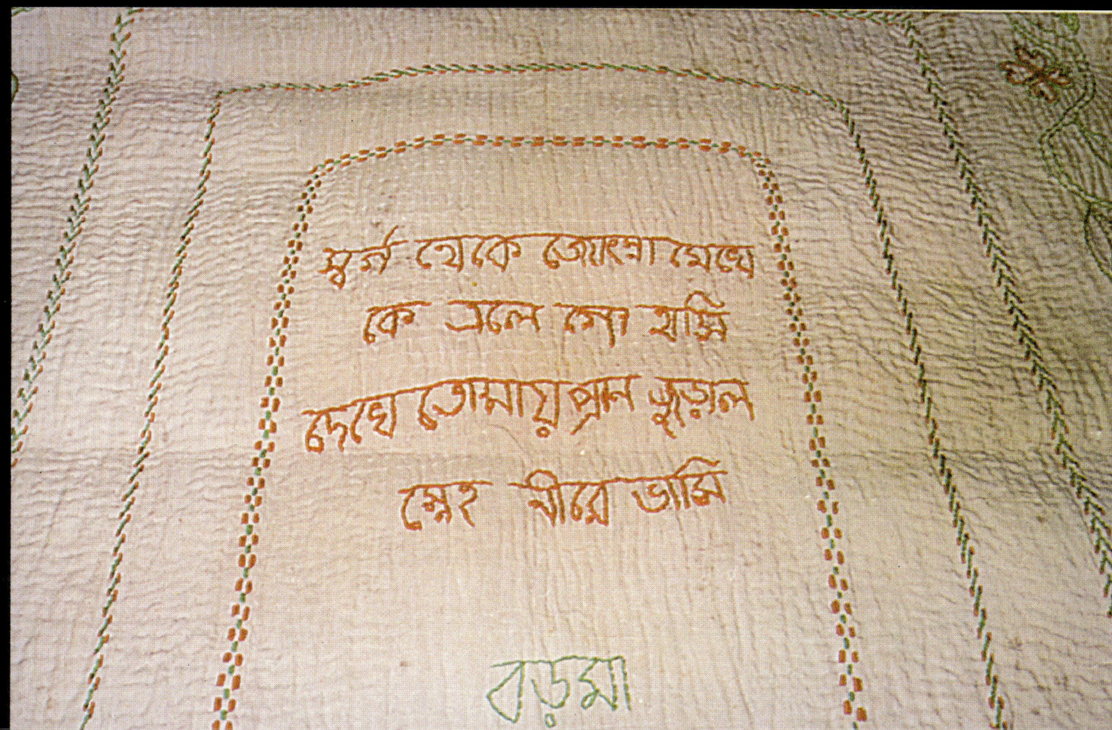

180. Blessings embroidered in kantha.

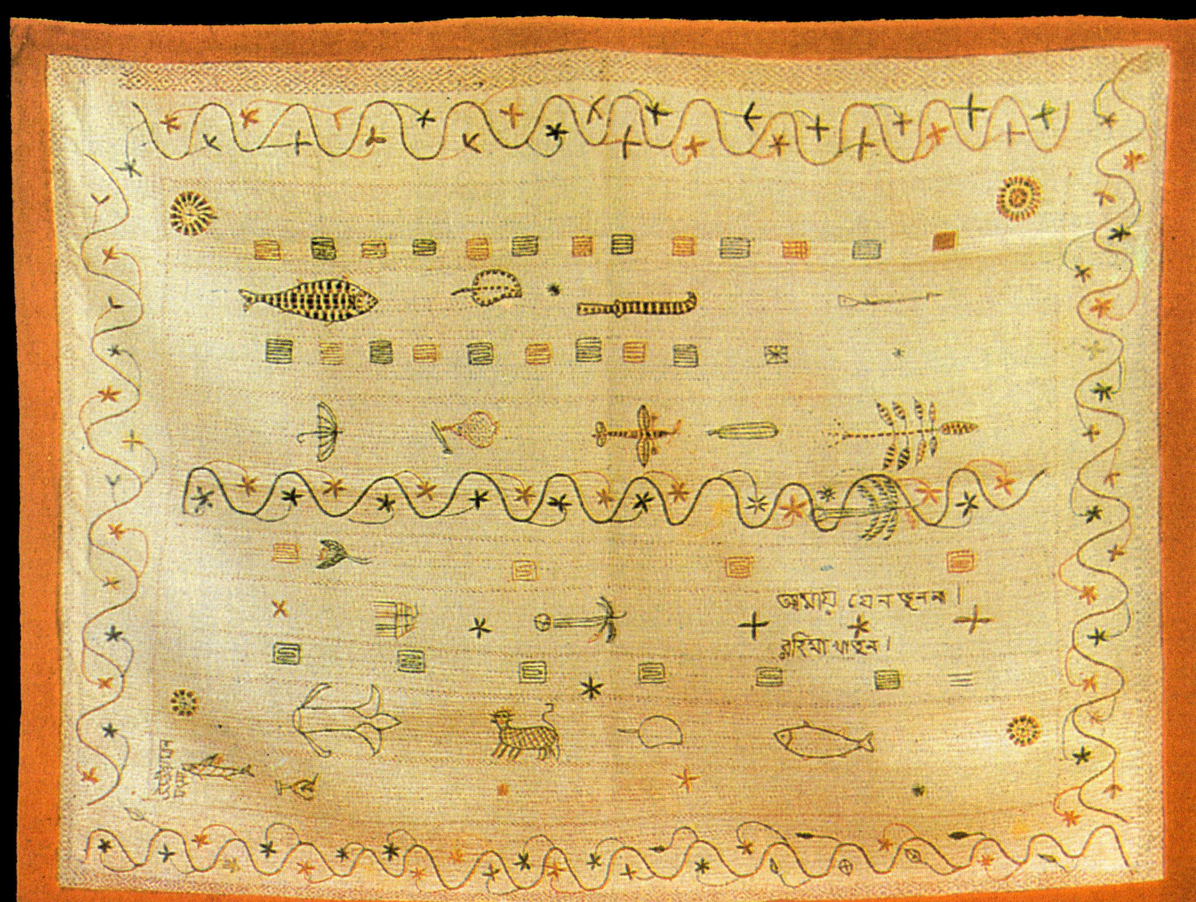

181. Kantha with wife's prayers.

182. Kantha with embroidery of Nakshi Kanthar Maath, Jasimuddin's poem.

Present Status

With the passage of time the kantha has ceased to be as essential an item in the household as in the past. Today it is made more as an art object enjoying commercial prospects. To the red, blue, yellow (not so much) and black threads have been added the green, majenta, mustard-yellow and orange. To the traditional 'run' and other stitches have been added the chain, herring-bone, double herring-bone and the cross. The cross stitched kanthas of Rajasthan are in keeping with modern art. Today the darning stitch is also being used in different ways. Provas Sen's comments in this regard are worth recalling:

"Some enterprising entrepreneurs and voluntary organisations devoted to the uplift of women, mostly based in Calcutta and Santiniketan, have organised units to produce what may be called non-traditional, commercial kanthas. They use the typical kantha stitch to embroider some stylised floral motifs picked up from old kanthas to produce a number of items for modern urban use like saris, stoles, table linen, furnishing fabrics etc. New cotton and silk materials are used, to produce these items and, excepting saris, most of the other items are layered like the traditional kantha. The designs and motifs embroidered are no longer the self-expression of individual craftswomen. They are dictated by professional designers and are copied by embroiderers for mass production".[1]

This mass production has opened new horizons and there is constant experimentation keeping in mind a market which has grown beyond national boundaries. The kantha today is used to make shawls, saris, kurtas, tea cosies, curtains, bags and such other items also. This has also helped in keeping alive a folk art. The Crafts Council of West Bengal has done a lot towards this end and Sujata Mitra and Ila Ghosh have for the last fifty years got the women around Santiniketan to continue with this art. Jamuna Sen, Sunanda Mukhopadhyaya, Deepa Roy, Mamata Bandopadhyaya, Mridula Sarkar and others are doing commendable work in this field in the Bolpur-Santiniketan area.

Other districts are also not lagging behind. The traditional kantha continues to be made at Raikhan Dighi village of Malda. At Aminabazar village or Murshidabad Shyamali Das and her Satavisha Social Welfare Society is busy getting forty women to make different things with the kantha stitches. In other villages also the nakshi kantha continues to be made. Takdira Begum, winner of state and national awards, is doing good work at Srikrishnapur village, under Kurumba police station, in Burdwan district as also Kanchan Chowdhury at Ukta village.

Amina Begum of Niramisha village under Deganga police station of North 24 Parganas is another artist who deserves mention... round 300 women are learning the art from her and she has received many prizes including the Presidents Award. In keeping with the times and depending on demand she also ventures into the field of stitches other than that of the kantha. At Barasat, Najimul Islam and Mohammed Sirajul Islam are two men engaged in teaching the art of kantha stitching to women of the surrounding areas.

In Calcutta similar work is going on at Ranu's Boutique under the guidance of Sujanta Sen who makes her own designs, Kamaladevi Kantha Centre where Rubi Palchowdhury has girls working on traditional kanthas, at Sasa, Lahari, Disha and other centres.

Outside West Bengal, in Agartala Professor Maya Mukhopadhyaya is doing good work with nakshi kantha. It is due to her efforts that needy women are today able to earn a little by making saris, cushion covers, bedcovers, kurtas etc. Already fifty women have been taught the art, some of whom are graduates and some others have not even been to school. Of them Putulrani Debnath has won awards for her work.

In Bangladesh several NGOs are taking a leading role in developing the kantha industry. The various organizations are, Bangladesh Rural Advancement Committee (BRAC), Kumudini Welfare Trust, Dhaka, Nijera Kari,[2] Dhaka, Banchte Sheikh,[3] Jessore, Karika, Dhaka, Aranya,[4] Dhaka, Prabartana,[5] Dhaka, Arshi,[6] Dhaka, Suraya Rahman is known for her designs which include scenes from Rabindranath's dance drama *Shyama*, Jasimuddin's *Sojan Badiyar Ghat*, as also hunting scenes in the Mughal days, scenes from Queen Victoria's regime, alpana etc. Here one must acknowledge the contribution of Syeda Rubi Gaznavi who had played a pioneering role in the rejuvenation of the kantha art in the eighties. Thanks to her the artists have full freedom in the matter of choosing their designs. Talking of the revival of the kanthas in Bangladesh, Henry Glassie has said:

"The art of the nakshi kantha, once meticulously contrived of scraps, was revived during the 1980s. Now there are kantha pillow covers and bedspreads and pictorial wall hangings that recycle used imagery, resembling old motifs: the artefacts of rural life, the chariot of the Hindu temple and especially the wedding procession that brings into conjunction the male and the female, urging diversity toward unity, just as the kantha did when its artist made a beautiful new thing out of old rags".[7]

Of the different organizations, BRAC has undertaken a massive programme to make modern kanthas without forgetting past traditions. Thanks to them many women have today gained recognition. BRAC has four centres all devoted to the making of the nakshi kantha. The Jamalpur centre has four sub-centres and under their direction many women make kanthas at home which they then bring to the centres. The Sherpur, Jessore and Kusthia centres also run many sub-centres. The quality is checked very carefully before these are sent out for marketing. BRAC has also developed an export market and today many village women have been able to stand on their feet.

A major departure from the past is the use of new clothes for kanthas with backings to make these hardy. In India such kanthas are being made in Bihar, Gujarat and Rajasthan also, apart from West Bengal. Because of a concerted effort, what was once an essentially folk art is fast becoming an industry and at the same time retaining the old beauty. The way batik has gained international recognition has kindled new hopes for the kantha.

References

1. Probhas Sen, *Crafts of West Bengal*, Ahmedabad, 1994. 2. Do it Ourselves. 3. Learning to Live. 4. Forest. 5. Beginning. 6. Mirror. 7. Henry Glassie, *Traditional Art of Dhaka*, 2000.

Appendix - A

Field Survey: West Bengal and Bangladesh

Field survey for the book had taken me to various villages in West Bengal and Bangladesh where the nakshi kantha continues to be made with great enthusiasm as part of a tradition whose glory has not been diminished by the touch of modernity. Mentioned below are the names and works of the artists. Survey conducted in 1999 and in Chittagong, 2000.

WEST BENGAL

Birbhum

1. Sakirpara village, Rajnagar police station.

Informant : Sakila Bibi (40), husband, Sheikh Rahamat, education nil, occupation, domestic work and kantha sewing during leisure hours.

Contact : Sheikh Alauddin

About 300 people live in the village. In almost every house the women stitch kanthas. The work takes between five and ten months, depending on the designs. For flowers red, blue, yellow, pink threads are used and green for leaves and branches. The flower is the main motif and closely embroidered. Small or 'guri' runs used for stitching.

2. Budpur village, Rajnagar P.S.

Infomant : Nuresa Bibi (35), husband, Sheikh Alauddin, education, slight, housewife.

Contact : Sheikh Habal.

Five hundred strong population, mostly Muslims, engaged in timber and biri trade. Women make nakshi kantha, known here as 'katha'. Sujni, Rumal, Jaynamaz made with chiffon thread, the stitching mostly beginning from the border. The designs are first outlined with pencil, and include different types of flowers, like jaba, anarkali. The 'run' stitch used here as also at Arali and Elotey villages.

3. Anchal village, Bolpur P.S.

Informant : Anwara Bibi (55), husband Marhum Goleman Sheikh, education nil, occupation, making kanthas.

Contact : Chandra Sarkar.

Sujni, Asan, pillow covers made here with DMC and Anchor thread. Kanthas called parata and roti are also made here. Kanthas gifted during a girl's marriage and also on other occasions. Dead bodies are covered with kanthas which are removed before burial.

4. Harisabha Para, Rampurhat, P.S.

Informant : Nehrunnissa Begum (38), husband, Mohammad Musa, education, read up to class X, Occupation needlework, particularly kantha making.

Contact : Manik Sengupta.

Muslim women have been doing this for generations here. Mother-in-law has a beautiful roti kantha, so named because of the round roti-shaped designs, made by Marhuma Fultun Bibi. Coloured threads use from the British days. Guri run called here Kuchki Dhaga, Sujni kantha takes two to six months to make. Learnt the art from grandmother, mother, aunts. The designs used are the of nacklaces, alpana, flowers and creepers. Coloured threads used.

5. Margram village, Margram P.S.

Informant : Kazi Kismotara, husband, Miraj Ali, education up to class X, housewife.

Contact : Naseem Azad.

Sixty percent Muslim population, mostly farmers also some engaged in plumbing work and in weaving or biri trade. Sixty per cent literate, play various games and organize seminars on science. No tension between villagers. Many bauls live here.

Sujni made here mostly during rainy season. Five-layered cloth used, ends secured first and designs outlined with pencils. Sari ends are often placed on borders, designs chosen by women themselves or sometimes others askd to do the job. Chiffon, crochette or DMC thread used. Minimum time taken to stitch kantha is one month. Both rich and poor woman make kanthas but never for money. Kanthas are gifted at weddings and other occasions.

6. Margram village (Kuthipara), Margram P.S.

Informant : Manjura Khatun (47), husband Kabir Hossain, education upto class IX, stitches kanthas in between domestic chores.

Contact : Aminul Maula

Kanthas stitched according to the other Margram village.

Nakshi kantha made on commercial basis at Sian, Nanur, Sinibejra, Labhpur villages and Jadavpur, four kms from Sriniketan. It is a commercial occupation but old motifs and designs have been retained.

7. Sanmat village, Bolpur P.S.

Informant : Almeera Bibi (42), husband Mir Nazrul, education, read upto class V housewife.

Informant : Habiba Bibi (70) husband, Mustafa Ali, education Nil, housewife.

Contact : Maya Chakravarty.

Six thousand people live in the village, majority Muslims. Farming is the main occupation. Women skilled at making nakshi kantha. Different types are made, like sujni, asan, dastarkhan, jaynamaz, arshilata, etc. Kanthas made during winter as during monsoon they make mats. Among threads used is hali brought from Assam. A distinctive design here is the 'maze'. The border designs vary from the rosogolla, baloon, rainbow, to flowers and creepers. A kantha often takes a year to be made. The kantha is not an object of commerce here. During weddings a minimum of four kanthas are given to the bride. Often more than one woman work on a kantha. The more beautiful kanthas here are made by the Muslims women.

183. Two artistes, Almira Bibi and Habiba Bibi.

8. Mahidapur village, Bolpur P.S.

Informant : Momena Khatun (38), husband, Sheikh Iliyas, education, read upto class IV, housewife.

Contact : Akbar.

Kanthas are generally made by the Muslims for their own use or for gifting to others. A large kantha takes eight to ten months, depending on design. Sari ends are often placed on borders.

9. Kendradangal village, Parui P.S.

Informant : Raushan Nihar Bibi (76), Husband, Marhum Haji Gulan Kibria, education nil, housewife.

184. Sitting room.

185. Bedroom.

186. Dining Room.

187. Sari-Ila Ghosh's organization.

188. Shawl-Sunanda Mukhopadhyaya's organization.

189. Sari-Satabhisa.

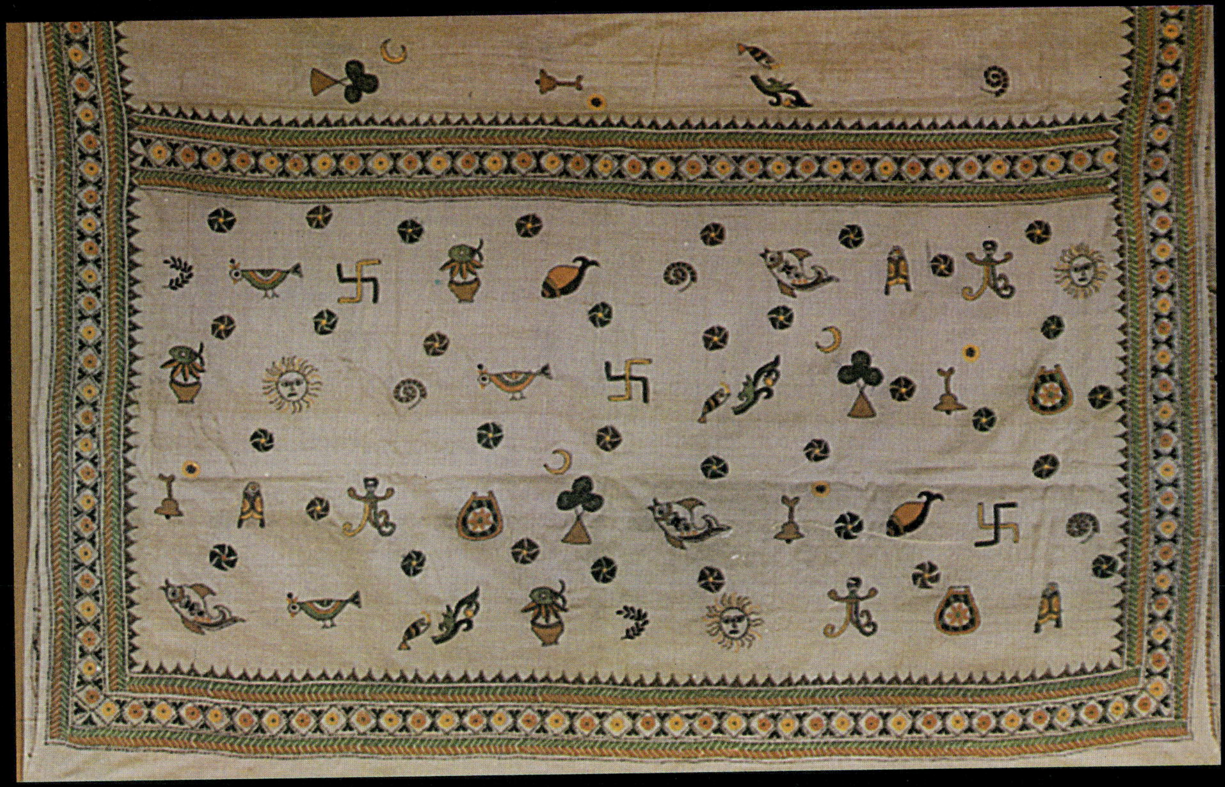

190. Sari-Ranus Boutique.

191. Kantha by Amina Begum.

192. Bedcover being made at Kamaladevi Kantha Centre.

193. Love of Krishna.

194. Fish motif on cushion cover-Suraiya Rahman.

195. Kantha stitching at BRAC.

196. Washing after stitching, BRAC.

197. Japanese Kantha made in the Bengal fashion.

Contact : Akbar.

Mostly farmers, forty percent of women are literate. Village is situated 14 kms from Bolpur.

Saw two beautiful sujni kanthas. One made jointly by Raushan Nihar Bibi and Marhuma Ayesha Khatun. Made from hali threads of the British days, the kantha is three-layered and stitched with 'guri' run. The twisted flower, peculiar to Birbhum, is seen in both kanthas. The other kantha is 120 years old and made by Hazi Jobeda Bibi who died at age of 100. It is a sujni with designs of moon, star, betel-leaf, ears of corn, geometric squares, kalka, large flowers etc.

10. Sriniketan block, Bolpur.

Informant : Maya Chakravarty (46), educational qualification, graduate, occupation, Gram Sevika (rural social worker).

Contact : Parichaya Rakshit.

Originally from Khulna, Bangladesh, kanthas used to be made at their home and given as gifts on special occasions. At her parents' wedding 12 kanthas had been given to her father and 17 to her mother. Kanthas used to be given at childbirth, male child getting less than the female.

Burdwan

1. Berenda village, Ausgram P.S.

Informant : Sufia Begum (55), educational qualification, nil, occupation needlework.

Contact : Safiul Alam .

2. Bhuera village, Pichkuri P.S.

Informant : Amina Bibi (40) husband, Sheikh Rasid, educational qualification nil, housewife.

Contact : Julekha Khatun.

Nakshi kantha is made in both villages. Sujni, asan etc. made. Designs range from flowers and plants to geometric patterns. Different types of stitches can be seen in the kanthas. For temples, the 'daant' (teeth) is used.

Nadia

1. Niramisha village, Nakasipara P.S.

Informant: Ashalata Dey (35), educational qualification, read upto class X, Sews during leisure hours.

Contact: Chandra Sarkar.

Most kanthas here are four-layered. Sujni, betan, asan, made. Different types of motifs and designs used., like flowers, circular alpana, geometric patterns etc. White, blue, yellow, red, orange, pink, green threads used.

North 24 Parganas

1. Niramisha village, Deganga P.S.

Informant : Amina Begum (45) husband Rabiul Huq, educational qualification, read upto class X, occupation, embroidery, Particularly kantha making.

Contact : Premendra Mazumdar.

Society is mainly agrarian. Amina Begum learnt kantha stitching from her grandmother and elder sister, recipient of many prizes. Kanthas are stitches here according to the traditional way, different stitches like chain, Kashmiri etc. are applied. Eight to ten types of threads are used and various designs are embroidered.

2. Kadambagachhi village, Deganga P.S.

Informant : Mohammad Nazimul Islam (30), occupation, needlework.

198. Artist Suniti Sarkar.

199. Momena Khatun

Contact : Premendra Mazumdar.

A special feature is the participation of men in the work of kantha stitching and designing. Mohammed Nazimul Islam and Mohammed Sirajul Islam are two such men. Various stitches are applied, like the Kashmiri, shallow, champa, spring etc. Abstract designs are noticed in the borders as also flowers and creepers and the motifs include Greek and Hindu mythological as also haystacks, mosques and animals. In the adjoining villages housewives stitch kanthas, the principal stitch being the 'run'. Coloured threads are used and the borders are variously designed.

South 24 Parganas

Ananda Palli, Champahati area, Baruipur P.S.

Informant : Suniti Sarkar (87), Husband Mahendranath Sarkar, educational qualification never been to school but can read, housewife whose hobby is kantha stitching.

Contact: Maya Dutta (Mazumdar).

Born in Faridpur, spent many years in Narail of Jessore, now stays at Champahati. Began stitching when she was around nine years old. Takes about eight months to make a kantha on old pieces of cloth and taking out threads from sari ends. Has stitched and designed many kanthas but now a little hampered by age.

Murshidabad

Aminabazar village, Jiagunge P.S.

Informant : Rupali Das (25), occupation needlework.

Contact : Shantanu Thakur.

Has been getting girls to make kanthas at Satavisha Welfare Society since 1993. The stitches used are, run, double run, herring-bone, chain, double chain for designing ears of corn, thatched roofs, pathways or grass. Sari, kurta, bag, bedcover,

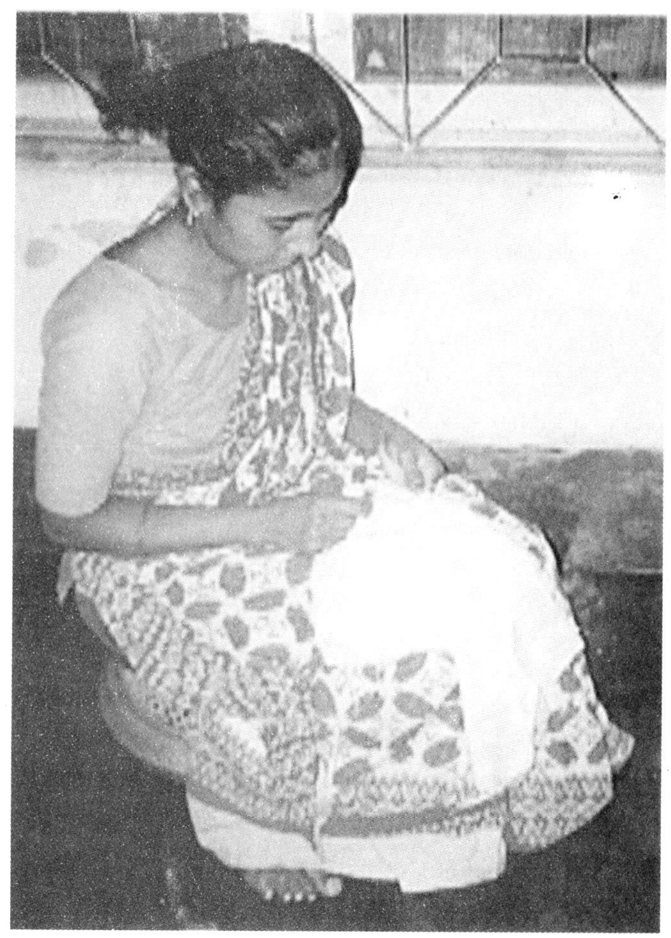

200. Sona Begum

201. Md. Nazmul Islam.

wall piece etc. made here. Kanthas are also made at Mukandabag, Shibtala under Jiagunge Bhagabangola police station.

BANGLADESH

Rajsahi

Dariapur village, Nawabganj P.S. Nawabganj District (formerly Champa nawabganj).

(*a*) **Informant :** Jahanara Begum (25) husband Rabiul Aul, educational qualification up to class V, occupation, housewife.

(*b*) **Informant :** Nurunessa Begum (23), husband Mahirul Islam, education, upto class IV, occupation, housewife.

(*c*) **Informant :** Nasima Khatun (20) Patner Abul Kashem, education, upto class IX, occupation needlework.

Contact : Mazharul Islam Taru.

Nakshi kantha here is known as carpet kantha. Different types are made like sujni lep, asan, coverlet, jaynamaz etc. The designs are many like hills, flowers, snails, crabs etc. Girls stitch kanthas throughout the year but mostly during the rainy season. The kanthas have three or five layers, girls make their own designs or buy these, rates varying from Rs. 3 to thirty rupees, depending on size of kantha. Lep or sujni takes six months, asan or pillow cover about a fortnight. The alpana is popular, particularly in lep kanthas, as also floral and geometric designs. The practice of gifting kanthas at the daughters' wedding is followed. Kantha making is a means of livelihood in these villages.

Jessore

1. City College Para, Kotwali P.S.

Informant : Shankari Roy (25), husband, Jiban Roy, education, passed SSC, occupation needlework.

Contact : Rabeya Khatun.

2. Manirampur village, Manirampur P.S.

Informant : Ruksana Parveen (23) husband, Shakil Ahmed, education, passed SSC, occupation needlework.

Contact : Rubeya Khatun.

Situated near Jessore town, both villages have mixed population though kanthas are made mostly by the Muslims. Kanthas made throughout the year. Rayon used and borders first outlined, then designs imprinted either by the women themselves or by somebody else. Designs and motifs are varied and so are the stitches.

3. Hanwar village, Manirampur P.S.

(*a*) **Informant :** Mafia Begum (45), husband, Tabibar Rahman, education, read up to class V, occupation, needlework.

(*b*) **Informant :** Sufia Begum (35), husband, Muntaj Sardar, education, nil, occupation, needlework.

(*c*) **Informant :** Kanij Fatema Baby (25), father

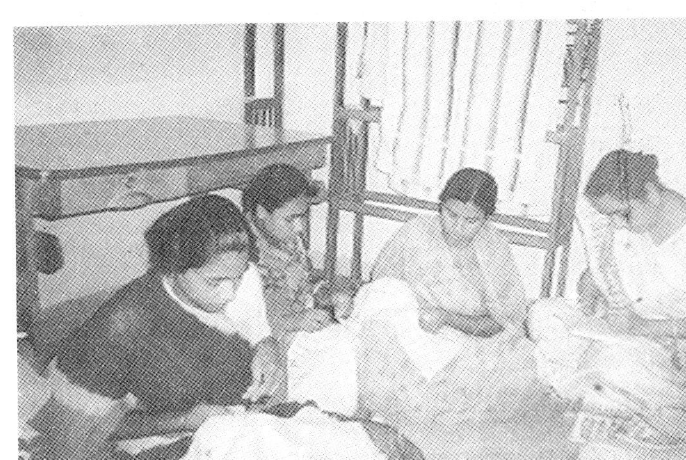

202. Artists at work, Jamalpur.

Gaji Mohammed Abdul Gaji, education, preparing for graduation, occupation needlework.

Contact : Aratirani Sarkar.

About 250 families live in Hanwar most of whom are Muslims. Women make nakshi kanthas during leisure hours, more during monsoon than other months. It is a means of livelihood particularly for the poor women, though kanthas are also gifted. The time taken to make one depends on size and design. The Hanwar Kanthas are renowned for their beauty.

Kusthia

Barkhada village, Sadar, Kusthia, P.S.

(a) **Informant :** Chhabia Begum (30) husband, Khairul Islam, education, can sign her name, occupation, housewife.

(b) **Informant :** Shilarani Ghosh (22), father Amarendranath Ghosh, education, read up to class X, occupation, needlework.

(c) **Informant :** Reena Begum (25), husband, Mansur, education, read upto class V, occupation, needlework.

Contact: Syed Ehsanuddin Ahmed.

Located near Kusthia town the village, like adjoining villages, has a mixed population. Muslims women, more than the Hindus, make kanthas and for some of them it is a means of livelihood. It is also customary to give kanthas as gifts. Like elsewhere here also the art has come down through generations. The designs are first drawn then embroidered with two types of thread. The threads are either 'multi' (red, blue, green, black, yellow, orange, violet) or 'vegetables' (light shades), for working inside the kantha. The kanthas here are three-layered, designs on the surface ranging from animals and flowers to fish on a plate. In Kusthia, good kanthas are to be had at Milpara, Barkhada, Baliapara, Swastipur, Lahini Para.

Khulna

Sheikhpara village, Chuadanga P.S.

Informant : Momena Khatun, (42), education nil, occupation needlework.

Contact: Imran

Mixed population, including Christian and Buddhists. Agriculture main occupation. Apart from needlework, fishing nets are also made with nylon. Criminal tendencies can be noticed, once the abode of armed 'Sheikhs', hence the name.

The kanthas of Khulna have their own characteristics. The borders are designed with pictures of scenic beauty. Kanthas are generally three-layered and two if the design is very heavy. The designs are first drawn. The motifs include houses, flowers and plants, deer, lotus, masjid etc. Earlier threads used to be drawn from sari borders, now bought from the fishermen and coloured. The kanthas are used in the homes and also gifted. It is the Muslim women who are more engaged in kantha making, learning the art from their elders.

Faridpur

Hijalbari village, Kotalipara P.S.

Informant : Usha Ojha (Mazumdar), husband Shyamalkanti Ojha, education B. Sc, occupation needlework.

Contact: Safiqul Islam.

Kanthas are made mostly by the poorer sections of the Muslim community as a means of livelihood. A fine sense of art helps them to embroider the design without drawing these first. Generally the border is first made. A large kantha takes six months if made by a single person or around two months if there are more than one working on it. Good nakshi kanthas are to be seen in the Rajbari area.

Jamalpur

Beltia village, Jamalpur P.S.

(a) **Informant :** Hamida Khatun (25), husband, Akhtar Uzzaman, education, nil, occupation, needlework.

(b) **Informant :** Anju Begum (35) husband, Abdul Halim, education, nil, occupation, needlework.

203. Kantha made by Raushan Nihar Bibi and Ayesha Khatun, Kendradangal, Birbhum.

204. Kantha made by Haji Jobeda Bibi, Birbhum.

205. Artist Usha Mazumdar, Hijalbari, Faridpur

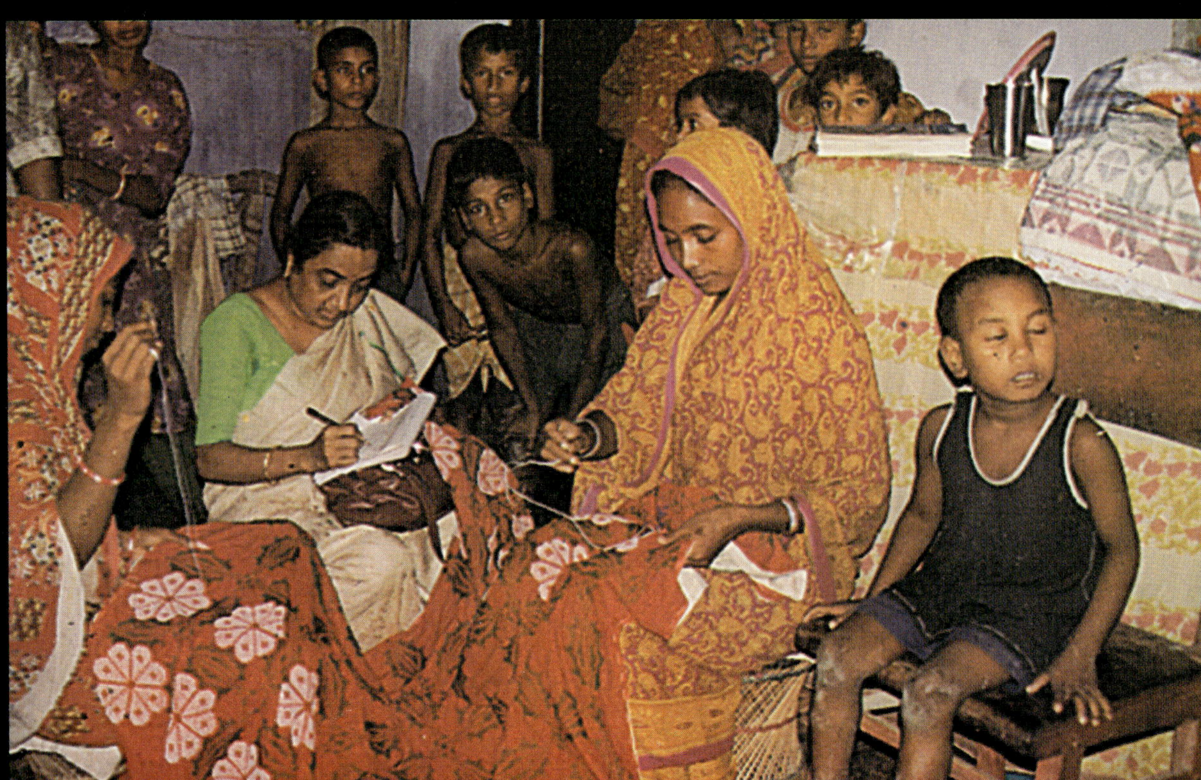

206.Jahanara Begum and Nurunessa Begum.
Dariapur. Champainababganj

207. Kantha by Rajia Bibi, Sansat, Birbhum.

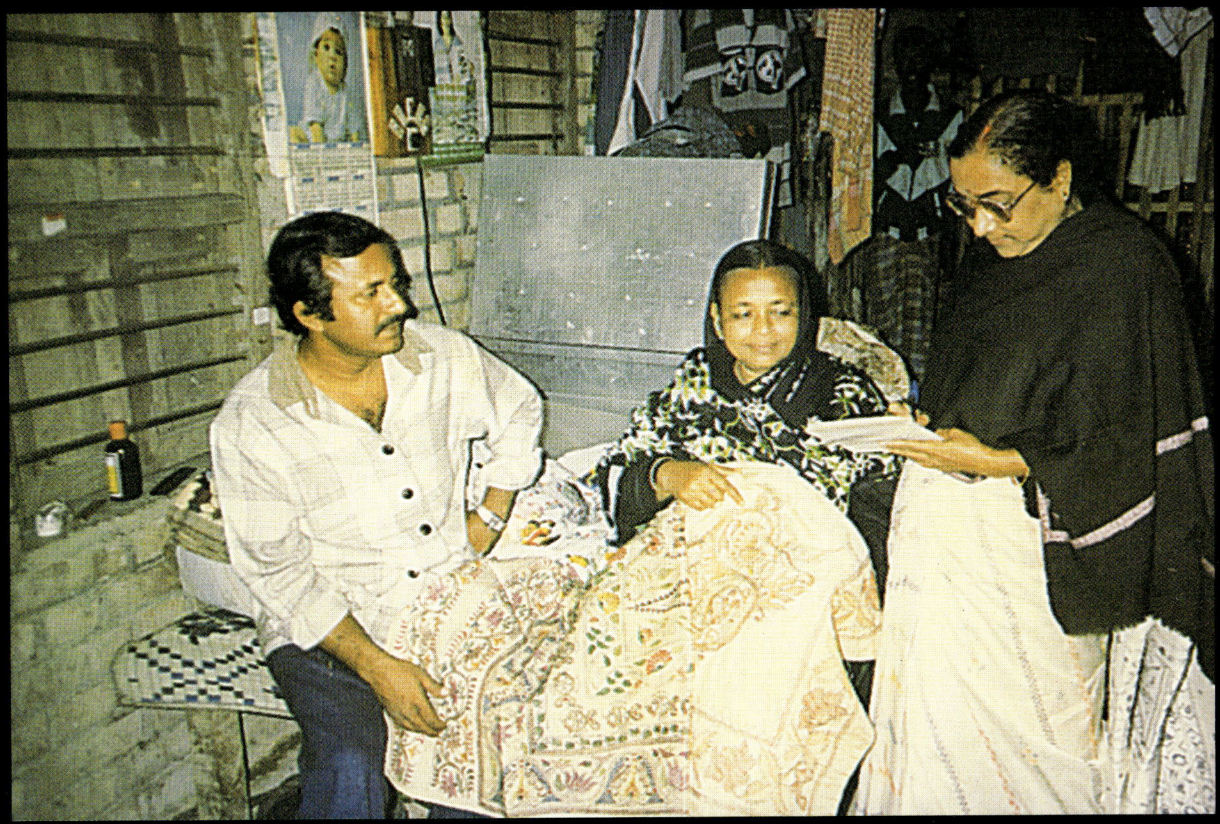

208. Amina Begum, Niramisa, North 24 Parganas.

209. Women making kantha, Hanwar village, Jessore.

210. Women making kantha, Beltia, Jamalpur.

211. Kantha-Nasima Khatun, Champainababganj.

212.Kantha-Alwara Bibi, Amina Bazar, Murshidabad.

213. Kantha-Momena Bibi, Mahidpur, Birbhum.

214. Kantha-Nanjura Khatun, Kuthipara, Birbhum.

215. Kantha-Rina Begum, Barkhada, Kushthia.

216. Kantha-Natu Saha, Chittagong.

217. Kantha-Amina Bibi, Bhuera, Burdwan.

218. Kantha-Ashalata Dey, Machpota, Nadia

219. Kantha-Mitali Das, Chechuria, Chittagong.

220. Kantha-Sakina Bibi, Saikir Para, Birbhum

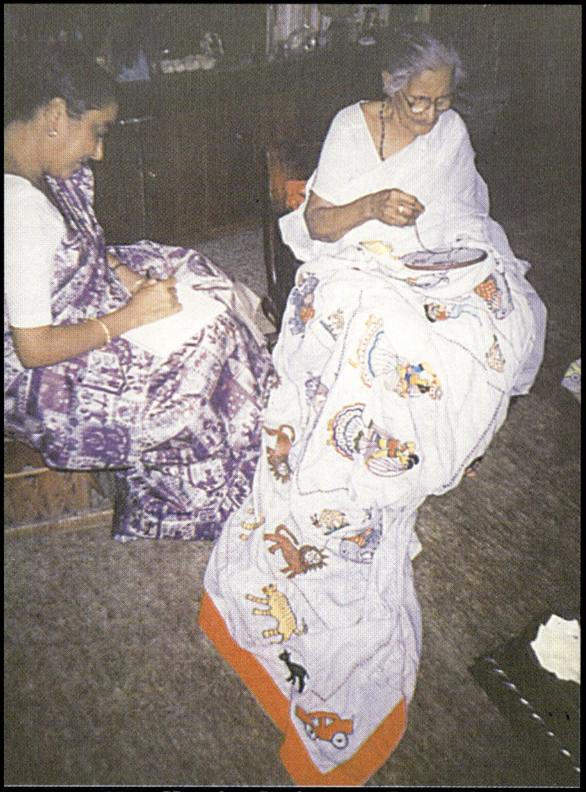

221. Kantha-Jinduprova Devi, Dhaka.

222. Kantha-Makhan and Begum Munia Bibi sherpur

223. Kantha-Fultun Bibi, Harisabhapara, Birbhum.

224. Kantha-Hasina Shahnaz, Margram, Birbhum

(c) **Informant :** Ratna Begum (25) husband, Bipul Hossain, education, nil, occupation, needlework.

Contact : Kamal Chakravarty.

Kantha making is widespread in Jamalpur. Here the women are particularly skilled and began stitching from a very early age. The kanthas are designed from the centre and the ends stitched with uneven 'run's or the 'taga'. The kanthas are generally of three layers with backing in between. Rayon and 'Sonamukhi' needle are used. Of the motifs the elephant is most popular, the others being horse, fish, snake, peacock, butterfly, kalka, the *chalta* flower (a kind of sour fruit, known locally as mushri—this motif is also highly popular), temple, mosque etc. Jamalpur's style of filling up the kantha is similar to Jessore and Kusthia but unlike Rajsahi where the cross stitch is more in vogue. In Jamalpur it is the 'run' which is seen more often. In the borders, the 'pati' is often seen designed, pati being a kind of mat made with the barks of trees.

Sherpur

Krishnapur Daripara village, Sherpur P.S.

Informant : Makhan Begum (35), husband Shahjahan Mistri, education, nil, occupation, needlework.

Contact : Rafiqul Islam.

Different designs and motifs are seen in the kanthas here. Many women engaged in the work here.

Rangpur

Mosudkhan Chowdhurani village, Pirgachha P.S.

Informant : Sona Begum (30), husband, Mohammed Yusuf Ali, education, nil, occupation, housewife.

Contact : Ishtiaque Hasan.

The stitches used are both even and uneven. Different types of designs and stitches can be seen.

Chittagong

Informant : Jinduprova Devi (87), husband, Hariranjan Chowdhury.

Contact : Chandrasekhar Saha.

Doing needlework from the age of 12, Jinduprova has won awards. The designs she embroiders are in keeping with the changing times. For instance her 'Khelna' kantha (toy kantha) which has motifs of different cars and animals. The marigold is sebn very commonly in kanthas here.

Chechuria village, Jaldi P.S.

Informant : Mitali Das (25), occupation, needlework.

Contact : Shubhra Chowdhury.

Mixed population, Muslim women generally make ordinary kanthas and Hindus the nakshi kantha. At least two kanthas are given when a girl gets married. Coverlets, bedcover, asan, pillow-covers are a source of income. The 'run' is the main stitch, known as 'shoja' (straight) in Chittagong. For asan, the cross stitch is also used. The designs include eye of the pineapple, sheaves or corn, *chalta* flower.

Shabek Rangunia village, Rangunia P.S.

Informant : Natu Saha (35) husband Kajal Saha, occupation, needlework when time permits.

Contact: Pakhi Saha.

Thick kanthas are used as quilts and also bedspread. Creepers, nuts, *chalta* flower, sheaves of corn and alpana at the centre can be seen in the kanthas here. Stitches are chain, cross, shadework.

Appendix - B

In Museums and Individual Collections

The search for the nakshi kantha took me beyond West Bengal, to other states and Bangladesh. The following is a list of kanthas that I found in museums and homes of individuals.

Gurusaday Museum, Calcutta

The museum has 201 Kanthas collected by Gurusaday Dutta between 1929 and 1940. There is also one made by Ms Marimuchi Suki of Japan. Of the 201 Kanths, 14 are Lep Kantha, 52 Sujni, 94 Betan, 19 Arshilata, 12 Durjani, 8 Handkerchiefs, three pillow- covers. Of these 161 are from districts like Jessore, Khulna, Faridpur, Rajsahi, Dhaka, which comprise the present Bangladesh and two from West Bengal. The origin of rest is unknown.

Five of the Kanthas are Dorokha:

GM 1841 Sujni, Khulna, by Manadasundari Dasya, approx. 19th century

GM 1514 Betan

GM 1532 Betan, Jessore

GM 1571, Sujni

GM 1579 Betan, Jessore

Five of the kanthas have the maker's name sewn on them. They are Anantabala Devi (GM 1428), Rahima Khatun (GM 1438), Chapalabala Roy (GM 1475), Manadasundari Dasya (GM 1481) and Shibani Bala (GM 1482).

Full details of the exhibits:

1. GM 1425 $8'11\frac{1}{2}''$ × $5'\frac{1}{2}''$, Lep Kantha, Jessore, early 20th century. Three lines of geometric pattern on white surface, embroidered lotus bud border and embroidered designs on four ends.
2. GM 1426 5′6″ × 4′1″, Sujni, Jessore, 19th century. Lotus at the centre and birds, elephants, boat, household items all over the surface. Geometric patterns in the borders.
3. GM 1427 5′2″ × 3′2″, Sujni, Jessore, approx. 19th century. Half moon border design, lotus at centre and motifs of animals, fish, birds, hand, fans, one mirror, one umbrella and nut cracker.
4. GM 1428 5′1″ × 3′10″, Sujni, Jessore, artiste Anantabala Devi, early 20th century. Lotus motif at centre and all around. Also birds, flowers, fish, human figures, trees, animals etc.
5. GM 1429 6′4″ × $4'4\frac{1}{2}''$, Sujni, Jessore, approx. 19th century. Circular alpana design with lotus and round floral designs round the lotus. Lotus also at four ends. Surface motifs include man on elephant, horse rider, man with fan in hand, peacock, umbrella etc.

6. GM 1430 6′4″ × 4′7″, Sujni, Khulna, approx. 19th century. Motifs of flowers, trees, animals and women in different pose.

7. GM 1431 $4'7\frac{1}{2}''$ × 3′2″, Sujni, Birbhum, early 20th century. Floral designs along the borders, lotus at centre and motifs of lotus, tiger, elephant etc. outlined.

8. GM 1432 2′7″ × 2′6″, Betan, Jessore, approx 19th century. Black thread used for designs on white surface.

9. GM 1433 $2'7\frac{1}{2}''$ × 2′6″, Betan. Lotus at centre, 12 geometric patterns in borders, motifs of pink peacock, fish, animals, small flowers etc.

10. GM 1434 4′8″ × $3'1\frac{1}{2}''$, Sujni, Khulna, approx. 19th century. Five types of geometric and floral designs in borders, lotus at centre, four wishing trees (myth) at four ends etc.

11. GM 1435 7′7″ × $4'2\frac{1}{2}''$, Lep, Jessore, early 20th century, Parallel floral designs on four sides; four embroideries, birds and flowers. Cosmic lotus at centre. Cows, horses, birds and dog on one side, human figures and man with bird.

12. GM 1436 7′1″ × 4′1″, Lep, Khulna, early 20th century. Geometric patterns on four sides tree with cosmic lotus at centre, four lotus at four ends, girl with bird, boy and girl sitting on bed, girl standing with sari end in hand. The motifs of girls resemble patas of Kalighat (pata: typical Bengali painting of women on clay).

13. GM 1437, 6′6″ × $4'4\frac{1}{2}''$, Sujni. Flower patterns on borders, white surface. Designs of 12 lines sewn with multicoloured threads.

14. GM 1438 $6'1\frac{1}{2}''$ × 4′7″, Sujni, Faridpur, early 20th century. Artiste Rahima Khatun. Written on kantha, "forget me not" — Rahima Khatun, Borders showing creepers, same in the middle, fish, bird, lion, tree, mango, flower, house, umbrella, aeroplane, knife, gun, flying bird (written flying fish).

15. GM 1439 $6\frac{1}{2}''$ × 3′9″ Sujni. Designed borders on four sides. Small square geometric designs all over, floral designs at centre and also on four sides.

16. GM 1440 5′8″ × $3'6\frac{1}{2}''$, Sujni. Lotus at centre, designed borders, four embroideries on four corners. Triangular creepers designed.

17. GM 1441 $5'1\frac{1}{2}''$ × $3'4\frac{1}{2}''$, Sujni. Five lines of floral, geometric and peacock designs. Lotus at centre and quare lotus motif at four corners. Many birds, tigers, fish, horses and human figures, elephant with howdah etc.

18. GM 1442 4′8″ × 3′, Sujni, Jessore. Different floral and geometric patterns on four sides. Lotus at centre and two kalkas embroidered together and many single kalka embroidered. Chariot, tree, wishing tree, horse, monkey, fish, peacock, tiger, lion, elephant, dog, girl between two elephants, man standing on lion etc. as motifs.

19. GM 1443 $5'4\frac{1}{2}''$ × 3′9″, Sujni, Jessore, approx 19th century. Borders with geometric patterns and four kalka embroidered on four corners.

20. GM 1444 6′11″ × 4′7″, Sujni, Jessore, early 20th century. Two lines of creepers designed all around. Tree with flowers and a peacock sitting on top at centre, round which are two lines of design and one-sided blossoming flowers with leaves on one side.

21. GM 1445 5′5″ × 4′, Sujni, Khulna, approx. 19th century. Row of birds in the middle and around it in three borders rows of horses and human figures, their hands above their heads.

22. GM 1446 5′1″ × $3'7\frac{1}{2}''$, Sujni, Faridpur, approx. 19th century. A tree in the middle

with two birds sitting on it. Four trees, one in each corner, borders with creeper designs.

23. GM 1447 $5'\frac{1}{2}''$ × 4′1″, Sujni, Jessore, early 20th century. Lotus in the centre, a tree in each of the four corners, a horse, human figures, small lotus, elephants, peacocks, fish and bird motif. Creeper designs outlined in borders.

24. GM 1448 $5'4\frac{1}{2}''$ × 3′4″, Sujni, Faridpur, approx. 19th century. Trees in four corners, three lotus standing straight in centre, round which are circular rings. On one side 15 fish and on other side different birds, animals and man on horseback, two hubble bubbles. Six cows and two dogs on one side and knife and spoon on the other, a pair of scissors etc.

25. GM 1449 $4'11\frac{1}{2}''$ × 3′1″, Sujni, Jessore, approx. 19th century. Three trees, many birds and kalka, hand fan, nutcracker, winnow, hand mirror etc. as motifs. Three lines of border at centre forming a square, three kalkas one at each end and nose ring as motif.

26. GM 1450 5′3″ × $3'5\frac{1}{2}''$, Sujni, Central lotus with trees in four corners, the whole surface has creeper designs. In addition floral patterns, many animals, peacock and fish, winnow, skull. Kalka design around the borders.

27. GM 1451 $4'10\frac{1}{2}''$, × 3′2″, Sujni, Jessore, early 20th century. Central lotus, round which rows of human figures, four flowers, four kalka at the ends. Four figures on one side and on other five wearing foreign clothes. Thin two-lined designs on two sides of the border. Human figures also at an angle with the border, kalka, flower, hat etc. as motif.

28. GM 1452 6′ × 3′8″, Sujni, Khulna, approx. 19th century. Very thin border. The whole divided into diamond shape and full of floral designs. Each portion has many kalka and birds.

29. GM 1453 $5'6\frac{1}{2}''$ × $3'7\frac{1}{2}''$, Sujni, Kalka on border on four sides, floral and geometric designs, flowers at centre with design shaped as human eye.

30. GM 1454 6′ × 3′9″, Sujni, Thin two lined border. Nineteen lines of flower and geometric patterns all over.

31. GM 1455 7′2″ × 4′6″, Lep, Jessore, approx. 19th century. Lotus centre, round which two lines of creepers and geometric designs. Kalka and lion at each of four corners, four floral designs.

32. GM 1456 $5'3\frac{1}{2}''$ × $3'5\frac{1}{2}''$, Sujni, Central lotus and kalka at corners. Five thread with flowers, betel-leaf, nut-cracker, winnow, fork and spoon, mattres, moon etc. Eight line border with kalka, fish, geometric patterns.

33. GM 1457 6′ × 4′2″, Sujni, Khulna, approx. 19th century. Small flowers and birds at centre, creeper designs in borders, horse, elephant, kalka etc.

34. GM 1458 6′7″ × 4′3″, Sujni, Khulna, approx. 19th century, kalka at centre, also in 12 lines at borders and different geometric patterns. Kalka in four corners. Bright red and black needlework on white surface and also yellow and blue designs.

35. GM 1459 5′3″ × 3′6″, Sujni, Jessore, approx. 19th century. Lotus at centre, round which elephant, human figures, peacock, horse, tiger, fish etc. Kalka at corners and on sides all around men on horseback, on elephants, birds, peacock, snake, fish and rows of men (perhaps soldiers), trees, kalka, floral designs, geometric patterns, a man with snakes on head and shoulders etc.

36. GM 1460 6′11″ × $5'8\frac{1}{2}''$, Sujni. Jessore, approx. 19th century. Two birds on either side, floral design at centre, kalka in corners and geometric patterns in border.

37. GM 1461, 6'8 $\frac{1}{2}$" × 4'8$\frac{1}{2}$", Sujni. Eighteen strips of designs, flowers and geometric patterns in borders.

38. GM 1462 6'6" × 4'8$\frac{1}{2}$", Sujni. Four kalka in corners, geometric patterns in borders.

39. GM 1463 4'6$\frac{1}{2}$" × 3'3$\frac{1}{2}$", Sujni. Jessore, approx. 19th century. Lotus at centre next to which men on elephant, cows, fish, horses, lions, dogs, cats, deer flowers, three men, many women etc.

40. GM 1464 6'3$\frac{1}{2}$" × 4'2", Sujni. Jessore, 19th century. Big lotus at centre, kalka at corners, human figures, men on elephants, peacock, wild boar, birds, lion, one strange figure – face of girl and body of animal. Kalka, fish and geometric patterns in eight lines in borders.

41. GM 1465 6'4$\frac{1}{2}$" × 4'3", Sujni, approx. 19th century. Central lotus with flowers all around, fish, geometric pattern, trees with birds on four corner, camel, elephant, man on horseback, winnow, peacock, kalkas with floral designs in four corners.

42. GM 14667 '$\frac{1}{2}$" × 4'10", Lep, Jessore, approx. 19th century. Girl with folded hands in centre, four kalka in four corners with flowers on either side. Geometric pattern in border.

43. GM 1467 5'8$\frac{1}{2}$" × 3'8", Sujni. Jessore, approx. 19th century. Central lotus, kalka in four corners, different motifs like man on elephant, man on horse, five human figures, snake and peacock, fish, monkey, tree with flowers. Geomeric and floral designs of five lines in border, lines of kalka, men with guns and dancing girls.

44. GM 1468 6'1$\frac{1}{2}$" × 4'1", Sujni. Central lotus and creeper designs divide the whole kantha into small squares.

45. GM 1469 5'10$\frac{1}{2}$" × 3'11$\frac{1}{2}$", Sujni. Central lotus round which are many flowers, four leaves one in each corner. Geometric designs round the border.

46. GM 1470 6'5" × 4', Sujni. Khulna, approx. 19th century. Kalka designs at centre, geometric and floral designs in borders.

47. GM 1471 5'9" × 4'5$\frac{1}{2}$", Sujni. Faridpur, approx. 19th century. Central lotus and birds around it. Animals, fish and human figures, peacock shaped boat, temple, chariot etc. outlines of design in borders.

48. GM 1472 6'5$\frac{1}{2}$" × 4'5$\frac{1}{2}$", Sujni. Central lotus with kalka in four corners, four elephants around lotus.

49. GM 1473 7'1$\frac{1}{2}$" × 4'9", Lep. Central lotus, around which conch shell creepers. Next this chariot, human figures, man on elephant. Many lotus, flowers, kalka and designs, birds, animals, tree in each corner and two lines of geometric pattern in border.

50. GM 1474 7'3" × 4'4" Lep. Jessore. The whole kantha is covered with outlines of creeper designs shaped as barfis.

51. GM 1475 6'4" × 4', Lep. Jessore approx. 19th century. White surface with artist's name, Chapalabala Roy, at centre. Four colourful kalkas, one at each corner, thin designs in borders. Red, white and black threads used and small runs stitched on the surface.

52. GM 1476 4'2$\frac{1}{2}$" × 2'10", Sujni. Jessore, approx. 20th century. Thin borders of geometric patterns, a girl worshipping at centre. On one said paddy being husked outside a hut, a holy man, elephant, goat and horse. On other sides, kitchen, cat, fish being sliced, elephant, horse, goat and two banana trees. Also bride and groom going in palanquin with musicians, a brahmin and people carrying gifts on their heads, curd seller etc.

53. GM 1477 5′9″ × 3′7$\frac{1}{2}$″, Sujni. Jessore, approx. 19th century. Central lotus, kalka with bird on each of four corners, Round the lotus, man, horse, man on horse, kalka, birds, peacock, man playing flute, feudal lord being fanned by a man, one standing with horn, two elephants fighting. Fish motif in one line of border and geometric pattern in the other.

54. GM 1478 4′7$\frac{1}{2}$″ × 3′8″, Sujni, Jessore, approx. 19th century. Central lotus, around it flowers, betel-leaf, fish, rows of elephants, soldiers, bird. Kalka in five lines in border also geometric patterns and creepers.

55. GM 1479 4′11″ × 3′6″, Sujni, Faridpur, approx. 19th century. Lotus in centre. Kantha divided into six parts. In first part, four girls with pitchers in arms. In second man and woman citting on chairs, one mendicant and one guard. In part three, man sitting, horse with rider, bird. In fourth landlord smoking, dog, wrestlers fighting monkey, dancing woman. In fifth, scene of hunter in a chariot, two with guns about to hunt animals. Tiger, buffalo, deer, cats, rats, peacock running away. In sixth part men fighting where Ramanikanta Ghosh is written. Flowers, kalka and geometric pattern in borders. On three corners blossoming flower, tree with leaves and on one corner flower and peacock.

56. GM 1480 5′$\frac{1}{2}$″ × 3′5$\frac{1}{2}$″, Sujni. Jessore, approx. 19th century. Central lotus with flower trees around it, peacock, bird, human figure, betel-leaf, nutcracker, pinri (wooden seat) etc. as motifs. Border have horse on one side, man on horse back, rows of elephants and birds on creepers on the other. Kalka on border on one side and opposite it geometric patterns.

57. GM 1481 5′6″ × 3′10″2′ Sujni, Khulna, approx 19th century. It is a Dorokha kantha made with exceptional skill. Well decorated lotus motif at centre, round which are rows of kalka and name of artiste: "This Sujni in made by me Manadasunder Dasya, daughter of Baradakanta Basu of Dangal Badhal. I have made it with my hands and gifted it with my respects to my father. Any faults may kindly be excused". The motifs and drawings in the kantha include rows of soldiers, girl sitting at window, horse drawn carriage, three men on elephant, lobster, tree, insect. Bird, feudal lord watching dancing girls, monkey. Kadam tree in each corner, floral and geometric pattern in border. Many motifs resemble the typical pictures of 'pat' or scroll paintings of Kalighat.

58. GM 1482, 6′5$\frac{1}{2}$″ × 4′4″, Lep, Faridpur, approx. 19th century. Kantha made by three generations. Central lotus and lotus on all sides, kalka on each corner. Inside mango trees, mirror, combs, umbrella, nutcracker, lamp holder, vessel for preparing colireum, sun, half moon and star, etc. as motif.

59. GM 1483 2′2$\frac{1}{2}$″ × 7$\frac{1}{2}$″, Arsilata, Dhaka, approx. 19th century. Three lengthwise lotus in centre, Durga on one side, Radha—Krishna on other side, bird in each corner and thin border.

60. GM 1484 11′$\frac{1}{2}$″ × 7$\frac{1}{2}$″, Sujni Jessore, approx. 20th century. Kantha made by Parulbala Sarkar. It has lotus and other motif.

61. GM 1485 8′$\frac{1}{2}$″ × 9$\frac{1}{2}$″, Rumal, Khulna, approx. 19th century. Flowers in centre, four fish on four sides. Many types of flowers and kalka. In four corner flower with two leaves and geometric pattern in border.

62. GM 1486 1′9″ × 7′, Arsilata, Faridpur, approx. 19th century. Four lotus on thin border. Geometric pattern and kalka on border at end.

63. GM 1487 2′10″ × 2′7$\frac{1}{2}$″, Betan, Faridpur, approx. 19th century. Central lotus, wish fulfilling tree in four corners, motifs of

elephant, lion, cow, small human figures, insects, peacock, mice around lotus, geometric design in border.

64. GM 1488 2′9″ × 2′6″, Betan, Faridpur, approx. 19th century. Central lotus, tree in four corners, human figures, elephant, chariot, two peacocks with snakes in mouth, mermaid, small tree, three human figures, many flowers.

65. GM 1489 2′5″ × $1''10\frac{1}{2}''$, Betan, Jessore, approx. 19th century. Creepers in centre four lines of geometric, floral and kalka designs in borders.

66. GM 1490 2′7″ × 2′, Betan, Jessore, approx. 19th century. Lines of creeper designs all over and geometric patterns in borders.

67. GM 1491 3′1″ × 2′11″, Betan , Jessore, approx. 19th century. Central lotus, around it scenes from the tales of Krishna and Radha, kalka in borders, geometric patterns in border.

68. GM 1492 2′8″ × $2'7\frac{1}{2}''$, Betan. Lotus in centre. Kalka in four corners, around lotus motifs of horse, elephant, goat, bird, pineapple, flowers etc. Floral and geometric patterns in borders.

69. GM 1493 2′9″ × $2'7\frac{1}{2}''$, Betan, Jessore, approx. 19th century. Central lotus, around it elephant with driver, dog, bird, peacock, fish, kalka, horse, lion, tree in two corners, rows of kalka and flower in border.

70. GM 1494 4′ × 3′ Betan. Lotus in centre and around it flower, trees, small lotuses, flower buds, mirror, knife, broad borders with geometric pattern.

71. GM 1495 $3'2\frac{1}{2}''$ × $1'9\frac{1}{2}''$, Betan, Jessore. A triangular kantha, wish fulfilling tree in centre and around it motifs of creeper, flowers and birds. Fish designed in four corners.

72. GM 1496 2′7″ × 2′7″, Betan, Jessore. Central lotus, around it peacock on kalka, horse, man on elephant, peacock, betel-leaf, box of vermilion, lines of flower.

73. GM 1497 2′9″ × $2'11\frac{1}{2}''$, Betan, Jessore, approx. 19th century. Lotus in centre and geometric patterns in four borders.

74. GM 1498 2′10″ × 2′10″, Betan, Khulna, approx. 19th century. Lotus in centre and around it kalka, elephant, lion, small insects, fox, cow, peacock, fish, tiger, bird, man with animal cubs, squirrel, geometric patterns in border.

75. GM 1499 2′9″ × $2'5\frac{1}{2}''$, Betan, Faridpur, approx. 19th century, Lotus in centre and around it elephant, bird, lion, cow, tree, bear with rope round noose, flower shaped kalka in four corners and geometric pattern in border.

76. GM 1500 1′7″ × $1'7\frac{1}{2}''$, Betan, Khulna, approx. 19th century, Lotus in centre, around it four fish, four birds, four kalkas one in each corner, geometric pattern in borders.

77. GM 1501 $2'4\frac{1}{2}''$ × $2'3\frac{1}{2}''$, Betan, Khulna, approx. 19th century, Lotus in centre, around it kalka, trees, lines of flowers and fish, geometric patterns in border.

78. GM 1502 $2'9\frac{1}{2}''$ × $2'\frac{1}{2}''$, Betan, Jessore, approx. 19th century, one line of geometric pattern at centre. Six lines of border with rows of elephant in two, geometric pattern in one, floral designs in one and rows of elephants in remaining two lines.

79. GM 1503 $1'10\frac{1}{2}''$ × 1′9″, Betan. Central lotus, fish, peacock, tree and flower around it, kalka in each corner and broad border with rows of kalka.

80. GM 1504 3′ × 2′10″, Betan, Khulna, approx. 19th century. Lotus in centre, around it chariot, fish, peacock, kalka, tree, elephant, Bhagirath ushering in Ganga, (myth) man on horseback, wish fulfilling tree in four corners, kalka and floral design in two borders.

81. GM 1505 2′5″ × 2′5″, Betan, Jessore, approx. 19th century, Lotus in centre, around it human figures, butterfly etc. Lotus motif in four corners. Borders on three sides of central motif have motifs of elephant, horse, bird and lotus. In one border geometric patterns in black thread.

82. GM 1506 2′6″ × 2′2″, Betan, Jessore. Triangular pattern, lotus in centre, around it four decorated kalkas, peacock, fish around lotus, creeper and geometric patterns in borders.

83. GM 1507 2′10″ × 2′9″ , Betan, Faridpur, Central lotus, kalka in four corners, floral, creeper and kalka designs on border.

84. GM 1508 2′9″ × 2′ $6\frac{1}{2}$″, Betan, Faridpur. Lotus in centre, wish fulfilling tree in four corners, around lotus tree with flowers, leaves and other motif, floral and geometric pattern in borders.

85. GM 1509 2′3″ × 2′3″, Betan, Faridpur, approx. 19th century. Lotus in centre, around it motifs of knife,winnow, spoon, fan, betel-leaf, elephant etc. of four trees in corners three have identical leaves. Geometric pattern in borders.

86. GM 1510 1′$10\frac{1}{2}$″ × 1′6″, Betan. Borders have red sari borders and lotus design embroidered with white thread all over.

87. GM 1511 3′ × 3′, Betan, Jessore. Lotus in centre, peacocks in four corners and around lotus figures of primitive man, fish, figures in European style, elephant, man on horseback, rows of elephants. Kalka, floral and geometric patterns in borders.

88. GM 1512 3′3″ × 2′11″, Betan, Faridpur, approx 19th century. Lotus in centre, wish fulfilling tree in four corners, lotus, fish, bird, elephant, man on horseback, peacock, human figures, monkeys and floral designs in borders.

89. GM 1513 2′10″ × 2′9′, Betan, Jessore. Lotus in centre, flower in four corners, around lotus, fish, bird, big lotus, ape, dog, crocodile, man on horseback, elephant, flower, Shiva linga in temple, hanging lantern, winnow, mother and child, guard with stick, man sitting on bed with umbrella in hand, three boatmen, landlord with hookah, two in peacock shaped boat. Thin borders with geometric patterns.

90. GM 1514 3′6″ × 3′, Betan. Lotus in centre, around it birds, man with drum, archer, fish, Shive linga in temple, man on elephant, tiger, human figure, kalka, man with sword, dog sitting on horse, peacock, man sitting on chair etc. Floral and geometric patterns in borders.

91. GM 1515 2′$6\frac{1}{2}$″ × 1′11″, Betan, Khulna, approx. 19th century. Lengthwise floral, kalka and geometric patterns, floral and geometric patterns in borders.

92. GM 1516 2′10″ × 2′9″, Betan, Khulna, approx. 19th century. Temple in the square portion in the centre, man standing on horse facing man standing on tiger. Creeper and geometric patterns in border and also tiger and crocodile motif outlined.

93. GM 1517 1′11″ × 1′$9\frac{1}{2}$″, Betan, Faridpur. Lotus in centre, kalka in four corners, around lotus rows of fish and birds, floral and geometric patterns in borders.

94. GM 1518 2′2″ × 2″, Betan, approx. 19th century. Circular arrangement of flowers in centre, all around man with whip on horseback, gun, horse, dog, boar, man on elephant, running fox, peacock, snake, figures of man and woman, boy and girl facing each other, face of girl, geometric patterns outlined in borders.

95. GM 1519 2′10″ × 2′10″, Betan, Khulna. Lotus in centre, two kalkas in two corners and wish fulfilling tree in two others. Around lotus figures of four men, motifs of peacock etc. Creeper designs and rows of horses in borders.

96. GM 1520 2′9″ × 2′7″ , Betan, Jessore. The whole kantha divided into squares with geometric patterns. Kalka in four corners and

in one border. Geometric patterns in three other borders. Bright yellow colour amidst red and blue.

97. GM 1521 3′3″ × 2′11″, Betan, Rajsahi, early 20th century. Central lotus, flower in four corners, lines of geometric patterns in the middle with kalkas at each end. Shiva linga inside temple, flag in front of elephant, boar, shark, banana tree, lion, tiger, sitting man with hookah, dog, fish, umbrella, hunting bird, floral designs outlined. Geometric patterns in borders.

98. GM 1522 3′ $2\frac{1}{2}$″ × 3′1″, Betan, Khulna. Lotus in centre, trees all around. At one corner Krishna and Radha. King and queen sitting on thrones in a temple and people playing drum and cymbals before them. Horse with rider and men standing, severed hand of man, birds, peacock, frog, fish, elephant, etc. as motifs. Floral and geometric patterns in border.

99. GM 1523 2′ × 1′9″, Betan, Jessore, early 20th century. Red and black threads have made this kantha bright and colourful. Circular designs of flowers at centre, four kalkas at the square portion in the middle, two trains on two sides and two fish and four flowers in other two sides. Creeper designs with flowers in borders and geometric pattern in one border, black and light orange threads used. Red, black, orange and yellow threads used on the white surface of the kantha, as also grey thread.

100. GM 1524 $2\frac{1}{2}$″ × 2′, Betan, Faridpur. Central lotus, kalka, one in each corner, rows of fish and birds, kalka-shaped creepers on four sides and floral and geometric patterns in borders.

101. GM 1525 2′4″ × 1′10″, Betan, Jessore, early 20th century. Four lotus designed in centre, four kadam tree one in each corner, borders of geometric patterns.

102. GM 1526 2′9″ × 2′5″, Betan, Jessore, early 20th century. Lotus in centre, tree in corners, two kalka, one on each side, one fish on one side and three on other side.

103. GM 1527 2′3″ × 1′8″, Betan, Jessore, early 20th century. Lines of geometric patterns cover the whole kantha.

104. GM 1528 4′ $5\frac{1}{2}$″ × $3'2\frac{1}{2}$″, Betan. Lotus at centre, trees all around and borders of geometric patterns.

105. GM 1529 2′9″ × 2′5″, Betan, Khulna. Lotus at centre, Krishna under Kadam tree in corner. Round it geometric patterns, peacock , man on horseback, figure, crocodile, tiger, fish, man with gun, female figure, birds and deities like Kali, Ganga, Brahma.

106. GM 1530 2′18″ × $1'9\frac{1}{2}$″ , Betan , Jessore. Lotus at centre, decorated kalka on four corners, floral and geometric patterns in borders.

107. GM 1531 $2'10\frac{1}{2}$″ × 2′9″, Betan, Jessore, approx. 19th century. Central lotus and of four sides, parallel desigs of half lotus. One line of elephants and one of lotus and geometric patterns in borders.

108. GM 1532 2′10″ × $2'8\frac{1}{2}$″, Betan, Jessore, approx. 19th century. Lotus at centre and tree on all sides, peacock and snake. Trees on top of the border, Krishna coiled by snake, kalka, flower tree, birds, horse, man on elephant, chariot, bird, peacock, lion, crocodile, cow, creeper, woman and man at window, owl, crow, rats and king and queen on elephant back as motifs.

109. GM 1533 $2'6\frac{1}{2}$″ × 2′6″, Betan, Jessore, approx. 19th century. Lotus in centre, butterfly in four corners. Lines of elephant in one side, horses and lotus on the other sides.

110. GM 1534 2′ 8″ × 2′5″, Betan, Jessore, approx. 19th century. Lotus in centre, geometric patterns in border.

111. GM 1535 2′10″ × $2'5\frac{1}{2}''$, Betan. Lotus in centre, trees in four corners. Also standing figure of man and man on peacock, elephant and horse, man lying down. Deities include Kali, Mahadev, Durga on lion's back, Human figure and horses as motif. Borders have floral designs and motifs of tiger-lion and chariot.

112. GM 1536 2′8″ × 2′8″, Betan Khulna. Lotus in centre, tree on four corners. Also motifs of peacock, horse, butterfly, fish, flower and kalka. On four sides borders of parallel geometric patterns.

113. GM 1537 2′7″ × 2′1″, Betan Jessore, approx. 19th century. Four horses with wings (myth) at centre, around these creeper designs with lotus and kalka.

114. GM 1538 $3'2\frac{1}{2}''$ × 2′9″, Betan. Beautiful lotus designed at centre, trees in four corners, two birds, many fish. Four birds in four corners of the kantha. Borders designed with floral and geometric patterns.

115. GM 1539 $1'10\frac{1}{2}''$ × 1′10″, Betan, Jessore. Lotus in centre and motifs include three peacocks, many birds, fish, flower. Round the lotus three lines of geometric patterns.

116. GM 1540 3′8″ × 3′2″, Betan. Two flowers, four kalka and lotus at centre. On two sides of this creepers designed like conch-shells and fish.

117. GM 1541 $2'7\frac{1}{2}''$ × $2'6\frac{1}{2}''$, Betan, Khulna. Lotus in centre, kalka in four corners and many birds, elephant, cow, crocodile, lion with face like a man. Borders of four sides with geometric patterns.

118. GM 1542 2′11″ × 2′9″, Betan, Faridpur, approx. 19th century. Lotus in centre with three all around, also bird sitting on a branch, bird, peacock, king and queen, flower, fish, human figure, floral and geometric patterns in border.

119. GM 1543 3′ × 3′, Betan Jessore, approx. 19th century. Very bright and colourful kantha. Circular designs of flower at centre. Also multicoloured flowers. For kalkas one in each corner, two pictures of man on horseback, peacock, elephant, tiger, bird, fish, figures of man and woman, Shiva linga in temple etc. Geometric patterns in borders. Red, black, blue, green, yellow, sky blue, light orange threads used.

120. GM 1544 2′8″ × $2'6\frac{1}{2}''$, Betan, Khulna, approx. 19th century. Varied designs sewn with orange, black, ash coloured threads. Lotus in centre and square around it has trees, peacock on elephant, one big chariot, running horse, peacock with plumes spread, little chariot and flowers. Border has one fish and one kalka in one line and 16 such fish and kalkas made. In other border lines of geometric patterns.

121. GM 1545 2′10″ × $2'8\frac{1}{2}''$, Betan, Khulna. Lotus in centre, trees with borders in four corners. Lakshminarayan, man with child on shoulder, old woman, Ram and Sita, Lakshman, Radha-Krishna, peacock, tortoise, fish, elephant, and man on horseback, snake, bear etc. Creepers resembling geometric patterns in border.

122. GM 1546 $2'4\frac{1}{2}''$ × 2′7″, Betan, Faridpur, approx. 19th century. Lotus in centre, trees in four corners, knife, winnow, betel-leaf, two scissors, spoon, chair etc. Border has geometric patterns and fish-shaped creepers.

123. GM 1547 $2'\frac{1}{2}''$ × $1'11\frac{1}{2}''$, Betan, Jessore, early 20th century. Lotus in centre, trees in four corners flowers and a pair of fish on either side. On other two sides kalka. Geometric patterns in borders.

124. GM 1548 $3'4\frac{1}{2}''$ × 3′2″, Betan. Lotus in centre, tree in four corners. Also, chariot, peacock, elephant, fish, temple two Shiva lingas, Kali idol, budding flowers. One line

of geometric pattern in border and another of kalka, next line floral and then another line of geometric patterns.

125. GM 1549 2′ × 1′5″, cover, Jessore, approx. 19th century. Geometric patterns along three lines in centre and in borders on four sides.

126. GM 1550 4′5″ × 2′7$\frac{1}{2}$″, Betan. Triangular in shape with lotus in centre. Two flowers, butterfly, fish, horse, sheep, bird, deer, monkey, tiger, peacock, elephant, cow etc. Creeper designs on two sides of border and geometric patterns.

127. GM 1551 2′9$\frac{1}{2}$″ × 2′4$\frac{1}{2}$″, Betan, large lotus motif in centre, trees and Shiva linga, pair of peacocks and snake, tiger with man's head between jaws, elephant, birds, running horse, snake etc. Wide geometric patterns in border.

128. GM 1552 2′10$\frac{1}{2}$″ × 2′7$\frac{1}{2}$″, Betan. Lotus in centre, trees in four corners, Shiva Linga in temple, chariot, flower, tree, elephant, horse etc. Geometric patterns in border.

129. GM 1553 2′5″ × 2′4″, Betan, Khulna. Lotus in centre, four kalka one in each corner, two birds, one line of kalka creepers and another line of birds.

130. GM 1554 3′ 3$\frac{1}{2}$″ × 3′1″, Betan, Khulna. Lotus in centre, trees in two corners, one landlord sitting and being banned by one man and a guard standing, Durga image, Chandi with four hands killing Asura (demon), Kali with *dakini*, *yogini* (witch and demi goddess), pig, bird, hookah, lion and an European figure etc. Wide border on one side has geometric and conch-shell patterns.

131. GM 1555 3′ 2$\frac{1}{2}$″ × 2′5$\frac{1}{2}$″, Betan. Lotus in centre and lotus creepers round it, trees in four corners, two kalkas on two sides, and borders on four sides of creepers and geometric patterns.

132. GM 1556 3′ × 3′, Betan, Faridpur, approx. 19th century. Lotus in centre, kalka in four corners, two men on horseback, man with umbrella, man on horseback, man in standing pose, two men sitting on chairs, two Shiva linga, peacock, fish, tiger, flower tree, flower etc. Geometric pattern in one border.

133. GM 1557 3′9″ × 2′6″, Betan, Jessore. Lotus in centre of triangular kantha. Geometric patterns in four triangular borders parallel to one another. Rows of horses on two sides. Kalka and geometric patterns in one border.

134. GM 1558 2′6″ × 2′6″, Betan, Faridpur, approx. 19th century. Lotus in centre and around it figures like Krishna and Balaram with guns in hands. Figure of European man in boat with gun in hand, European woman, running horse, boar, peacock, lion, bird, fish, flower, tree, elephant and man on horseback, man sitting on chair etc. as motif. Creeper designs on one side of border and sari ends on other.

135. GM 1559 2′9″ × 2′7″, Betan, Jessore, approx. 19th century. Lotus in centre, bird sitting on half lotus in four corners. Also fish, snake, bird, kalka, etc. as motif. Geometric and creeper designs in border.

136. GM 1560 4′5$\frac{1}{2}$″ × 3′1″, Betan, Faridpur. Triangular kantha with lotus in centre, trees in four corners, row of birds in one side and kalka on other side, geometric patterns on border.

137. GM 1561 3′9$\frac{1}{2}$″ × 3′8″, Betan, Rajsahi, early 20th century. Small lotus in centre, motif of rhino in one creeper at centre and that of buffalo in another creeper, geometric patterns in third line, decorated kalka in four corners, line of elephants between centre and corner kalka, line of buffaloes, of tigers and of camels. Kalka lines on four sides and flower in creeper designs as also butterfly. Cut-work fringes in border.

138. GM 1562 3′ × 2′10″, Betan, Faridpur, approx. 19th century. Lotus in centre and human figures in different pose, kalka in four corners. Flower, Shiva linga, Radha Krishna, sitting Hanuman (monkey god), camel, elephant, horse, snake, bull, a man holding horse's reins, man on horseback, winnow, etc. as motif and creeper designs in border.

139. GM 1563 2′10″ × 2′7″, Betan, Jessore, approx. 19th century. Lotus in centre, tree in one corner, man on elephant, bird, camel, shark, horse, crown, two figures of man, fish, etc. and two lines of geometric pattern in border.

140. GM 1564 4′3″ × 2′10″, Betan, Jessore. Lotus in centre, man fighting with tiger, two tigers, three figures of men standing with legs crossed, boar, elephant, monkey, three trees in three corners, Hanuman (myth), peacock, bird, winnow, deer, horse, man on elephant and geometric patterns in border.

141. GM 1565 2′9″ × 2′5″, Betan, Faridpur, approx. 19th century. Lotus in centre, floral design in four corners, sari ends in border.

142. GM 1566 2′9″ × 2′8$\frac{1}{2}$″, Betan, Jessore, approx. 19th century. Lotus in centre, two peacocks on kalka in four corners. Also bird, elephant, horse, fish, flower, spoon, creeper designs of fish and geometric patterns in last lines of border.

143. GM 1567 2′3″ × 2′2$\frac{1}{2}$″, Betan, Lotus in square portion at centre and geometric pattern in two parallel borders.

144. GM 1568 2′10$\frac{1}{2}$″ × 2′10$\frac{1}{2}$″, Betan, Khulna, approx. 19th century. Lotus in centre, trees in four corners, on four sides fish, birds, frog, peacock, butterfly etc. Floral and geometric patterns in six lines of border.

145. GM 1569 3′7″ × 3′1″, Betan, Shiva sitting on his bull at centre, Krishna, Radha, Baraiburid, (liason between Krishna and Radha) Hanuman, small birds, peacock, flower, butterfly, archer, kalka etc, kalka and human figures in border and floral designs.

146. GM 1570 8′2″ × 5′2 ″, Lep, Jessore, approx. 19th century. Kalka in four corners, also along three lines in border, lotus and geometric patterns.

147. GM 1571 7′9$\frac{1}{2}$″ × 4′7$\frac{1}{2}$″, Sujni. Designs along wide borders, rows of kalka, kalka umbrella in four corners. Cutlined designs all over the kantha.

148. GM 1572 6′8″ × 4′10″, Sujni, early 20th century. Kalka in four corners, lotus in centre, round it creeper designs. Border with beautiful flowers and geometric patterns.

149. GM 1573 6′11$\frac{1}{2}$″ × 4′7″, Lep Jessore, approx. 19th century. A colourful kantha, circular floral designs in centre, 16 kalkas in four corners, four in each, two Jeevan Briksha (Tree of Life), four elephants, two on each side, five tigers on each side, motifs of bird, flower, butterfly etc. Kalka lines around border, two lines have similar designs on either side and different designs on other side, geometric patterns in the last border. Red, yellow, brown threads used in the kantha.

150. GM 1574 8′ × 4′10″, Lep, Jessore, approx. 19th century. Lotus in centre, four kalkas in different coloured threads bunched in each of four corners, rest stitched with white thread.

151. GM 1575 6′5$\frac{1}{2}$″ × 4′2″, Lep, Khulna, approx. 19th century. Lotus in centre and on four sides of it chariots, trees, rows of fish, lion, bird, butterfly, figures of men, elephant, and man on horseback, peacock, cow, human figure in European dress etc. Kalka and geometric pattern in border.

152. GM 1576 6′3″ × 4′1″, Sujni, Lotus in centre, wish-fulfilling tree on two corners of it, lotus and bird, kalka on four corners—on four sides of it peacock, cow, horse, human figures, box of betel-leaves, winnow, bird, fish, elephant etc. Floral and geometric patterns in borders.

153. GM 1577, 6′1″ × 4′2″, Sujni, Jessore, approx. 19th century. Lotus in centre and around it flowers, birds, kalka, leaves etc. as motif. Floral and geometric patterns in border. Red, blue, yellow, green, threads used on white surface of kantha.

154. GM 1578 6′6″ × 3′11″, Sujni, Khulna, approx. 19th century. Four different types of peacock in each of four corners, birds, 10 lines of kalka, floral designs on four sides, then five lines of kalka, four lines of circular lotus, six lines of kalka, boy sitting on chair at side. In the next line boy with kite, one kalka, one peacock, and three kalkas, line of flowers in middle. Next line shows horse with syce, five kalka, next line has six kalkas, then line of leaves, next four lines of lotus motif, five kalkas, on the top ten lines of kalka, 21 kalka on one end of the broad side (one in red another in blue thread) and 19 kalkas in red on other side. Geometric patterns in border.

155. GM 1579 2′11″ × $2'9\frac{1}{2}''$, Betan, Jessore, approx. 19th century. Lotus in centre with kalka in four corners, chariot, bird, fish, tiger, human figure, makar (a mythological acquatine animal— Capricorn (astrol.) in the remaining space and borders of geometric patterns.

156. GM 1580 $2'7\frac{1}{2}''$ × 2′7″, Betan, Jessore, approx. 19th century. Lines of kalka and human figures all over the kantha. Circular lotus in centre, round which designs of leaves. Geometric pattern at end. The kantha is marked by close stitching.

157. GM 1581 2′10″ × $1'10\frac{1}{2}''$, Betan, Jessore, early 20th century. Triangular kantha with geometric patterns in borders on four sides. Kalka in four corners and in the remaining part floral motifs.

158. GM 1582 $2'\ 7\frac{1}{2}''$ × $2'\ 6\frac{1}{2}''$, Betan, Khulna, approx. 19th century. Kantha made by Shrimati Shibani Bala. Lotus in centre and round it chariots, human figures, peacocks, tigers, birds sitting on tree, horse, cow, elephant, fish, lines of human figures in circle, kalka in four corners, geometric patterns in borders on two sides.

159. GM 1583 $3'4\frac{1}{2}''$ × 3′11″, Betan, Faridpur, approx. 19th century. Large lotus in centre flowers in full bloom in four corners and parallel geometric patterns in seven borders.

160. GM 1584 $3'\ 1\frac{1}{2}''$ × $2'\ 6\frac{1}{2}''$, Betan, Jessore. Lotus in centre, kalka in four corners, boat filled with passengers, monkey, elephant with hookah and mahut (driver), one man with umbrella above head holding on to a cow, man, etc. Geometric patterns in borders on four sides.

161. GM 1585 $2'10\frac{1}{2}''$ × $2'9\frac{1}{2}''$, Betan, Khulna, approx. 19th century. Full of motifs. Lotus in centre, kalka in four corners. Different motifs around the lotus— Radha, Krishna, garuda (mythical bird), gopini (milkmaid), Ganesha, Kartick, chariot, priest, girl sitting in a room, landlord, man smoking the hookah, man resembling foreigner sitting on chair, half statue of soldier, five girls on back of monkey like figure, girl fanning landlord, tiger, snake, girl wearing skirt, and five girls in same dress standing in a dancing pose (foreign influence) elephant and tortoise, fish, locked in terrible contest, severed head, pitcher, one paying respect to idol, hookah etc. Geometric pattern in border.

162. GM 1586 2′9″ × 2′8″, Betan, Khulna, early 20th century. Lotus in centre, leaves on four corners, lines of fish and kalka in four borders and also of geometric patterns.

163. GM 1587 $3'7\frac{1}{2}''$ × 3′, Betan, Khulna, approx. 19th century. Lotus in centre, kalka in four corners, twin peacocks, flower laden tree, elephant, horse, fish etc. as motif, geometric pattern in border.

164. GM 1588 $1'6\frac{1}{2}''$ × $11\frac{1}{2}''$, Cover, Jessore, approx. 19th century. Very bright kantha, borders designed with orange, blue, green and yellow and black threads. The borders show kalka, diamond, jamdani and geometric patterns. Borders designed on surface with white thread and small 'run' stitches in vacant space.

165. GM 1589 $1'5\frac{1}{2}''$ × 1'4" , Rumal, Khulna, approx. 19th century. Lotus in centre, wish fulfilling tree in four corners, two boats, elephant, horse, lion, bird, human torso, mirror, fish, flower etc. Three lines of geometric pattern in border.

166. GM 1590 $1'10\frac{1}{2}''$ × $1'4\frac{1}{2}''$, Cover, Designed with borders on four sides and geometric patterns running parallel along three lines in border.

167. GM 1591 $1'7\frac{1}{2}''$ × 1'5", Rumal, Jessore, approx. 19th century. Lotus in centre and four kalka on two sides of it. On other two sides, human figures, one resembling a *rakshasa* (demon-myth) another a *brahmadaitya* (a form of ghost). Four wish fulfilling trees in four corners. Motifs of fish, flower etc. Thin geometric pattern in border.

168. GM 1592 $1'6\frac{1}{2}''$ × $1'6\frac{1}{2}''$, Rumal, Khulna. Lotus in centre and also four corners. Around this human figures, fish, birds, small kalka etc. Kalka lines in borders on four sides.

169. GM 1593 $1'1\frac{1}{2}''$ × 1', Rumal, Lotus in centre, creeper designs of flowers and leaves, kalka and geometric patterns in borders on four sides.

170. GM 1594 $1'6\frac{1}{2}''$ × $1'6\frac{1}{2}''$, Rumal, Rajsahi. Lotus in centre, different types of flowers in four corners and kalka and geometric patterns running parallel in borders.

171. GM 1595 $1'4\frac{1}{2}''$ × $1'\frac{3}{4}''$, Rumal, Jessore, approx. 19th century. Lotus in centre and around it four squares with kalka in each. In addition butterfly, tree flower, fish etc. as motif. Borders of three lines along four sides containing geometric patterns. On white surface red, black, yellow, and ash coloured threads used.

172. GM 1596 1'9" × $8\frac{1}{2}''$, Arsilata, Khulna, approx. 19th century, Designs embroidered with blue thread on white surface. A snake coiled around five lines flower in middle and ten kalkas. Three lines of geometric pattern and one line of ear of corn in border.

173. GM 1597 $1'\ 8\frac{1}{2}''$ × $7\frac{1}{4}''$, Arsilata, Jessore, approx. 19th century. The kantha has floral and creeper designs and geometric patterns in borders on two sides.

174. GM 1598 $1'5\frac{1}{2}''$ × $7\frac{1}{2}''$, Arsilata, Faridpur. Lotus motif in five squares and kalka and geometric patterns in borders on two sides.

175. GM 1599 1'5" × $7\frac{1}{2}''$, Arsilata, Jessore, approx. 19th century. The kantha has creepers, geometric and floral designs arranged like in a border.

176. GM 1600 $1'5\frac{1}{2}''$ × $6\frac{1}{2}''$, Arsilata, Faridpur. Three lotuses in three squares and geometric patterns in borders on four sides.

177. GM 1601 1'8" × 6", Arsilata, Khulna, approx. 19th century. Designs of two flower buds on nine hearts type designs at centre. Around the centre two lines of kalka and three of fish. Barfi lines on four sides and geometric patterns in borders.

178. GM 1602 $11\frac{1}{2}''$ × $5\frac{1}{4}''$, Arsilata, Khulna. Lotus in centre and flowers on two sides and human figures on one side. The kantha has two flowery trees, on one side of which one tree without flowers and on other side a man's figure. Geometric patterns in borders.

179. GM 1603, 9″ × 2″, Arsilata, Rajsahi. Three horses in one line running lengthwise and six butterflies in another line. Geometric patterns and heart shaded like on other side and kalkas, in four corners.

180. GM 1604 2′1″ × $7\frac{1}{4}$″, Arsilata, Khulna, approx. 19th century. The kantha has been divided into three parts. In the middle part lotus, kalka and bird. In other two parts trees with flowers and leaves, fish and birds. Geometric patterns in borders on four sides.

181. GM 1605 1′$4\frac{1}{2}$″ × 7″, Arsilata, Faridpur, approx. 19th century. Lotus in centre and on two sides of it two wish fulfillig trees. Geometric patterns in borders on four sides.

182. GM 1606 1′4″ × 7 ″, Arsilata, Khulna, approx. 19th century. A tree with flowers and geometric patterns in borders.

183. GM 1607 1′10″ × 8″, Arsilata, Faridpur. Lotus and four peacocks in centre, on other two sides designs of flowers and leaves. Geometric patterns in borders.

184. GM 1608 2′3″ × 9″, Arsilata, Faridpur. Wish fulfilling tree at centre, Radha, Krishna, on one side and Ram, Sita and Lakshman standing at the back, birds, fish, flowers, on other sides wish fulfilling trees. Geometric pattern along thin borders.

185. GM 1609 1′$2\frac{1}{2}$″ × $7\frac{1}{2}$″, Durjani, Jessore, approx. 19th century. On one side kalka and geometric patterns and lotus on the other.

186. GM 1610 11′$\frac{1}{2}$″ × $4\frac{1}{4}$″, Durjani, Jessore. Kalka, floral and geometric designs.

187. GM 1611 1′1″ × 9″, Durjani, Faridpur. Designs of small flowers.

188. GM 1612 1′ × $1\frac{1}{2}$″, Durjani, Jessore, approx. 19th century. Very bright kantha, stitched with red and yellow threads. Lotus in centre, kalka and geometric designs in border.

189. GM 1613 $10\frac{1}{2}$″ × 7″, Durjani, Khulna. Lotus in centre and geometric patterns in border. Designs outlined all over the kantha.

190. GM 1614 9″ × 6″, Durjani, Jessore, approx. 19th century. Lotus motif at square portion in the middle, small flowers in corner, geometric patterns in borders on four sides.

191. GM 2126 1′11″ × $10\frac{1}{2}$″, Arsilata, Faridpur. Lotus, kalka, flower laden tree and flowers and geometric pattern in borders.

192. GM 2127 1′9″ × 7″, Arsilata, Faridpur. Lotus and tree motifs.

193. GM 2128 1′8″ × 6″, Arsilata, Faridpur. Kantha divided into seven parts. Three girls in three parts and four boys in four parts. Geometric pattern in borders.

194. GM 2129 1′11″ × 7″, Arsilata, Khulna, approx. 19th century. Colourful kantha divided into four parts each containing different type of circular lotus motif. Also many floral designs. Geometric pattern in border and on white surface, orange, green, red, black, yellow, ash and light blue threads used.

195. GM 2130 $9\frac{1}{2}$″ × $6\frac{1}{2}$″, Durjani, Jessore. Designs of Lotus and other motifs.

196. GM 2131 7″ × $4\frac{1}{2}$″, Durjani, Faridpur. Kantha made by Shrimati Nirmalasundari Saha, Kamargram Mahila Samity. Lotus and other designs embroidered with wool.

197. GM 2132 $7\frac{1}{2}$″ × $4\frac{1}{2}$″, Durjani, Jessore. Lotus and other designs.

198. GM 2133 $6\frac{1}{2}$″ × 4″, Durjani, Jessore. Lotus and other designs.

199. GM 2201 $9\frac{1}{2}$″ × $6\frac{1}{2}$″, Durjani, Faridpur, approx. 19th century. Artist, Nirmalasundari Saha. Main motif one large lotus, below which and on top floral and geometric patterns.

Orange and green threads used on white surface.

200. GM 1/63 $6'10\frac{1}{2}''$ × 4′7″, Lep, Khulna. Lotus motif in a triangle in centre and four flowers. Geometric pattern in borders.

201. GM 2/63 $1'3\frac{1}{2}''$ × $9\frac{1}{2}''$, Rumal, Khulna. Geometric patterns all over.

202. GM 129/91 4′4″ × $3'5\frac{1}{2}''$, Betan, Japan. Designs of Japanese home. White thread used for small 'run' stitch on white surface. Artist's name, Marimuchi Suki. Inspired by Bengal kanthas she stitched it and donated it to Gurusaday Museum in 1991.

Asutosh Museum, Calcutta University

There are about 200 nakshi kanthas in this museum. Descriptions of some are given below:

1. Accession No. 86. 252/0937, Coverlet, Jessore 4 × $2\frac{1}{2}''$ hands. Lotus in circular alpana design in centre and other flowers. Three kalkas in a bunch in four corners two men on elephant between kalkas on the wide side, man with umbrella. One big and one small horse length-wise, man with kite. On another side peacock with plumes, men, flowers. Lengthwise on another side big and small fish, birds, flowers, man sitting with drum. On the broad side after thin border, 7 plus 7 same flower. One corner top and bottom, red, blue, yellow, and green threads used to make same flower. Kalka line on four sides. Eight designs in thin border. Guri run stitches on vacant portions of white surface.

2. Accession No. 86. 252/10938, Bongaon, Asan kantha, $2\frac{1}{4}''$ × $2\frac{1}{2}''$ hands. Kantha with many motifs. Guri run stitches on white surface. Designs made with red, black, yellow, leaf green threads. At centre lotus and tree with flowers, round it circular alpana design and on four sides of it sari end designs. Four peacocks and four flowers in four corners. Next to rows of flowery trees, peacocks in a circle. After this seven designs of borders. Kalka in four corners of main kantha.

   Breadthwide the kantha is divided into six parts. In the first part, two peacocks on top and bottom of kalka. In second part two men and a woman in between carrying things on head. Two flowers on top and bottom of this. In third part, chariot and man and woman sitting in chariot. In fourth part two girls wearing skirts and holding up hands, holding handkerchief. In middle of fifth part one Tree of Life, below which on two sides two fish and on top two peacocks sitting on tree. In the sixth part kalka designs. Lengthwise kantha divided into four parts. In the first bird in cage, two men and women, one holding up hand and the other with hands on waist. It bottom Tree of Life and flower. In second part chariot with flag, two peacocks on top facing inwards.

   In third part sahib sitting in chair and servant giving him the hubble-bubble. In addition motifs of fish, flower, peacock. In fourth part Tree of Life, fish, peacock.

   Breadthwise in the top the kantha divided into five parts. In the first part kalka, three girls in the second with things, chariot in the third, girl standing in the fourth, Tree of Life in the fifth.

   Lengthwise another side divided into four parts. Kalka in the first part, one girl in the second, Krishana playing the flute with Radha, chariot in the third and man sitting on horse with whip in hand in fourth. Two peacocks at the top and one at the near of the horse and one man standing with hand on horse's face. Below horse fish, at the side kadam flowers on top and bottom of peacock.

3. Coverlet, Jessore. A long kantha. Guri run stitches on white surface. Designs with many coloured threads. Alpana design at centre, Tree of Life in each corner, multicoloured flowers in

the kantha, kalka rows along four sides, broad designs at border.

4. Accession No. T 041. Asan kantha, Narail, Jessore. Very old kantha and colours have faded. Designs with red, blue, green, pink threads on white surface. Lotus in centre and round it rows of flower, twisted flowers and kalka. Tree of Life in each of four corners. On one side four women and one man standing in boat, five girls sitting and on one corner kartick sitting on peacock. On another side man on tiger, with two in front and rear standing with handkerchief in hand. On another side mother with child and another girls holding on to baby, on another side girl standing in a dancing pose, next to her man with hat on, Krishna standing with legs crossed. Below Radha sitting, holding on to his feet. Next, line of flowers made with red and pink thread.

5. Accession No. T 8994, Coverlet, Jessore. Designs on white surface with coloured threads. Inside 'guri run' stitches. Alpana design at centre and on four sides, kalka, flower and fish. In four corners same kalka embroidered

6. Asan kantha, Khulna. White surface, 'guri run' stitches with red and yellow threads. Designs embroidered all over with red, black, yellow threads. Alpana design at centre, next to it rows of flowers. Then border designs with red and black threads, rows of kalka, round flowers. Kalka in four corners.

7. Accession No. T 5607. Big Lep kantha, Dhaka, Carpet designs in light coloured threads. Alpana design at centre with coloured threads. Three kalkas in bunch in four corners. 'Benki' (bending) design and fish scales designed in border.

8. Accession No. T 126. Sujni kantha, Khulna. On white surface 'guri run' stitches with white threads. Red half-inch sari end in border and then 'run' stitches with coloured threads. Alpana design in centre, round it different motifs. Most motifs outlined, some filled.

9. Accession No. T 131. Asan kanthas khulna. Coloured designs on white surface. Alpana design in centre, round it on four sides many types of branches, filled flower and four kalkas in four corners differently embroidered. Row of kalka in border.

10. Accession No. 86.124/1080. Sujni kantha, Sripur, Jessore. Guri run stitched with white thread on white surface, different designs with coloured threads. Alpana design at centre round it tops of chariots, smoke coming out of railway engine, balloon on top of engine, Tree of Life, horse. Four big kalkas one in each corner and round border rows of medium kalkas.

11. Arsilata, Jessore. Guri run stitched on white surface with white thread. Designs of flowers with red and blue threads. Small run stitches in borders.

12. Arsilata, Lower Bengal. Main surface white with designs in red and black thread. Kalka lines on four sides.

13. Joth Kantha, Faridpur. Long and thin kantha. Designs in red and black threads.

14. Joth kantha, Lower Bengal. Long and thin with square designs in red, black, yellow and white threads.

15. Arsilata, Jessore. Red and black threads used for designs on white surface.

16. Accession No. T 2654. Batua, Barisal. White surface with designs in red, sky blue and yellow threads.

17. Accession No.126/10811. Sujni kantha, Jessore. Designs in red, orange, black, blue and light green threads on white surface. Alpana design in centre and on four corners Tree of Life in coloured threads. Also elephant, tortoise, twisted flower, peacock, fish, bird, Shiva temple with Shiva linga designed. Flowers and wavy designs in border.

18. Sujni Kantha, Jessore. Small runs with white thread on white surface. Designs embroidered with black, light blue and light

orange threads. Alpana in centre. Also designs of different flowers.

19. Accession No. 86/129/10814, Sujni, Jessore. Red, black, pink, blue threads used to embroider designs on white surface. Large alpana in centre, Tree of Life in two corners and alpana in two others. Also four kalkas and on two sides men on elephants and horses. Also other motifs, man on horseback with umbrella in one hand, two peacocks facing each other. Man on elephant back, man standing before elephant with umbrella, handfan etc.

20. Sujni, Jessore. Designs with red, black, blue threads used for designs, small leaves, alpana in centre and multicoloured kalka in four corners.

21. Accession No. T 3352. Sujni, Jessore. Colourful kantha. Threads used red, blue and white. Circular lotus design in centre, kalka, flower, human figures on two sides. Rows of horses on all four sides, nine black boars in one line and many flowers in the next. After this row of elephants.

22. Asa, Lower Bengal. Designs with red, black, blue, sky blue threads on white surface.

23. Asan, Jessore. Closely knit like carpets. Designs with many coloured threads on white surface. Alpana in centre, four kalkas, each different from other, in four corners. Tree of Life in middle of each kalka, borders designed like sari ends.

24. Asan, Khulna. Designs with red, black, light yellow, light green threads on white surface. Circular alpana designs at centre, round it circular designs with bending (benki) stitches. Motifs of fish, man with different kinds of things, man on horseback, elephant, tiger. Stretched designs of lotus in borders.

25. Accession No. 86.251/10936, Sujni, Jessore. Smapp 'run' stitches with white thread on white surface, inside designs embroidered with red, blue, yellow and black threads. Alpana in centre. Three elephants with two men on each in the wide part, peacock, man on horseback, fish, five girls holding hands. Designs of round flowers on two sides and rows of 44 kalkas on four sides. Designs of feet in borders.

26. Asan, Jessore. Small run on white surface with white thread and inside designs embroidered with red, light red, sky blue and yellow threads. Alpana in centre. Fish, peacock, men and women in different poses and a sitting dog. Motifs of elephant, birds, Tree of Life etc. Motifs and borders not filled up by stitched with small 'runs', only part of central design filled up with yellow and red threads. Eight lines of border have different designs.

27. Sujni, Jessore, approx. early 20th century. Designs with red and yellow threads on white surface. Forty-two designs resembling flower petals and four others designed with blue thread on white and stitched with small 'run's.

28. Rumal, kalka and flower designs.

29. Rumal, Radha and Krishna in small portion at centre and below Durga on lion with Kartick and Ganesha on right and left of her.

Indian Museum, Calcutta

About twelve kanthas here of which five are from Bengal.

1. Accession No. A.T. 84/ 620 approx. 19th century Bengal kantha. Designs with red, blue, green and orange threads on white surface. Motifs of Tree of Life, trees, chariot, flower, fish, man on deer, on dog, on peacock. Many scenes embroidered such as, girl slicing fish outside her hut, ratha yatra mela, goddess Lakshmi, temple, Dakshineswer temple, old man smoking hookah, grand-daughter and cow tethered early.

2. Accession No. A.T. 83/ 570, approx. 19th century. Lotus in centre. Round it rows of five types of kalka, kalka and fish in borders, elephant in one corner and many flowers, chariot etc. as motifs. In other two corners,

motif of figure and that of flower and figure. Scenes like girl standing on dead body and fox. Designs with brown and white threads on white surface.

3. Accession No. A.T. 83/576, Faridpur, approx. 19th century. Radha, Krishna motif. Red, blue, black, light yellow threads used for designs. The central lotus in the square portion and on four corners of it kalka and round the centre Radha Krishna motif. In the next part kalkas bunched in there in three in each corner. Again Radha-Krishna motif. Six types of designs in the borders. Around the last border, geometric patterns, then small runs, then creeper designs, again small run and then floral design. Then small runs with flowers and geometric designs alternately.

4. Accession No. 83/580 approx. 19th century. A thick kantha with wavy small runs all over. Lotus in centre, round it 15 motifs of witches in a circle. Betel-leaf, half moon in four corners, inside birds, flowers etc. as motifs. White thread used for the small runs and red, yellow, blue, green, purple, brown threads used for designs.

5. Accession No. 14987, Jessore, approx. 18th century. Very thick and old kantha. Small 'run' stitches all over the white surface in white thread. Designs with blue and light red threads. Lotus in centre, round it on two sides four chariots. On one side the chariot has horse attached to it and syce holding its reins. In the middle Tree of Life and another between two chariots on one side, four people on top and bottom of tree. Four peacocks, two on top and bottom of Tree of Life, two on top of two chariots, and on other side one large peacock each on top of two chariots. On one side of border, two lines of boys and girls in different poses. Four elephants on two sides of the line, and floral designs in geometric patterns. Then in three lines of the border designs of sari ends.

Victoria Memorial Hall, Calcutta

The kantha mentioned below is in the Calcutta Gallery of Victoria Memorial Hall: The kantha is of Magura (Jessore) areas. Made in 1891, measures 5 × 4 hands. Made by Balasundari Dasi. Lotus in the centre, round it two four large twisted flowers. Border has rows of sari ends designs, kalka, row of 27 horses and 27 elephants, human figures in a row, (one boy and one girl). Four kalkas in four corners. Large kalka in right and left and rows of swan and fish. In addition, tiger, butterfly, Tree of Life, house and people, boy and girl, dog, monkey, deer, flower, train, twisted flower, sun, chariot, flag, butterfly, two lions, two bears, peacock, big chariot, house, man with umbrella, monkey with tail twisted up, crocodile, comb, flower, aeroplane, Tree of Life. After big kalka, rows of flowers with branches. Designs of butterfly, border designs, household items. On right of centre a Tree of Life, next to it many small butterflies. On the left two chariots. Chariots on the sides of the chariot also. One hundred figures of human beings on two sides of the border. On the right rows of 30 kalkas, on top fifty five kalkas. Small 'run' stitches on white surface, red, blue, yellow, green, ash and sky blue threads used for designs.

Academy of Fine Arts

Here there are four kanthas.

1. Sujni Kantha, 4.0″×5.11″. Small run's stitched with white thread on white surface. On one side of broad side and on other side two large Tree of Life. White, yellow, blue, red, green threads used. Many flowers designed. Lotus in centre and round it flowers in geometric patterns. Three peacocks each on either side of this. On one side a peacock with plumes spread. Rows of fish, 10 each, on either side and kalkas in the next line. One horse, conch-shell lines on top and bottom and borders stitched with threads of different colours. Then a row of ear so of corn. Kantha gifted by Shrimati Rama Dutta.

2. Asan Kantha 3.0″×2.9″. The red colour dominates, blue used slightly at the centre

and borders. Kalkas in four corner and tree with branches. The flower in the tree resembles sunflower. Other motifs are, boy and girl, peacock, duck, fish, flower etc. 'Barfi' design in the border, then a line of flowers and leaves.

3. Asan Kantha, 2.6″×2.8″. Lotus in centre and round it circular design of 'barfi'. Four different Tree of life on four sides, kalka in four corners. Border made with black thread and button-hole stitch. Fish scales designed with red thread, then leaves and small kalkas. Angular designs of leaves in rest of the kantha, red and blue threads in alternate lines.

4. Rabindra Gallery has a Sujni kantha that was used by Rabindranath. It is a thick kantha with small 'run' stitched in white thread on white surface, four large kalkas stitched in red and black in corners and similar but smaller kalkas in borders.

Government Industrial and Commercial Museum, Calcutta

Five kanthas kept here.

1. Sujni kantha, 4 hands, seven fingers long and three hands, three fingers broad. It carries name and address of maker, Hemalini Biswas, Chakdaha, Payaradanga, Nadia. At the centre is a picture of Gandhiji and the word 'Bapuji' embroidered. On either side of the picture, the National Flag and flowers in pots. In addition lotus and conch-shells designed. From the National Flag it is evident that the kantha was made after independence.

2. Sujni kantha, Faridpur, 3 hands 17 fingers long and two hands 16 fingers wide. White surface on which different motifs embroidered with coloured threads. Border design resembles the Jamdani of Dhaka. Lotus in centre, around it flowers. Tree of Life, kalka. Rows of fish on the broad side. Different fruits, twisted flower, tree, scissors, horse designed lengthwise like glass panes.

3. Dhakna Kantha, 3 hands and nine fingers long and two hands, 11 fingers wide. White surface and on it different designs embroidered with coloured thread. Lotus in centre. Other motifs, peacock, horse with syce, girl with hands raised, Tree of Life, betel-leaf, flower etc. Kalka in border.

4. Sujni Kantha, Barisal, 4 hands 12 fingers long, two hands, three fingers wide. Four fingers of fringe on two sides. Chakra in centre, kalka, nine on top and 11 below. Large kalkas in border on wide side. Slokas written lengthwise on one side.

5. Batua Kantha, 19 fingers long and 11 fingers wide below and six fingers on top. Resembles a shoulder bag. White surface closely filled up. Lotus and leaves designed with many coloured threads.

Regional Design and Technical Development Centre, Calcutta

There are eight kanthas here of which one is small and torn.

1. Accession No. 703, Arsilata, 1 hand long, 1 span wide. Red and blue threads used on white surface. Floral designs at centre and around. Alpana design in centre, round which four small peacocks—this is the central portion. Four Tree of Life in one portion of one side.

2. Accession No. 667. Asan Kantha, Faridpur, 2′5″ × 2′5″. Coloured design on white surface. Lotus in centre and alpana designed in circular manner round it. Kalka in four corners, two Trees of Life on two sides with flowers around. Elephant with flowers below and peacock and fish on top. At the top on another side, elephant, fish, flower and eye designed below with blue thread.

3. Accession No. 600. Asan Kantha, 150 × 123 cms. Jessore. Lotus in centre and two floral lines. Twisted flowers in four corners, fish and rows of soldiers and birds. In bottom kalka, horse and horses on four sides also. Threads of many colours used.

4. Accession No. 693. Lep kantha, 214 × 152 cms. Colour motifs like elephant, fish, horse, flower etc.

5. Accession No. 865. Asan kantha, 150 × 140 cms. Designs with coloured threads on white surface. Alpana in centre, next many motifs of animals. In one corner a man and a woman, man putting crown on woman's head. On another side a horse and tiger, man with stick and two with handkerchiefs and candles. On other side elephant and peacock facing each other. Fish on top of peacock. Border has fish, flower and kalka.

6. Accession No. 662. Asan kantha, 78 × 84 cms. Embroideries with white and other threads on white surface. Inside small run stitches with white thread. Designs mostly outlined, only parts filled. Floral alpana design at centre. Kalka in three corners. On one corner next to kalka three man with guns, one policeman. Twisted and other flowers. On other side two elephants with armed man on one and another sitting in hookah on other. On other side two horses standing with riders wearing European clothes. On another side Jagannath in chariot, next to which a girl with fan and flowers. Next, man wearing hat, mongoose (bottom), memsahib, maulvi, many kalka all around at bottom and border design.

7. Accesssion No. 694. Lep kantha, 220×154 cms, Midnapore. Circular colored alpana design at centre, round which four kalka on four sides. Flower and fish on sides of kalka. Then design of eyes in orders which are half inch wide. Lengthwise border design of four inches, small 'run' then half inch of eye design, kalka, red on top and yellow at bottom. Wide border designed inside and towards the bottom designs with white and black threads. Then designs like eyes of pineapples, pitchers, ears of corn.

Birla Academy of Art and Culture

Only one kantha 118×185 cms. Made towards end of 19th century. Embroidered on kantha is the sensational affair of Mohanta Madhabgiri and Elokesi that had rocked contemporary society and found its place in the 'oat' paintings also.

Rabindra Bhavan, Viswa Bharati, Santiniketan.

Tagore got it as a present at Silaidaha. Many motifs on light cream surface. Motifs include, fish, betel-leaf, camel, lotus, horse, elephant etc. These have been oulined and vacant spaces of designs have the wavy 'kuchi taga' stitches. Thick kantha with floral designs in border.

Kala Bhavan, Viswa Bharati, Santiniketan

There are 33 kanthas here.

1. Accession No. 2681, Sujni kantha, 5 × 3 hands. Kantha got from Tamluk. It is a dorokha with designs made in various coloured threads. At the centre is a lotus with 12 petals and circular lines of flowers. Next 14 parrots in a circle and kalka in corner. Then motifs such as lobster, horses, soldier's figure, saheb and two women and four men wearing foreign clothes. One sweeper, girl with fan in hand, one sitting with umbrella, one memsahib and three elephants. All these in one single panel.

   In the next line a girl with a catherine wheel in hand, two male sweepers, two women, fish, flower. Geometric patterns in border with red and blue threads, then row of flowers and line of kalka.

2. Accession No. 2663. Dhakna kantha, 3 × 3 hands, Jessore. A dorokha with motifs of animals. Designs embroidered with light red and blue threads. A lotus like flower in centre, next to it eleven triangular designs. On three sides creepers and figures on the other side. Tree of Life in four corners, next to which motifs like monkey, horse, human figure, birds with long beaks. Nineteen kalkas in next line then the shefali flower and triangular designs.

3. Accession No. 2682. Lep kantha, 6 × $3\frac{1}{2}$ hands. Two Trees of Life in centre and twisted flowers on top and bottom of trees.

Border has lamp like designs on all sides. In the border thin geometric patterns, then again lamps.

4. Sujni kantha, 5×3 hands. Lotus in centre, kalkas, many flowers and Tree of Life. Kalka in rows in border, followed by line of figures. Flowers in the next line then creeper designs. On the right of the centre many motifs of figures like, musician, a palanquin being carried, two on horseback, many girls, train, old people with sticks, sahib and a girl with a pitcher. On the other side many animals with twisted flowers in-between.

5. Accession No. 2665. Sujni, $4\frac{1}{2} \times 2\frac{1}{2}$ hands. Heart shaped designs in border, kalka in four corners, kantha looks like a designed shawl. Kalkas embroidered with red, yellow, green threads, small 'run' stitched with white thread.

6. Accession No. 2671. Sujni, $4 \times 2\frac{1}{2}$ hands. A dorokha, it has written on it, Bamasundart Dasya, price three rupees. Many motifs resembling terracotta and pat paintings. Designs made on white surface with coloured threads. These include, snake fighting peacock, dog, lion, sahib smoking while a girl is dancing, memsahib, stork, elephants fighting, gecko, cock fighting etc.

7. Accession No. 2669. Sujni kantha, 4 × 2 hands. Artist's name given as, Shri Sarbasundari Dasi Chowdhurani. Lotus in centre, many elephants all around. In addition peacock, elephant, lion, horse, human figure etc. Red and blue threads used for designs and white for small run stitches.

8. Accession No. 2666. Sujni kantha, 5 × 3 hands. Designs on white surface with red and black threads. Motifs of elephant, horse, fish, kalka, flower. Written upside down is Jagatchandra Chakravarty.

9. Accession No. 2684. Sujni kantha, $4\frac{1}{2} \times 2\frac{1}{2}$ hands. Collected from Lohagar village in Birbhum district. Lotus in centre, Tree of Life in four corners and motifs of horse, bird. hand fan, three fish with one head. Sari ends in border.

10. Accession No. 2668. Dhakna Dak kantha, 2 × 1 hand. Two roses, two elephants with creepers on top. In the bottom two Trees of Life and one fish.

11. Accession No. 2677. Asan kantha, 1 × 1 hand. Three squares in middle made with different threads. Next creeper designs.

12. Accession No. 2607. Sujni kantha, 4 × 2 hands. Twelve-petalled lotus in centre, next to it different designs in circular fashion.

13. Accession No. 2595. Arsilata, $1\frac{1}{2} \times 1$ hand. Designs with red, blue, yellow threads. Lotus in centre. Also ant, elephant, snake, horse and floral designs. Two kalkas on broad side and creepers in border.

14. Accession No. 2661. Sujni, Pabna, 5 × 3 hands. Twelve lotuses in the entire kantha. Flower in centre, next to it leaves, Tree of Life etc. Designs in red and black.

15. Accession No. 2670. Sujni kantha, 5 × 3 hands. Squares all over the kanthas with twisted flowers in each. Floral design at centre, Trees of Life around it, creepers in border.

16. Sujni kantha (no number). Beautiful but old and torn. Four kalkas in four centres, also in centre, designs of flowers and fish. Different coloured threads used.

17. Accession No. 2672. Sujni kantha, $5 \times 3\frac{1}{2}$ hands. Beautiful kantha with a motif. Seen in the kantha are fish, flowers, tortoise, elephant, peacock, girls pulling chariot etc.

18. Accession No. 2659. Sujni kantha, $4 \times 2\frac{1}{2}$ hands. Floral designs throughout. Touch of modernity can be seen.

19. Accession No. 2683. Sujni kantha, 4 × 2 hands. Belongs to end 19th century. Four kalkas in four corners and dots designed.

20. Accession No. 2658. Dhakna kantha, $1\frac{1}{2} \times 1$ hand. Used as pillow cover.

21. Accession No. 2656. Pillow cover, $1\frac{1}{2} \times 1$ hand.

22. Accession No. 2679. Small pillow cover, $1\frac{1}{2} \times 1$ hand.

23. Accession No. 2692. Same as above. Eye designed with black thread.

24. Accession No. 2676. Same as above. Lotus with red, black threads.

25. Accession No. 2668. Same as above. 'Barfi' designs with twisted flowers inside.

26. Accession No. 2667. Small sujni kantha, $3\frac{1}{2} \times 2$ hands. Chain stitch used for embroidery. Motifs include two bodies with single head, also elephant, bull etc.

27. Accession No. 2652. Part of small, longish kantha. Designs of small kalka and flowers.

28. Accession No. 2674. Dhakna kantha, $1\frac{1}{2} \times 1$ hands. Floral designs.

29. Accession No. 2680. Dhakna kantha, $1\frac{1}{2} \times 1$ hands. Floral designs.

30. Accession No. 2673. Sujni kantha, 4 × 2 hands. Very old and stains have appeared. Motifs include elephant and peacock.

31. Accession No. 4.2.38, Asan kantha, 3 × 3 hands. Made by Bulbul and bought from Sriniketan Shilpa Utsav for three rupees. Shows Shakuntala with deer at hermit's ashram, round which are kalka designs.

32. Accession No. 6.10.2. Silk kantha with designs of the temple at Puri, chariot etc.

33. Accession No. 2654. Dhakna kantha, $2 \times \frac{1}{2}$ hands. Small with kalka, lotus, peacock and different flowers designed.

Bangiya Sahitya Parishad

There is only one kantha made by Kadambari Devi. It is a carpet kantha made with cross stitch and presented by her to poet Biharilal Chakravarti. Embroidered in the kantha is a line from the poet's poem Saradamangal. Designs of red, yellow, purple and light green on green surface. On top of the poem's line, at the kantha's centre, are Bengali alphabets are also in the side. Leaves around the central portion. Designs with yellow thread in the border.

Ramakrishna Mission Institute of Culture

There are six kanthas here, four large and two batuas (small bag).

1. Sujni kantha, 3×2 hands, one hundred years old. Small run stitches with red, black, blue, green and yellow threads on white surface. Lotus in centre, round it circular floral design, five types of designs around the borders. On the broad side 18 twisted flowers, Trees of Life in four corners. On the one side a man between two trees, on the other side peacock and fish. Lengthwise man on horseback on one side, dog below and on other side one girl in dancing pose.

2. Asan kantha, 2×2 hands, 100 years old. Designs on white surface with coloured threads, small 'run' stitches with white thread. Line of twisted flowers along the border, in four corners four leaves, seven flowers, two elephants between two trees, two men between the elephants, one has one hand held up and the other both. Two other men on the other side and a child between them. Peacock eating snake, Krishna in two poses, Shiva linga. Two horses on another side.

3. Gilaf, eight inches long. Red, black, yellow and ash thread on white surface. Designs of flowers and creepers and geometric patterns in border.

4. Gilaf, three inches long. Lotus in centre and around it floral designs. Designs embroidered with red and black thread on white surface.

5. Sujni kantha, 4 × 3 hands. Designs embroidered with multicoloured threads on light mulberry coloured surface. Designs made with filling stitches. Row of flowers and creeper designs around border, then small kalka in next line. Four large kalkas, flowers, creepers in four corners. On two sides along the width two big trees. Lotus

floating in water in centre and round it a line of nine big fish. In the next line small lotuses. Then a thin circular border. Ducks below the trees and on top two birds, flowers in branches and butterflies above flowers. On four sides of trees, four peacocks, their plumes spread. Lengthwise four conch-shells.

6. Asan kantha, $1\frac{1}{2} \times 1\frac{1}{2}$ hands, one hundred years old. Designs with coloured threads on white surface. 'run' stitches in spaces between the designs. Lotus in centre, round it floral designs, three kalkas in each of four corners and deer munching grass next to it a peacock and butterfly. On other side one girl with handkerchief standing in dancing pose. Next a butterfly and peacock. On other side one elephant, peacock, butterfly. On another side two boys with a cycle like thing, hands raised holding a dumb-bell. Geometric patterns in three lines of border. Eight twisted flowers in the broad side and lengthwise lines of round flowers on two sides. Then three lines of borders with geometric patterns.

State Archaeological Museum, Calcutta

The museum has three kanthas.

1. Betan, Murshidabad, 20th century. Deep sky blue, it resembles a sataranji, that is spread on the floor for people to sit. Red shalu round the border. Four corners filled with designs in coloured thread. Designs in white thread above. Large flower in red thread in centre and round it designs in white thread.
2. Sujni kantha, 6′ long and 4′ wide. A red kantha with floral designs embroidered in white. Two circular alpana designs in centre and in four corners designs made with white threads.
3. As a Asan kantha, 2′×2′. Ash coloured thread used for designs in border. Deep brown thread used all over the kantha. 'Run' stitches in white threads.

Karu Angan, Salt Lake, Calcutta

There are 10 kanthas here.

1. Arsilata, $1\frac{1}{2}$ hands and two span long 1 hand 1 span wide. Designs, in coloured thread on white surface. Artist, Nishabala Dey, embroidered in English. It is a tray cover. Motifs include kalka and joss stick-holders. Creeper designs in border. Laced on all sides.
2. Arsilata, $1\frac{3}{4}$ hands long 1 span wide. Mainly red thread used, also light orange and green. Alpana and kalka designs.
3. Pillow cover, 2 hands long, 1 hand and a span wide. Coloured threads used for designs on white surface. Two lotus in centre. Tree of Life in four corners, flowers resemble twisted flowers. Many motifs in the kantha. Artist's name given in kantha as Rajeshwari Mondal, Govindpur.
4. Sujni kantha, contemporary, Birbhum. Small 'run' stitched on violet surface. Designs with coloured threads. Main design resembles a fish bone and embroidered in white thread.
5. Sujni kantha. Round alpana at centre. Small run stitches give it a wavy look. Motifs of ears of corn and lotus petals, kalka etc.
6. Sujni kantha. Colourful kantha. Small 'run' stitches, designs with many coloured threads. It was made in Mymensingh one hundred years ago by Umarani Biswas. At centre lotus inside alpana design, birds on Tree of Life in four corners. Four pineapples along the breadth and eight lenghtwise. The lotus centric alpana designs below central design looks like that in a dastarkhan, as does the top part. Kalkas, trees (23) around the central design. Twisted flowers between trees, round which creepers designed.
7. Sujni kantha, end 19th century. Special feature are the designs of sahibs and memsahibs. One such girl in the lower half of the kantha, lengthwise. Breadthwise designs

of creepers going up like a snake, crocodile, man in crocodile's tummy (as in pat designs), human face, men on elephants, sun, creepers, Tree of Life. Then memsahib on horseback, twisted flower, leaves. In the top designs of human beings, monkey, peacock, Trees of Life. Then flowers and mat like designs.

8. Baby's kantha. White small 'run' stitches, designs with red thread on two-inch thick border.
9. Baby's kantha. This is a 'paar' designs kantha. Red and blue threads used. Four types of designs in border.
10. Sujni, designs embroidered with coloured threads on white surface.

Sunderbans Anchalik Sangrahasala, Baruipur, South 24 Parganas

There are four kanthas here.

1. Asan kantha, 1 hand, 1 span × 1 hand. Thick kantha, white surface with small 'run' stitches. Designs embroidered with red, green, yellow threads. A tree with branches in centre and three flowers. Creeper designs in borders.
2. Asan kantha, 2 hands × 1 hand. Small run stitches with white thread between coloured threads on white surface. Designs made with different coloured threads. Circular lotus in centre, round which are four peacocks and small twisted flowers. Six types of designs in border, made with different coloured threads in different lines.
3. Lep kantha, 6 hands×4 hands. Thick kantha, with designs in black, red and green threads. 'Barfi' designs in border, small 'runs' for two inches and then designs in red threads. Designs alternately in red, blue and green threads.
4. Sujni kantha, 4 hands×1span×3 hands. Whole kantha separated into small squares each of which has twisted flowers in two types of threads. Other designs are eyes, ears of corn and flowers. Borders have designs measuring 5 ½″ × 3 ½″. White, black, red, light yellow threads used all over.

Lokasanskriti Museum, Kalyani University, Kalyani

The museum has four kanthas.

1. Betan kantha, $1\frac{1}{2} \times 1\frac{1}{2}$ hands, dorokha stitched, made by Radharani Devi of Chakdaha, Nadia, in early 20th century.

   White surface and embroideries with coloured threads. Central design is that of lotus and four peacocks in four corners. Kalka and floral designs, girls, Tree of Life, man on elephant, two on horseback. Two peacocks above elephant one on each side, flower and half moon at the bottom.
2. Sujni kantha, Jessore, $5\frac{1}{2} \times 3\frac{1}{2}$ hands, pre-20th century, made by three women. White surface with small 'run' stitches in white thread.Circular floral design at centre with petals like that of the lotus. Threads of many colours used.
3. Sujni kantha, 4×3 hands, Midnapore, late 20th century. Presented to somebody described as 'Saiful', embroidered in kantha. Motifs include Tree of Life, flowers, creeper etc. White surface.
4. Wall-hanging, 2×2 hands, Sonargaon, Narayanganj, late 20th century. White surface and coloured threads used to make borders of the eye, snail and vegetable designs. At the centre is a map of India, coloured threads outlining the different states and space filled up with small 'run' stitches. Word INDIA made with green, red, yellow and sky blue threads, map outlined with black thread.

Akshaykumar Maitreya and Raja Rajaram Museum, Siliguri

The museum has one kantha.

Accession No. 7A P 7A AR O, Betan kantha 85× 52 cms, West Dinajpore, approx. 19th century, artist Mankumari Devi, collected by Satyahari Dutta and Namita Dutta of West Dinajpore.

Small 'run' stitches with white threads on white surface, motifs made with red thread. Thin button-holes with red and black threads in border, then creepers. In the middle fish, birds, ducks, nutcracker, conch-shell, elephants, tigers. Tree of Life etc.

Acharya Jogesh Chandra Museum, Bangiya Sahitya Parishad, Bishnupur Branch, Bankura

There are two kanthas here.

1. Sujni kanthas of the district's Simlipal areas, 4 hands 4 fingers × 2 hands 10 fingers, 20th century, donated by Phanibushan Pannigrahi, artist a Brahmin from Orissa. Dorokha kantha with small 'run' stitches inside and designs made with coloured threads. Motifs include, Tree of Life, monkey with tail curled up. Lamp, betel-leaf, fish, dog, peacock, boar, fox and other animals. Many types of flowers.
2. Sujni kantha, a little small in size, white surface with floral designs in red, blue, black threads.

Ananda Niketan Kirtishala, Bagnan, Howrah

There are 13 kanthas here.

1. Sujni kantha. Floral designs in one-half with red, green and yellow threads and in cream, yellow and green threads in the other. Rows of kalka all around.
2. Lep kantha, $4 \times 3\frac{1}{2}$ hands, Shyampur, Howrah, 19th century. Colour has fade, leaves designed on white surface. The designs are outlined and other leaves and palm of a hand fill the space inside. Alpana all around.
3. Betan kantha, 2×2 hands, Jessore, 19th century. White surface circular designs of flowers and kalka. Also, man with pigtail, bull, tiger, fish, flower, elephant, twin kalkas in corner and also above border. Round flowers in four corners.
4. Betan kantha, 2×2 hands, Faridpur, 19th century, artist, Kadambini Dasi. Very colourful, divided into three at top, bottom and side. Kalka and flower at bottom square portion. At middle syce holding horse and artists name embroidered. Three headed man next to horse. Also elephants, human figures in red and yellow and legs and hats is blue threads. On the other side tiger and Tree of Life. On one side three more human figures, one girl and two men on either side in vaulting pose. At top Tree of Life, birds and peacock and in middle 'paar' design in red thread.
5. Betan kantha, $4\frac{1}{2} \times 2\frac{1}{2}$ hands. Designs on white surface with many coloured threads. Lotus at centre, half of border has kalka and the other half creepers.
6. Sujni kantha, 4×3 hands, motifs include, Tree of Life, temple, peacocks, tree in cross stitch. At the centre circular design of flowers. Lengthwise, horse, cycle, boat on one side, on the other boy with fan and umbrella, two carrying palanquin, betel-leaf, nutcracker, fish.
7. Sujni kantha, $4\frac{1}{2}$ hands × $2\frac{1}{2}$ hands. Eight petalled lotus other flowers in centre, butterflies, peacocks, tree, deer etc. The 'Chokh (eye) Taga' design before the border. Kalkas in many colours.
8. Lep kantha 6×4 hands. The 'paar' design on white surface. Small 'run' stitches.
9. Sujni kantha $5 \times 3\frac{1}{2}$ hands. Outlines in red, black, yellow on white surface. Seven fish, kalka shaped leaves and flowers designed.
10. Betan kantha $2\frac{1}{2} \times 2$ hands. Small 'run' stitches in white thread, creepers in border. Ears of corn and flowers in red and green. At centre is a four line rhyme obviously addressed to a child— "Who is it that has come laughing through the clouds, to fill my heart and flood me with tears of love".
11. Baby's Kantha, 2 × 1 hand. Circular alpana in middle with lotus in centre. Footprints of Lakshmi embroidered in lotus, and also elsewhere, in all ten, Cocount trees in four corners in green thread and huts below in mustard colour.

12. Baby's kantha, 2 × 1 hand. Different designs woven in red, pink, brown, yellow, black and green threads. Flowers and creepers in borders. Kalkas, conch- shell and temples designed.
13. Baby's kantha, $2\frac{1}{2}''$ × $1\frac{1}{2}''$ hands. Outline on white surface with 'run' stitches using red, blue, green stitches. Two parrots lengthwise. Conch-shells in border.

Tripura Govt. Museum, Agartala

There are 23 kanthas here, 21 of which had been collected by Dinesh Chandra Sen from different parts of East Bengal (now Bangladesh) and presented to Raja Bir Bikram of Tripura. One was collected by Bipulkanti Saha from Udaypur, Tripura, and the other donated by the artist's daughter Malabika Dasgupta.

1. Text 1, Lep kantha, 164 × 100 cms, 19th century. Very old kantha, round floral design at centre, two leaves and long flower in four corners and geometric patterns in border. Written at one end, Sri Hari.
2. Text 2, Betan kantha, 76 × 82 cms, 19th century. Designs with red, yellow, sky blue threads. Circular floral motif in centre, figures of men on horses and elephants, flowers.
3. Text 3, Sujni kantha, 134 × 80 cms, 19th century. Small run stitches in white thread. Closely designed with coloured threads. Circular floral design in centre, trees in four corners, geometric patterns in borders.
4. Text 4, Asan kantha, 86 × 85 cms, 19th century. Run and Satin stitches used. Designs on white surface with coloured threads. Four types of designs in borders. Also flower, tiger, lion, bird, elephant, human figures.
5. Text 5, Sujni kantha, 145 × 95 cms, 19th century. Coloured threads on white surface for embroidery. Rows of elephants, flowers, lotus in centre, circular floral design and next to it lines of birds and fish.
6. Text 6, Asan kantha, 63 × 62 cms, 19th century. Very old kantha, Round floral designs, geometric patterns, Tree of Life.
7. Text 7, Dhakna kantha, 71 × 45 cms, 19th century. Very thick kantha, Twelve round floral designs in geometric manner with coloured threads.
8. Text 8, Asan kantha, 90 × 85 cms, 19th century. Red, blue, green, yellow threads used. Circular floral design at centre, also elephant, horse, human figures, Trees of Life. Written below, Balai, Kadamba (type of flower) Briksha (tree), Sri Krishna Brindabanlila (Krishna at play at Brindaban), Sri Ram Raja (King Rama of Ramayana).
9. Text 9, Dhakna kantha, 75 × 44 cms, 19th century. Red, blue, yellow, black threads used. Circular flower and creeper designs at centre, Four gorgeous kalkas in corners.
10. Text 10, Lep kantha, 165 × 110 cms, 19th century. Flowers, small Trees of Life in corners, also Shiva Linga, Krishna, elephant and man on horseback. Many coloured threads used.
11. Text 11, Asan kantha, 71 × 45 cms, 19th century. Large Tree of Life at centre made with red, blue, black threads. Geometric pattern in border.
12. Text 12, Sujni kantha, 105 × 95 cms, 19th century. Very thick kantha like a wrapper. The 'bakheya' stitch used on white surface.
13. Text 13, Sujni kantha, 176 × 137 cms, 19th century. Divided into eight parts with red, black, sky blue and pink threads. Each part linked with a geometric floral design, geometric flower inside each part.
14. Text 14, Dhakna kantha, 76 × 71 cms, 19th century. Aeroplanes, butterflies, birds and bees with coloured threads, rose trees in corners, floral design at centre.
15. Text 15, Asan kantha, 92 × 90 cms, 19th century. Designs on white with red and blue threads. Elephant, horse, lion, bird, peacock, chariot, hookah, human figures etc. The middle is crumpled because of bad stitching.

16. Text 16, Asan kantha, 92 × 89 cms, 19th century. Designed with red, blue, yellow, sky blue threads. Eleven lines of designs in border, round flower, kalka, horse and elephant as motifs.
17. Text 17, Sujni kantha, 100 × 72 cms, 19th century. Very thick kantha, coloured threads used to make design like temple tower, 'V' shaped design at centre.
18. Text 18, Sujni kantha, 100 × 80 cms, 19th century. Circular floral design, our trees of life in corners, four types of kalka and one large round flower between two kalkas.
19. Text 19, Sujni kantha, 169 × 134 cms, 19th century. Embroidered in colour thread. Kalka, horse, peacock, women in different poses, two girls on horseback. Lotus in centre and chessboard patterns.
20. Text 20, Sujni kantha, 150 × 116 cms, 19th century. Light brown and light blue threads used for designs. Ears of corn in border. Small panels all over the kantha, twisted flower in each.
21. Text 21, Sujni kantha,167 × 110 cms, 19th century. Lotus in centre, geometric patterns in border and motifs of dog, peacock, bird, horse, fish. Four elephants on one side and four horses on other. Four Trees of Life in corners and round creeper designs.
22. Text 22, Sujni kantha, 147 × 97 cms, 20th century, collected from Udaypur in Tripura. Brown, black, yellow, red, orange and green threads used. Twisted flowers in borders, Trees of Life, lotus in centre, also elephant, horse and human figures. Line of 30 kalkas.
23. Text 23, Dhakna kantha, 35 × 19 cms, 20th century, collected from Agartala. Red, black, sky blue, yellowish green threads used, kalka and flowers designed. Thin 'paar' designed at the middle.

Crafts Museum, New Delhi

There are about 40 kanthas here, collected from different states. Some are discussed here:

1. Accession 4/463, Dhakna kantha, 81 × 46 cms. Kalka in four corners, many flowers in centre in circular manner. Twisted flowers on two sides of circle. Red, blue, black, yellow threads used for designs.
2. Accession 7/4799, Betan kantha, 183 × 108 cms. Two squares at centre with flower in each, trees of centre in middle, creepers, elephants breadthwise, horses lengthwise.
3. Accession 4/338, large Asan kantha, 121 × 123 cms. Kantha has name, Bidhukumar Das, embroidered. Circular alpana design at centre, inside man on horse and elephant, soldiers, human figures, floral designs.
4. Accession 7/429 Sujni kantha, 178 × 114 cms. Divided into squares. In border below, nine girls standing in row in dance pose and rows of girls from bottom to centre where there is the lotus.
5. Accession 7/4777, Sujni kantha, 152 × 112 cms. Battle scenes embroidered in Mughal art style. Soldiers, chariots, horse and 14 elephants dressed for battle.
6. Accession 4/463, Asan kantha, 88 × 98 cms. Circular alpana at centre, many flowers, human figures, designs with red and black threads in border and of round flowers.
7. Accession 80/174, Asan kantha, 84 × 93 cms. Kantha divided in four parts, kalka at corner in each. Over one kalka is written, Shri Trailakya Nath Mitra, Kadampur.
8. Accession HBF/48, Asan kantha, 75 × 81 cms. Alpana in centre and human figures.
9. Accession 7/2414 Sujni kantha, 74 × 247 cms. Floral designs, lotus with six petals in centre, three lines in half moon shape in four corners, betel-leaves in different sizes.
10. Accession 7/4778, Large Asan kantha, 84 × 92 cms. Human figure in centre, face like Hanuman, three-petalled lotus hanging from two hands.
11. Accession 7/6120 Sujni kantha, 193 × 130 cms. Designs in coloured thread on white surface. Kalka in four corners, stretched designs in border.
12. Accession 49/7772, large Asan kantha, 82 × 84 cms. Round alpana design in centre,

motifs of flower, kalka, bird. Name written in top.

13. Accession 4/3893, Sujni kantha 167 × 187 cms. Many motifs, man sitting on horse in boat.

14. Accession 7/1332, (3), Sujni kantha 165 × 348 cms. Kalka in four corners, inside two men in chariots, fighting with bows and arrows.

    Bottom, court scene, Sakuntala standing before Dushyanta with hands raised, she-demon with open hair standing with stick.

National Museum, New Delhi

Description of 10 kanthas.

1. Accession 89.13, Sujni kantha. Alpana in centre, four big flower round it, Trees of Life. Motifs include girl sitting at window. Hanuman with tail curled up, two on an elephant, woman on horse, man on horse, tigers. Rows of flower in border.

2. Accession 89.62 Sujni. Pineapple like design with coloured threads in centre, Trees of Life, kalka.

3. Accession 89.61, Sujni kantha. Flowers designed like alpana in centre, reverse kalkas in border, net row of fish. Kalka and flowers throughout the kantha.

4. Accession 88.300, Sujni kantha. Round alpana design in centre, kalka and creepers. Three squares in middle.

5. Accession 89.31, Sujni kantha. Designs in borders and inside with coloured thread on white surface, kalka in four corners, trees in-between, four birds, flowers in trees.

6. Accession 89.44 Sujni kantha. Creeper designs in coloured thread from top to bottom with flowers inside — kadam, twisted flowers, chalta.

7. Accession 89.45 Sujni kantha. Small squares made with 'run' stitches. Inside these floral designs. Kalka in four corners, lotus in square at centre. The kalkas are exceptionally bright and colourful.

8. Accession 89.25, large Asan kantha. Rows of kalka and floral designs in borders. In the centre two girls in dancing pose, dog below them. Other motifs include, bird, lion, cat, girls, goat, elephant, camel and peacock.

9. Accession 89.11, Sujni kantha. Flowers and many kalka all over. Round flower designed in centre, small lots in border and small kalka along a line. In the top portion is written, covering all four sides are words lamenting a girl's spinster status. Motifs include elephant, fish, two girls their hands raised, boy with arms raised, Shiva, bull etc.

10. Accession 63.214, Sujni kantha. Round alpana design at centre. Flowers and creepers in border. Next, rows of fish. Also running horse, birds, peacock with plumes spread, cow, deer, grasshopper, flowers.

Calico Museum of Textiles, Ahmedabad

1. Accession 1058, Asan kantha, 47.7 × 95.3 cms, Bengal, 19th century. Run, double run, darning, double darning, botton-hole stitches used. Coloured threads used for designs on white surface. Nine chambers in the kantha. In the middle one woman playing Veena sitting on lotus (Saraswati). Other chambers have leopards, horse, elephant, peacock, and donkey. In four chambers leopards have human faces.

2. Accession 1499, Asan kantha, 87.2 × 82.2 cms, Bengal 19th century, Kalka in four corners, girl sitting at window, elephants, an idol, with a man with pigtails standing with folded hands, peacock, horse, a sitting girl, another in dancing pose. Many coloured threads used and darning, satin, hem, chain stitches used.

3. Accession 459, Asan kantha. 83.8 × 83.8 cms, Bengal, 19th century. Run, darning, double run, satin stitches used. Floral design at centre. Trees of Life in four corners. In bottom half girls dancing, boy in the pose of a musician, one standing with child on shoulder, a boy standing in front of him, hands folded. Top, man on horseback, girl in a chair, fisherman with net, fish boy and girl in boat with another pulling the oar and

such other motifs, all in red and black threads. Kalka in border.

4. Accession 1046, Sujni kantha, 165.2 × 116.9 cms, Bengal, 19th century. Run, double run, darning stitches used. Tiger and horse with syce and rider as motifs, floral designs, geometric patterns in border.

5. Accession 3856, Sujni kantha, Bengal, 19th century. Alpana at centre, different flowers and birds seen. Run, darning, hem, botton-hole stitches used.

6. Accession 1048, Sujni kantha, 102.9 × 94.4 cms, Bengal, 19th century. Red, black, orange and ash coloured threads used, stitches being run, double run, darning, double darning. Flower designed at centre, kalka in corners and elephant, fish, peacocks, peacock on horse and small kalkas designed.

7. Accession 1062, Sujni kantha, 94 × 102.9 cms, Bengal, 19th century, Row of fish in order. Kantha divided into 25 square parts. Kalka in four corners. Then bodies of two elephants in one square and head in the adjoining one. Lions and flower on one side of elephant and buffalo and horse on another, with neck like giraffe, tiger, bison, hanuman, man with horns and stick in hand, dog and pup, goats, woolly lamb, flower, camel, deer with horns, flowers and creepers.

8. Accession S.F. 1698, Sujni kantha, Bengal, 20th century. Red, black, green, yellow threads used. Motifs of boy, girl, tiger, man on horseback, sun, etc. Geometric patterns in border with red and black threads. Run, darning, double darning stitches used.

9. Accession 1079, Lep kantha, 238.9 × 123.3 cms, Bengal, 19th century. Designs on white surface with bright red, black, blue, green, brown, threads. Geometric flower in centre in a square, kalka in two if its corners and birds and small animals in two others. Human figures, animals, fish, birds, flowery, trees, snake charmer etc. in two parts of the kantha. Light 'run' stitch used.

10. Accession 579, Sujni kantha, 194.4 × 139.7 cms, Bengal, 19th century. Divided into 24 parts with a motifs in each. Alpana between four panels in centre, flowers and leaves all round. The motifs include, camel, deer, lion, elephant, horse, man on horseback, fish, flowers, birds. One panel has man dressed in dhoti, chadar (cotton wrapper), sandals with toes turned up (nagra) and fancy sticks, representing the 'baboo culture'. Run, double run, darning stitches used.

11. Accession 1057, Sujni kantha, 135.3 × 101.7 cms, Bengal, 19th century. Run and darning stitches used. Many types of leaves, flower, household items, cow fodling its calf etc. Designs of sari end along border.

12. Accession 1045, Sujni kantha, 188.1 × 128.4 cms, Bengal, 19th century. Run, chain, darning, herring-bone stitches used. Divided into seven parts lengthwise, five of which have Arabic designs and betel-leaf motifs. Geometric patterns in centre. Rows of peacocks in one part. Kalkas in three corners, tiger and peacocks in the side.

13. Accession 1059, Sujni kantha, 149 × 86 cms, Bengal, 20th century. Motif of three stars in centre, round it designs of fish and flowers. Motifs of elephants and horse inside and around border strips of old black cloth attached.

14. Accession 1060, Asan kantha, 79 × 81.9 cms, Bengal, 19th century. Small 'run' stitches with white thread and orange, red, pink, green threads used for designs. Run, double run, darning stitches used. Lotus motif in centre deep coloured threads used for kalkas in three corners. Also, flower, fish, birds, animals, human figures and European soldiers in blue coats and tall red hats. Leaves and flower all over, rows of kalka round border.

15. Accession 811, Lep kantha, 208.4 × 147.4 cms, Bengal, 19th century. Designs made with run, darning stitches and red, white blue threads. Parallel geometric designs run down the kantha. Geometric patterns around the border in blue threads.

16. Accession 1047, Sujni kantha, 177.9 × 161.9 cms, Bengal, 19th century. Leaf motif in centre, flower trees in four corners, inside motif of animals, birds, flowers, old sari ends in border and on this broad floral designs. Designs made with 'run' double run, darning stitches and red and black threads.

17. Accession 1500, Sujni kantha, 129.8 × 89 cms, Bengal, 20th century. Designs made with run, chain, herring-bone stitches and many coloured threads. European influence noticeable in the intermingling of many needlework traditions.

    The central theme is battle. One scene has a soldier being honoured with garlands, below man with gun waiting for palanquin, on the right of this man with shut umbrella among others and another with gun. Men on horseback, archers and many birds. Many human figures stitched with run and darning stitches.

Bangladesh National Museum, Dhaka.

Description of five exhibited kantha. Total number in museum 937.

1. Index N. 68.16, Sujni kantha, Khulna, 20th century. Many 'barfi' designs, designs with coloured threads in kalkas. Motifs include, aeroplane, scissors, nutcrackers, hookah, palanquin, ships, winnow, boat, flag, horse, mirror, earrings, coconut and banana trees, flowers.

2. Index 77.1942, Sujni kantha, Faridpur, 20th century. Many designs with coloured threads on white surface.

3. Index 77.1903, Sujni kantha, Faridpur, 20th century. Six elephants, five deer and nawab on elephants shown in kantha.

4. Index 77.1809, Dastarkhan, Faridpur, 20th century. Over five hands long and 14 fingers wide. Motifs are, nutcracker, mango leaf, lotus, twisted flower, comb, rolled leaf fan, 'barfi' design in border.

5. Sujni kantha, Jessore, 19th century. Kantha has different idols and their motifs, like Durga on lion, Indra on elephant (Airabat), Durga with family. Flower, Tree of Life, festival scene, chariot, Krishna under kadam tree, Kartick on horseback and Shiva on bull.

Lok Aitihya Sangrahashala (Folk Tradition Museum), Bangla Acadmey, Dhaka

There are seven kanthas here.

1. Nakshi kantha, collected by Nurul Huq Mullah from Faridpur, 1968. White surface, lotus in centre, kalka in four corners. Next to kalka a tree with leaves, small 'run' stitched with white thread and green thread used for designs. Red thread used for border.

2. Tribal designs, collected by Mohammed Saidur from Rangamati in 1974. Resembles handloom cloth. Red and black threads used on surface.

3. Nakshi kantha, collected by Aldur Rahman Thakur from Ghior in 1965. Lotus in centre, creeper designs all around. Motifs include fish, betel-leaf, flower, rose. Name, Abinash embroidered in kantha. White, yellow, red, black, blue, pink threads used in kantha.

4. Nakshi kantha, collected by Mohammed Saidur from Narail in 1968. Lotus in centre, flower inside, 15 girls holding a rope, two chariots with people standing inside in different poses, peacocks (10) and Trees of Life (28). Many coloured threads used.

5. Nakshi Asan, collected from Bagerhat, Khulna. Two tigers facing each other in centre, next to it geometric patterns and twin leaves. Deep pink, green and blue threads used.

6. Asan kantha, collected by Mohammed Saidur from Narail in 1983. Border designed with red, black threads yellow.

7. Dastarkhan, collected by Mohammed Saidur from Gopalganj (Faridpur) in 1968. Two circles and semi- circles designed. Threads used, red, green, black, purple, orange, ash and mustard coloured.

Bangladesh Lok Karushilpa Foundation, Sonargaon, Narayanganj

Description of 109 nakshi kanthas in museum. Total number 800.

1. Accession 76(3)2, Sujni kantha, 199 × 111 cms, Rajsahi, mid-20th century. Designs in cross stitches with red, green, yellow threads. Flower in centre around which motifs of duck, peacock, deer, elephant. Geometric patterned flowers around border, Lace fringes.
2. Accession 76(3)3, Sujni kantha, 148 × 110 cms, Khulna, end 19th century. Coloured threads used to make rectangular 'paar' designs.
3. Accession 76(3)4, Sujni kantha, 162 × 99 cms, Khulna, end 19th century. White surface and 'paar' designs with coloured threads.
4. Accession 76(3)5, Bachka kantha, 87 × 84 cms, Khulna, mid-19th century. Designs with red, blue, green, yellow threads on white surface. Lotus in centre and four semi-circular petals. Twisted flowers on four sides and on top of border different twisted flowers. Three lines of leaves above this.
5. Accession 76(3)6, Asan kantha, 76 × 76 cms, Khulna mid-20th century. Red, green, blue, yellow threads used for desings, lotus in four corners and in centre. Mosque motif round centre, also tree, leaf, bird, fish etc.
6. Accession 76(3)7, Sujni kantha, 180 × 112 cms, Khulna, end 20th century. Designs in cross stitches and border designed with 'anarasi' (pineapple smell) flower. Artist's name embroidered as Mini.
7. Accession 76(3)8, Sujni kantha, 162 × 107 cms, Khulna end 19th century. Floral designs all along the surface with coloured threads.
8. Accession 76(3)10, Nakshi bag, 22 × 13 cms, Khulna mid-19th century. Red, black, white threads used. 'Barfi' design at centre also row of ants. Twisted flowers designed with black thread in front portion.
9. Accession 76(3)11, Nakshi bag, 20 × 12 cms. Khulna, mid-19th century. Designs with white, red, black designs. Central motif is a thatched roof.
10. Accession 76(3)13, Asan, kantha, 46 × 43 cms, Rajsahi, end 19th century. Red, blue, green, brown threads used. Lotus in centre, four trees in corners. Moon and star and creepers designed on either side. Stretched flowers in border.
11. Accession 76(3)16, Sujni kantha, 115 × 109 cms. Rajsahi, mid-19th century. Cloured threads used on white surface to make motifs of flower and ducks. Geometric pattern in border.
12. Accession 76(3)18, Sujni kantha, 167 × 108 cms, Khulna, mid-19th century. Red, green, yellow threads used. Chokh taga (eye border) in centre and amulets and nose rings designed in border.
13. Accession 76(3)19, Sujni kantha, 165 × 104 cms, Khulna, end 19th-century. Red, green, deep blue threads used on white surface. The 'anarasi' flower motif in the border design.
14. Accession 76(3)20, Sujni kantha, 167 × 100 cms, Khulna, early 20th century. Red, black, purple, green threads used. Floral designs all over.
15. Accession 76(3)21, Sujni kantha, 182 × 129 cms, Khulna, end 19th century. 'Paar' designs in rectangular form all over the kantha.
16. Accession 76(3)22, Arsilata, 59 × 20 cms, Khulna, early 20th century. Red, green, blue, light yellow threads used. Tree in centre and four corners. Four trees with branches round border and five lines of 'paar' design.
17. Accession 76(3)23, Arsilata, 41 × 22 cms, Khulna, early 20th century. Designs with coloured threads 'anarasi' flower as motif.
18. Accession 76(3)24, Sujni kantha. 153 × 97 cms, Khulna, end 19th century. Red, green and white threads used. Betel-leaf motif in centre, on four sides motif of tree, flower,

green coconut, pan etc. Flower-leaf in four corners. Lines of leaves in red and green threads in square portion at centre.

19. Accession 76(3)26, Dastarkhan, 120 × 33 cms, Khulna, end 19th century. Four lotuses in the surface, two flags in the middle of one-lotus and three 'barfis'. Written on top in Arabic, Allah Ho Akbar. Bismilla written with green thread and nose rings in border.

20. Accession 76(3)27, Bochka kantha, 96 × 94 cms, Khulna, early 20th century. Lotus with red and black threads and eye designed in border. In one sari end panel measuring 30 cms.

21. Accession 76(3)30, Sujni kantha, 157 × 97 cms, Khulna, early 20th century. Red, blue, green threads used for border designs on all sides. Flower designs in border.

22. Accession 77(3)29, Lep kantha, 183 × 129 cms, Khulna, end 19th century. Divided into 15 squares with a flower in each.

23. Accession 77(3)32, Sujni kantha, 170 × 122 cms, Khulna, end 19th century. Floral designs at centre, 'paar' designs in rectangular shape.

24. Accession 77(3)33, Sujni kantha, 180 × 115 cms, Khulna, early 20th century. 'Anarasi' flowers designed in whole kantha.

25. Accession 77(3)35, Sujni kantha, 148 × 106 cms, Khulna, early 20th century. Anarasi flower in 'paar' designs with coloured threads.

26. Accession 77(3)36, Dastarkhan, 109 × 33 cms. Khulna, end 19th century. Kantha divided lengthwise in three parts and in centre the lotus motif. In four corners designs of semi-circular leaves.

27. Accession 77(3)37, Sujni kantha, 162 × 97 cms, Khulna end 19th century. Red, blue and purple threads used for 'paar' designs throughout the kantha.

28. Accession 77(3)38, Asan kantha, 53 × 49 cms, Khulna, early 20th century. Lotus in centre. On four sides four flowers with 4 petals and one with three petals. Flowers with branches in four corners, geometric pattern in border. Red and green threads used.

29. Accession 77(3)39, Dastarkhan, 170 × 33 cms, Khulna, end 19th century. Six lotus lengthwise and 70 small kalka as motifs.

30. Accession 77(3)41, Sujni kantha, 159.99 cms, Khulna, early 20th century. 'Paar' designs on all four sides with black thread and fringes with red thread.

31. Accession 77(3)42, Arsilata, 86 × 31 cms, Khulna, end 19th century. Flowery tree in centre and on all four sides designs of 'Kalmilata' (edible acquatic plant) flower.

32. Accession 78(3)43, Sujni kantha, 178.132 cms, Jessore, late 19th century. Designs made with coloured threads. Lotus in centre, Tree of Life in four corners, floral patterns in border and the end of which old sari ends stitched.

33. Accession 78(3)46, Dastarkhan, 228.44 cms, Khulna, end 19th century. Eight petalled lotus in centre, round it flowers, creepers and 'anarasi' flower. Written on kantha, Mafuja Khatun.

34. Accession 78(3)47, Asan kantha, 92.86 cms, Kusthia, early 20th century. Tree, peacocks, flowers embroidered in cross stitch.

35. Accession 78(3)49, Asan kantha, 68.56 cms, Kusthia, early 20th century. Flower in centre and floral designs. Silk fringes at border.

36. Accession 78(3)50, Pillow-cover, 44.28 cms, Mymensingh, early 20th century. Banana tree, flowers, birds etc. as motif made with red and green threads.

37. Accession 78(3)51, Pillow-cover, 98.41 cms, Mymensingh, early 20th century. Two flowery trees in centre and creepers designed all around.

38. Accession 79(3)52, Bochka kantha, 112×94 cms, Khulna, end 19th century. Lotus in centre and all around designs of elephant,

fish, peacock, bird, wheel, human figures etc. Flowery trees in four corners.

39. Accession 80(3)54, Lep kantha, 202 × 152 cms, Kishoreganj, end 19th century. Flower in centre and all over, designed with red, black, blue, yellow, green, brown, orange threads on white surface.

40. Accession 80(3)55, Jaynamaz, 9 × $4\frac{1}{2}$ cms. Mymensingh, end 19th century. Large Tree of Life in centre and 18 lotus motifs.

41. Accession 80(3)57, Sujni kantha, 152 × 160 cms, Mymensingh, late 19th century. Red, black and mustard coloured threads used. Tree of Life in centre and stretched flowers designed. Amulet motif designed.

42. Accession 80(3)59, Sujni kantha, 162 × 104 cms, Mymensingh, early 20th century. 'Paar' designed throughout the kantha. Eye design in centre, date palm tree, horse ring and flower in border. Four stems of flowers in red thread in four corners.

43. Accession 80(3)60, Arsilata, 59 × 26 cms, Mymensingh, early 20th century. Tree of Life in centre and on two sides of it fish, duck, elephant, swastika kalmilata flowers.

44. Accession 80(3)61, Arsilata, 43 × 20 cms, Mymensingh, early 20th century. Kantha filled with two Trees of Life facing opposite directions.

45. Accession 80(3)64, Sujni kantha, 148 × 109 cms, Mymensingh, early 20th century. Red, blue, green threads used. Hundred petalled lotus in centre Designs of fish, flowery tree, flower, leaf, Kalmilata and snails.

46. Accession 80(3)65, Asan kantha, 46 × 46 cms, Mymensingh, late 19th century. Lotus in centre, Tree of Life in four corners. Designs of Kalmilata all around and flower and duck motifs in border. Old sari ends round the border.

47. Accession 80(3)67, Dastarkhan, 76 × 34 cms, Mymensingh, early 20th century. Red, yellow, leaf-green, deep blue threads used. Lotus in centre and three more lotus motifs. Kalmilata designed in border.

48. Accession 80(3)68, Arsilata, 51 × 18 cms, Mymensingh, early 20th century. Red, blue, green, vermilion coloured threads used. Tree with flowers in centre, found it moon and stars, leaves, butterfly and flower buds designed.

49. Accession 80(3)69, Arsilata, 40 × 18 cms, Mymensingh, early 20th century. Tree in centre and round it thin 'paar' designs.

50. Accession 80(3)70, Pillow-cover, 40 × 29 cms, Mymensingh, early 20th century. Flowery tree in centre, in four corners trees with three flowers each and other small flowers.

51. Accession 80(3)71, Pillow-cover, 40 × 33 cms, Mymensingh, early 20th century. Many coloured threads on write surface. Flowery trees facing away in centre and round these floral designs.

52. Accession 80(3)73, Pillow-cover, 44 × 29 cms, Mymensingh, early 20th century. Red, blue, yellow, green threads on white surface. Inside 18 divisions, each with a flower, round it kalmilata flower designed.

53. Accession 80(3)74, Pillow-cover 43 × 33 cms, Mymensingh, early 20th century. Lotus in centres and in four corners, four branches and flowers with leaves. Geometric patterns in border.

54. Accession 80(3)75, Pillow-cover, 43 × 31 cms, Mymensingh, early 20th century. Geometric patterns all over, 'benki' designs in border.

55. Accession 80(3)76, Pillow-cover, 42 × 33 cms, Mymensingh, early 20th century. Flowery tree in centre and motif of flowers and leaves.

56. Accession 80(3)77, Pollow-cover, 43 × 33 cms, Mymensingh, early 20th century. Red, black, blue threads used. Fifteen squares, twisted flowers in 12 and floral designs in three.

57. Accession 80(3)78, Pillow-cover, 43×34 cms, Mymensingh, early 20th century. Flowers and leaves designed with red, yellow, green threads. Flower in centre floral designs all

around and four corners. Designs of banana tree leaves and flowers on four sides. Ears of corn in border.

58. Accession 80(3)80, Asan kantha, 40 × 36 cms, Mymensingh, early 20th century. Lotus in centre, flowers on four sides of it and 'shapla' (aquatic plant) designs in four corners.

59. Accession 80(3)82, Asan kantha, 38 × 38 cms, Kishoreganj, early 20th century. Flower in centre, round it four flowers and two flowery trees. For four different flowery trees in four corners. Sankhalata (type of plant) in border.

60. Accession 80(3)83, Arsilata, 68 × 24 cms, Kishoreganj, late 19th century. Four lotus designed lengthwise, flowers and kalmilata designed. Old sari ends in border.

61. Accession 80(3)87, Pillow-cover, 43 × 33 cms, Kishoreganj, early 20th century. Geometric patterns in kantha, star shaped flowers in these and designs of stretched flowers on four sides.

62. Accession 80(3)88, Pillow-cover, 43 × 36 cms, Kishoreganj, early 20th century. Lotus in centre, trees with flowers and leaves in four corners.

63. Accession 80(3)90. Pillow-cover, 61.34 cms, Kishoreganj, early 20th century. Red, green, mustard coloured threads used to design flowers, nose-ring in border.

64. Accession 80(3)91, Pillow-cover, 53 × 83 cms, Mymensingh, early 20th century. 'Paar' design covers entire kantha, 'benki' design in border with red and green threads.

65. Accession 80(3)94, Pillow-cover, 43 × 36 cms, Kishoreganj, early 20th century. Large tree in border, all round stretched designs of flowers and leaves. Button-hole stitch in border, many coloured threads used.

66. Accession 80(3)95, Pillow-cover, 41 × 31 cms, Kishoreganj, early 20th century. Lotus in centre on four sides twisted flowers and geometric patterns. Trees in four corners. Red, green, mustard coloured threads used.

67. Accession 80(3)96, Pillow-cover, 46 × 28 cms, Kishoreganj, mid-20th century. Anarasi flower designed all over with red and green threads.

68. Accession 80(3)97, Pillow-cover, 41 × 31 cms, Kishoreganj, mid-20th century. Thatched roof in centre, each layer of roof has triangle designed, four in all, and a flower designed in each triangle. Red and yellow thread used.

69. Accession 80(3)99, Pillow-cover, 43 × 34 cms, Kishoreganj, early 20th century. Flower in centre round it other flowers and leaves, motifs of stretched flowers and betel-leaf in border.

70. Accession 80(3)100, Pillow-cover, 43 × 31 cms, Mymensingh, early 20th century. Fruit tree in centre and round it nose-ring, fish designed.

71. Accession 80(3)107, Lep kantha, 219 × 170 cms, Sherpur, end 19th century. Geometric patterns in kantha.

72. Accession 80(3)128, Lep kantha, 203 × 122 cms. Rajsahi, mid-20th century. Red surface has rows of fish, pitcher, winnow, flower and tree designed in white thread. Lace of red thread in border.

73. Accession 80(3)129, Sujni kantha, 118 × 84 cms, Rajsahi, mid-20th century. Bright, colourful kantha, yellow and green thread used. Designs on red 'shalu', a kind of cotton fabric. Eleven flowers in a row in centre. Designs of fish, flower, birds etc.

74. Accession 80(3)132, Sujni kantha, 198 × 170 cms, Kishoreganj, end 19th century. Twisted flower in centre, round it four of the same, and also in border.

75. Accession 80(3)139, Sujni kantha, 180 × 158 cms, Jamalpur, end 19th century. Triangular design in centre. Twisted and other flowers designed.

76. Accession 80(3)141, Sujni kantha, 143 × 100 cms, Jamalpur, end 19th century. Twisted flower and wheel in centre and amulet designed in border. Fringes with coloured thread.

77. Accession 80(3)151, Pillow-cover, 38 × 27 cms, Jamalpur, mid-20th century. Green, yellow, brown threads used. Three rows of fish and flowers, kalmilata flower in border. In the middle 40 squares and in eight rows of flowers, two rows of fish, two rows of flowers.

78. Accession 80(3)152, Dastarkhan, 125 × 31 cms, Jamalpur early 20th century. Three lotuses and four trees as motifs.

79. Accession 80(3)153, Arsilata, 59 × 23 cms, Jamalpur, mid-20th century. Two trees facing opposite ways in centre, round these designs of stretched flowers, lace in the border.

80. Accession 80(3)154, Nakshi bag, 36 × 22 cms, Jamalpur, end 19th century. Twisted thread designed in front measuring 31 cms, whole kantha has the *Kachu* (edible root) leaves as motif.

81. Accession 80(3)159, Dastarkhan, 114 × 30 cms, Kishoreganj, end 19th century. Three lotus, trees with leaves in four corners, two trees with flowers on two sided of the centre.

82. Accession 80(3)160, Dastarkhan, 143 × 22 cms, Mymensingh, end 19th century. Lotus in centre and on two sides circular flowers. Motifs include fish, nutcracker, twisted flower, star, leaf. Border has creeper design.

83. Accession 80(3)161, Arsilata, 58 × 18 cms, Kishoreganj, early 20th century. Red, blue, black, green threads used. Four lotus in centre and border thinly designed.

84. Accession 81(3)164, Jaynamaz, 89 × 70 cms, Tangail, early 20th century. Red, black, green, yellow threads used. Church motif in centre, next to it moon and star. Flower trees both at top and bottom. Round border, 'benki' design.

85. Accession 81(3)168, Dastarkhan, 116 × 27 cms, Tangail, mid-20th century. Three lotuses, two trees with leaves, two Trees of Life, star shaped flower and creeper design in border.

86. Accession 81(3)184, Dastarkhan, 81 × 23 cms, Kusthia, early 20th century. Red, green and yellow threads used on white surface. Three large circular flowers, two Trees of Life, stretched flowers in border and on the side of border triangular lace attached.

87. Accession 81(3)186, Arsilata, 51 × 24 cms, Kusthia, late 19th century. Red and black threads used, Tree of Life in centre and motifs a rows of ants and fish in border.

88. Accession 81(3)187, Arsilata, 34 × 19 cms, Kusthia, early 20th century. Coloured threads used on white surface. Large tree with six leaves in centre and designs around it and in border. Motifs of seven leaves on either side and geometric patterns.

89. Accession 81(3)188, Arsilata, 55 × 23 cms, Kusthia, early 20th century. Red and green threads used, flower in middle, semi-circular design and rows of fish round border and nose-ring designed.

90. Accession 81(3)191. Sujni kantha, 188 × 127 cms, Kusthia, end 19th century. Twenty-one squares in middle and round it 14 circular lotuses. Old sari ends in border.

91. Accession 81(3)193, Nakshi bag, 57 ×2 3 cms, Kusthia, early 20th century. In front an owl in red and green threads, and kachu leaves designed all over.

92. Accession 81(3)195, Nakshi bag, 37 × 23 cms, Kusthia, end 19th century. Designs of kachu leaves. An owl measuring 41 cms and torn parts stitched again with green threads.

93. Accession 81(3)198, Nakshi beg, 33×19 cms, Kusthia, early 20th century. Same design as above and owl in deep blue in front.

94. Accession 81(3)199, Nakshi bag, 31 × 19 cms, Kusthia, early 20th century. Kachu leaves designed and 'paar' in top and bottom corners.

95. Nakshi kantha (map of Bangladesh), Khulna (at present Satkgira) end 20th century. Different threads used to show borders of districts. Also floral designs. Made by Lady

Aminur Nahar, Alipur Village, Khulna. Written on kantha, "We Bengalis live in this pilgrim centre of Bengal". Kantha made from 1971 to 1978.

96. Jaynamaz, Tangail, mid-20th century.
97. Jaynamaz, Jamalpur, end 19th century.
98. Asan kantha, Khulna, end 19th century .
99. Bochka kantha, Gopalganj, end 19th century.
100. Same as above.
101. Asan kantha, Narail, Jessore, end-19th century.
102. Asan kantha, Kushtia, mid-20th century.
103. Same as above.
104. Asan kantha, Jessore, mid-20th century.
105. Same as above.
106. Bochka kantha, Gopalganj, mid-20th century.
107. Bochka kantha, Faridpur, early 20th century.
108. Asan kantha, Mymensingh, end 19th century.
109. Dastarkhan, Dhaka, moral lessons in red, blue, black threads.

Bangla Ghar, Dhaka, Bangladesh

Seventeen nakshi kantha collected by Tofail Ahmed.

1. Coverlet, Goalanda, 'Paar' design kantha, stitches in red, black, green threads.
2. Large Sujni, Chuadanga, different border designs in the kantha. Artist, Momena Khatun.
3. Pan-panchani, Rangpur, nearly 100 years old.
4. Palki (palanquin) kantha, Chalanbil, Natore. Designs symbolising the virtues.
5. Arsilata, Badarganj Union.
6. Betan kantha, Sankhalata (creeper) design.
7. Same as above.
8. Betan kantha, Mujibnagar. 'barfi' design.
9. Betan kantha, Bogura, Betbari.
10. Betan kantha, Rajbari.
11. Betan kantha, Bogura, Betbari.
12. Betan katha, Bogura Shibganj.
13. Carpet kantha, Rajsahi, Nababganj.
14. Batua, Rajsahi.
15. Khincha (small purse) Chalanbil, Natore.
16. Gift kantha on black surface.
17. Same as above.

Chittagong University Museum, Bangladash

Only one kantha, collected by Syed Majibur Rahman. Sujni kantha, 6′ 4″ × 4′ Chittagong, mid-20th century. Red, black, yellow, light blue threads used. Flowery tree in centre. Divided into 27 parts with the 'barfi' design. Each part has different flowers. Written along two sides of the centre is, 'This cloth belongs to Md. M.A.M. estd 1949.' Floral designs along sides of border.

The Victoria and Albert Museum, London

Quite a few kanthas are there in this museum. Six are discussed here.

1. 616-1886, kantha, Bengal, 16th century. Got from the Portuguese market. Hunting scene depicted on yellow silk with fine stitching. Hunter about to spear down a deer, a dog and motifs of other animals. Flowers in a circular arrangement.
2. I.S. 157-1853, kantha, Bengal, early 17th century. Got from the Portuguese market. Beautifully embroidered scene of hunters with guns and animals running away. Also had motifs of flower trees.
3. I.S. 22-1983. Sujni kantha, Jessore, early 20th century. Threads of very light colour used. Circular alpana design in centre, on its two sides chariots, on other two sides Trees of Life. Also human figures, dogs, fish, flowers, peacocks, tiger, elephant etc. as motifs. Different designs in borders on four sides.
4. I.S. 62-1981, Sujni kantha, Faridpur, end 19th century. Designs with red and ash coloured threads on white surface. One set of kalkas in two borders and another set in other two. Rows of leaves above the kalkas and 27 flowers inside.

5. I.S. 61-1981, Asan kantha, Bangladesh, early 20th century. Blue, red, mustard-yellow, light green and ash coloured threads used beautifully on white surface. Lotus motif in centre. Four types of kalka in four corners on both sides of which smaller kalkas on creepers. Motifs of peacock, bird and fish. Around the border ears of corn, kalka, geometric patterns and stretched flowers have been designed.
6. I.S. 13-1996, Asan kantha, West Bengal, late 20th century. Designs with red and ash threads on white surface. Whole kantha divided into 36 parts and in each flowers designed alternately with red and ash threads. Twisted flower in white thread between each division.

Philadelphia Museum of Art, USA

Fifty kanthas here including those collected by Stella Kramrisch. Described here are 18 of those.

1. Accession 1968-184-2, Lep kantha, East Bengal, second half of 19th century. Coloured threads used on white surface, circular lotus design at centre, round it alpana. Trees of Life in the corners of the central square portion, four peacocks on either side of it, leaves in the kantha's corners and thin border design.
2. Accession 1968-184-3, Sujni kantha, Bengal, approx. end 19th century. Designs with coloured thread on white surface. Circular flower in centre, birds all around, kalka in corners and dhoti and designed in border.
3. Accession 1968-184-4, Sujni kantha, Jessore, 19th century. A longish kantha. Motifs include elephant, fish, twisted flowers, human figures, peacocks. Creepers designed in border.
4. Accession 1968-184-5, Lep kantha, Faridpur, early 20th century. Many motifs with coloured threads like twisted flowers. Trees of Life, Krishna playing the flute sitting on a tree or holding hands with Radha, men and women in a boat. Thin design in border, above it kalkas.
5. Accession 1968-184-6. Asan kantha, Faridpur, late 19th or early 20th century. Motifs include peacock, big snake devouring smaller snake, Kali, Krishna, Radha, Shiva, cat, butterfly, leaves of the *asvathva* tree (Indian fig tree considered sacred). Written in the kantha, 'Bemal Kamini'
6. Accession 1968-184-7, Lep kantha, Faridpur, late 19th century. Alpana design in centre, stretched flowers in borders, Tree of Life in four corners, elephant, horse, Shiva Linga on one side and on the other, three men in different poses, severed heads, tortoise, fish. Next Shiva on tiger skin, two severed heads, snake and human figures.
7. Accession 1968-184-8, Lep kantha, Faridpur, 1875. Alpana in centre, Trees of Life in corners, Shiva and Parvati, man with two tails, syce and running horse, palace, Ram, Lakshman, Sita, Saraswati playing the veena, snakes, birds, flowers etc. as motifs.
8. Accession 1968-184-10. Sujni kantha, Faridpur, end 19th century. Three panels at centre. In one man and woman, horse, peacock, in another Krishna, fish, mongoose, Durga, hermit etc. Many other motifs length and breadthwise. Alpana at centre and kalka in four corners.
9. Accession 1968-184-11, Lep kantha, Jessore, second half of 19th century. Lotus in centre, round it circular alpana with flowers and kalka. On one side three women and a man, fish and on other sepoys with swords, horse, peacock, Also elephants, horses, women with swords on horseback.
10. Accession 1968-184-13, Lep kantha, Jessore, second half of 19th century. Alpana in centre, kalka in four corners, round which birds, flowers and betel leaves. Elephants and human figures on the broad side and horses and kalkas on the other.
11. Accession 1968-184-14, Sujni kantha, Jessore, late 19th century. Alpana in centre and motifs include, Durga with her family, syce on horseback, peacock, birds, horse and

elephant. Written on the kantha is, "Owner of this khata (as called in some places) is Shri Hiralal" and also a line singing the praise of the Almighty.

12. Accession 1968-184-14, Sujni kantha, East Bengal. second half of 19th century. Alpana in centre, kalkas in corners and border. Tree of Life birds, peacocks, horse, elephant, two syces with horses facing each other.

13. Accession 1968-184-17, Lep kantha, Faridpur, 19th century. Circular alpana design at centre, Tree of Life in four corners, many children with raised hands, a man in Western dress, fish, 14 men and women with swords.

14. Accession 1991-148-606, Sujni kantha, Khulna, approx. 19th century. Alpana design in centre, Tree of Life, chariot, girls with raised hands, horse, peacock, birds, elephant, tortoise, cat, many flowers.

15. Accession 1994-148-673, Sujni kantha, Bengal, approx. 19th century. Kalka and alpana with floral designs at centre. Many motifs including elephant, birds, man with hat on, woman on horseback, man sitting in chair etc.

16. Accession 1994-148-683, Sujni kantha, Bengal, approx. 19th century. Lotus in centre round it floral designs. On one side four girls in dancing pose, on the other three boys with raised hands holding branches of trees. Countless twisted flowers.

17. Accession 1994-148-684, Sujni kantha, Bengal, approx. 19th century. Alpana design in centre and on four corners of it four peacocks with spread plumes, flowers, Trees of Life. Four different kalkas in the kantha corners. In bottom panel on broadside, baboo sitting in a chair with hookah, boy standing with hat and another sitting in chair, five women with raised hands. Another botton panel has tiger, birds, fish and 10 in a peacock boat with head shaped liked peacock. Lengthwise a woman with a broom in one hand and holding a man by his hair, hunter on tiger, man on elephant etc. Many flowers and also two boars.

18. Accession 1994-148-715, Sujni kantha, Bengal, approx. 19th century. Looks a little different in that all designs have not been filled up but only outlined. Divided into 15 panels each with a separate design.

Personal Collections

Many people have kanthas in their possession. Here I have discussed some which I have seen or heard about.

Amitendranath Tagore, Calcutta. He has the kantha collected by Abanindranath Tagore. It has already been discussed in the chapter, 'Not Just Coverlets'.

Prasanta and Gita Das, Barasat, North 24 Parganas. Sujni dorokha kantha, 4 × 3 hands, about 200 years old and made by Jasoda Biswas. It is even better looking than the dorokhas found in the Hauli Damud region. Alpana in centre and kalkas, mostly outlined. The motifs are, horse, peacock, birds, human figures. In one corner two elephants facing each other, two horses in another, and in two other peacocks. Two large Trees of Life with wheel shaped flowers, smaller ones, twisted flowers. White thread used for small 'run' stitches and coloured for designs. Surface is white.

Sujata Mitra, Santiniketan

1. Bedspread (according to artists) over 100 years old. Made in Lohagar village, Birbhum, it is a thick kantha with small 'run' stitches between designs with white thread. Small flowers embroidered with yellow, red, green, black and other coloured threads.

2. A Birbhum kantha also over 100 years old. Designs made with coloured threads. Geometric patterns in border as also stretched flowers. The middle portion divided into 18 parts which have designs of the chalta flower and twisted flowers.

Indranath Mazumdar, Santiniketan

Nakshi bag, $9'' \times 4\frac{1}{2}''$ (in the middle) and an inch less in the top, Jessore, late 19th century.

Made by Jnada Mazumdar of Karandi village, Jessore. It has a broad base and tapers at the top. The bag was made after folding the cloth three times. The main surface is white on which many coloured threads have been used. Circular lotus in centre inside which are twisted flowers in a circle. Barfi designs in the border. Button holes made in the end with red thread.

Arun Nag, Santiniketan

Made by great grandmother (mother's side) of Arun Nag, in Rambhadrapur village, under Palang P.S. of Faridpur district. One hundred and twenty years old kantha, it was made with 'run' stitches from top to bottom. Black thread used on white surface. Kalkas in four corners and pineapple designs in border, followed by geometric patterns.

Sunanda Mukhopadhyaya, Bolpur

Sujni kantha made 60 years ago in Siwan by Safia. Designs made with threads from sari ends. Border has sari ends then designed creepers followed by peacocks and flowers. In the middle two Trees of Life, made with green and red threads. Peacocks made with red and blue threads. Butterfly in one corner.

Anath Nath Das, Santiniketan

1. Dhakna kantha, collected by Pulinbehari Sen. Made in Mymensingh, two hands long and a little over one hand broad. Made over 120 years ago. Small 'run' stitches on white surface and coloured thread used for designs.
2. Arsilata, Tangail, over 100 years old, made by Saralabala Sen. The 'eye' design in border. Flower designed in eye shaped panel in centre, three types of designs on all four sides. Red and blue threads used on white surface.
3. Baby's kantha, made over 80 years, different border designs on all four sides.

Bela Ghosh, Calcutta

1. Kusthia kantha over 100 years old. Four hands long and two hands and eight fingers wide. Many coloured threads used on white surface. Four colourful kalkas in four corners, threads used a little differently though design is the same. Many coloured threads used for dots inside. Kalka in black and red in border.
2. Sujni kantha, 6 hands long and four hands wide, 100 years old. Red, blue, sky blue, cream, brick coloured, purple, yellow threads used. Flowers and creepers in border four colourful kalka in four corners with small kalkas on top. Below leaves and flowers and leaves inside. At centre 16 leaves with branches round a big flower. Alphabets written in English like :

   K.K.D.M.I.D., R.A.N.C.H.

Satyajit Chowdhury, Naihati

1. Belongs approximately to early 1940s. Made by Soudamini Chowdhury, of Harinarayanpur village, Kusthia. A lep kantha, 7′ long and 4′ wide. Small 'run' stitches with white thread on white surface. Flowers and Trees of Life embroidered with red and light blue threads.
2. Asan kantha, $3\frac{1}{2}' \times 2'$, artist. Kshetradasi Chakravarty, Nimta, North 24 Parganas, 1930. White surface, coloured threads used to make peacock. In the corner flowers in pot.

Anita Sarkar, Lalbagh, Murshidabad

Four kanthas, all made in Lalbagh by late Sarojini Bag.

1. Sujni kantha, 5′10″ × 4′8″ Lotus in centre and small 'run' stitches with white thread. Fifteen lotus next to centre, elephants and peacocks on either side. Motifs betel leaf, owl, bird. Over 130 years old, took more than a year to make.
2. Sujni kantha, 5′10″ × 3′10″. Big lotus in centre and other lotus motifs. Sari end

threads used. Designs outlined with coloured threads.

3. Pillow-cover Kantha, 2′6″ × 11″. Small white kantha with designs embroidered in red and blue threads.
4. Arsilata, 1′1″ × 1″. Yellow and green threads used to make Chokh Taga (the eye border) designs.

Maya Mukhopadhyaya, Agartala, Tripura

1. This kantha received the National Merit Certificate in 1966. Two types of yellow, black, green snuff coloured threads used on white surface. It is made of three-layered cloth on which the 'run' stitch has been used in different ways. The theme is, rural scene and seen in the kantha are farmers working in the field, woodcutter chopping wood, potter making clay pots, date-palm juice being collected, fishermen, domestic scenes etc. Lotus in centre, round it domestic items, conch-shell, kalka, boat, sun, moon, elephant. The traditional ways of kantha making are noticeable.
2. Kantha made in 1996-97. Aspects of Krishna's life shown with fine embroidery.

Zainul Abedin, Chaka, Bangladesh

The renowned artist has 37 kanthas. Eight are discussed here.

1. Asan kantha, Jessore, Lakshmipasha P.S. One hundred and fifty two years old, white surface, many coloured threads used. Motifs include, dog, cock, flower, banana tree with man standing next to it, two on an elephant, human figures.
2. Asan kantha, Narail, Kalia P.S. Lotus with eight petals in centre, border designs on four sides, wild creepers in pot, chariot with flag and blossoming lotus on side, fish, betel-leaf, tree.
3. Asan kantha, Magura, Mohammedpur P.S. Lotus in centre with creepers all around, handfan, temple, fish, bird, elephant, running horse, tree.
4. Large Asan kantha, Faridpur. Bunch of flowers in centre, fish, kachu (edible root) trees in four corners, two star shaped flowers candles on all four sides.
5. Asan kantha. Designs in red and black thread on white surface. Flower in centre, on one side large scissor, nextcomb, fish, bird, flower, elephant, deer etc. Message in Bengali (spellings are the artist's own) urges all to remain well and says the kantha is fit for a 'badshah' (king) to sit on.
6. Sujni kantha, different motifs embroidered such as peacock, chariot, central lotus, tree, flower, dancer, fairies etc.
7. Sujni kantha 6′ × 3′. Thousand petalled lotus in centre, different creepers in border, designs of animals, man on horseback, dancing girl (nautch girl), demon, flowers etc.
8. Gatri (sack) kantha. Designs of flowers, creepers, kalka, household items, boat, wheel etc. Lotus in centre. Written on the kantha:

   Bandra (Bengali month) Tuesday Year 1316, 13 Magh (Year and month of Bengali calendar).

Mohammed Saidur, Kishoreganj, Bangladesh

Description of 100 of his 350 kanthas.

1. Dastarkhan, 5′2″ × 1″, Sherpur, 20th century, third decade. The kantha has the sun symbol, fish, creepers in the border followed by rows of ants and geometric patterns.
2. Asan kantha, 32″ × 32″, Faridpur, 20th century, third decade. Twenty-three conch-shell motifs on one side and four square designs on the other. Dates and sheaves of corn designed with different stitches. Conch-shell motif embroidered with yellow thread on red surface.
3. Asan kantha, 5′2″ × 1″ Kusthia, 20th century, fourth decade. Geometric patterns inside and on border with coloured threads. Red 'shalu' fringes in border which also has creepers designed.

4. Asan kantha, 47″ × 32″, Mymensingh, 20th century, scond decade. Six petalled lotus in centre, round it designs of sun. Deer and nine different types of flower. Red, yellow, black threads used for design on white surface.

5. Sujni kantha, 62″ × 52″, Kusthia, 20th century, third decade. Border has creepers between two rows of butterflies and on one side budding flower and creepers.

6. Lep kantha, 70″ × 64″, Rajsahi, 20th century, third decade. Squares in whole kantha with red and black threads and one round flower in each.

7. Asan kantha 32″ × 30″, Kusthia, 20th century, third decade. Diverse flowers in centre, rows of small flowers round it, then creeper designs and budding flowers. Geometric patterns in border.

8. Sujni kantha, 68″ × 50″, Magura, 20th century, fourth decade. Circular floral design in centre, half flowers with there petals in four corners. Below this human figures in different pose. Below Trees of Life, different figures. Thin geometric patterns in first line of border, then stretched flowers, again geometric patterns, next rows of kalka and more geometric patterns. Red, black, ash coloured threads used.

9. Asan kantha, 32″ × 32″, Jessore, end 19th century. Lotus in centre and around. Trees in four corners, amulet designs in border. Motifs of chariot, lamp, fish, fan etc.

10. Asan kantha, 16″ × $6\frac{1}{2}$″, Khulna, early 20th century. Lotus in centre, trees in corner, sun, deer etc.

11. Sujni kantha, 69″×51″, Rangpur, 20th century, second decade. Lotus in centre and creepers.

12. Asan kantha, 30″ × 31″, Faridpur, early 20th century. Thousand petalled lotus in centre, sun, wheel, fan, tree, betel-leaf on surface and eye design in border.

13. Asạn kantha, 33″ × 32″, Jessore, end 19th century. Eight petalled lotus in centre. Motifs include temple, nutcracker, mirror, birds, earrings, trees etc.

14. Asan kantha, Faridpur, end 19th century. Thousand petalled lotus in centre, trees in four corners, pitcher, betel-leaf, kalka on surface.

15. Asan kantha, 47″ × 31″, Mymensingh, 20th century, second decade. Hundred petalled lotus in centre, sari ends designs in border. Fish, wheel, ladle, nutcracker and flower. Trees in four corners.

16. Asan kantha, 37″×29″, Rangpur, 20th century, third decade. Hundred petalled lotus in centre, round it flowers, sun, trees in four corners.

17. Asan kantha, 26″ × 25″, Jessore, late 19th century. Lotus in centre, trees in four corners, also bird, nutcracker, etc. Ganga-Yamuna design in border.

18. Asan kantha, 37″ × 25″, Jamalpur, 20th century, third decade. Four leaves in centre, also six trees and creeper design in border.

19. Asan kantha, 29″ × 27″, Jessore, 20th century, second decade. Hundred petalled lotus in centre, trees in four corners, Ganga-Yamuna in border. Motifs, betel-leaf, peacock, fan, sun etc.

20. Khat kantha (for spreading inside palanquin), $25\frac{1}{2}$″ × 23″, Jamalpur, 20th century, third decade. Motifs, wheel, lotus, chain, tree, creepers designed.

21. Khat kantha, 19″ × 17″, Mymensingh, 20th century, third decade. Motifs, fan, wheel, tree, creepers designed.

22. Khat kantha, 19″ × 17″, Jamalpur, 50th century, third decade. Motifs, flower bud, leaf, nutcracker, seat, fish. Fringes on all sides.

23. Khat kantha, $18\frac{1}{2}$″ × 17″, Kusthia, 20th century, third decade. Hundred petalled lotus in centre, flower, elephant, wheel motif on four sides.

24. Khat kantha, 18″ × 17″ Tangail, 20th century, fourth decade. Six leaves in red at the middle, trees in four corners, floral designs.

25. Khat kantha, 20″ × 20″, Jamalpur, 20th century, third decade. Lotus in centre, also wheel, tree and flower motifs.

26. Khat kantha, 21″ × 21″, Tangail, 20th century, second decade. Lotus in centre, betel-leaf, swastik, stretched flowers and leaf motifs.

27. Khat kantha, 16″ × 15″, Jamalpur, 26th century, second decade. Sun, alpana design and fringes of printed cloth on four sides.

28. Khat kantha, 21″ × 20″, Mymensingh, 20th century, second decade. Lotus in centre, crow, fish, elephant, different birds, creepers in border.

29. Khat kantha, 17″ × 16″, Jessore, 20th century, second decade. Bird, three leaves, umbrella, red 'shalu' fringes in border.

30. Khat kantha, 15″ × $16\frac{1}{2}$″, Rangpur, 20th century, fourth decade. Thousand petalled lotus in centre, leaf, nutcracker, flower, creepers, red 'shalu' fringe in border. Written inside, Maletan Neha.

31. Khat kantha, 16″ × 18″, Jamalpur, 20th century, third decade. Lotus, bird, fish, wheel, red 'shalu' fringe.

32. Khat kantha, $15\frac{1}{2}$″ × $15\frac{1}{2}$″, Rangpur, 20th century, third decade. Lotus, wheel, flower, leaf, fish, bird, red 'shalu' fringe.

33. Khat kantha, $16\frac{1}{2}$″ × $15\frac{1}{2}$″, Rangpur, 20th century, third decade. Wheel, flower, stretched flowers in all sides, red 'shalu' fringe in border.

34. Khat kantha, 16″ × 15″, Jamalpur, 20th century, third decade. Leaf, tree, designs of sweet pie and written, Malek.

35. Bartan Dhakni (utensil cover), 13″ × $12\frac{1}{2}$″, Mymensingh, 20th century, third decade. Hundred petalled lotus in centre and four sides. stretched flowers in border.

36. Bartan Dhakni, 18″ × $17\frac{1}{2}$″, Jamalpur, 20th century, third decade. Four creepers with flowers hards in centre floral designs on four sides.

37. Bartan Dhakni, $15\frac{1}{2}$″ × $12\frac{1}{2}$″, Rangpur, 20th century, second decade. Designs of creeper, fish, nose-ring etc.

38. Bartan Dhakni, 18″×15 ″, Jamalpur, 20th century, third decade. Sun in centre and four trees on on four sides.

39. Asan kantha, $17\frac{1}{2}$″ × 15″, Jamalpur, 20th century. Designs in white with coloured threads. Creepers, flowers, lotus, bird, nutcracker, fish etc. Artist's name, Khadiran Benwa.

40. Arsilata, 38″ × 13″, Jamalpur, 20th century. Embroidered in red, blue, green threads. Leaves in centre, different motif. Artist, Khadiran Benwa.

41. Asan kantha, 16″×16″, Jamalpur, 20th century. Desings made with coloured threads. Sun in centre on two sides betel-leaves and small leaves on other two sides. Artist, Rahima Khatun.

42. Bartan Dhakni, $13\frac{1}{2}$″ × $12\frac{1}{2}$″, Jamalpur, 20th century. Sari end designs are in border, stretched flowers, lotus in centre. Artist, Rahima Khatun.

43. Asan kantha, 17″ × 15″, Jamalpur, 20th century. Lotus in Centre on four sides fish, nutcracker, fan. Red 'shalu' fringe with creepers designed inside. Artist, Rahima Khatun.

44. Asan kantha, 18″ × 18″, Jamalpur, 20th century. Designed with coloured threads. Four flowers with leaves in centre, leafy trees in four corners. Artist Sajennesa Khatun.

45. Asan kantha, 20″× 17″, Khulna, 20th century. Embroidery in many coloured threads.

Flower with leaves in centre, around it in a circle fish, trees in the side. Fifteen birds around the border. Artist Sajennesa Khatun.

46. Arsilata, 20″ × 8″, Khulna, 20th century. Length-wise leaves in the centre, creepers on four sides. Artist Netunnesa Khatun.

47. Arsilata, 20″ × 8″, Khulna, 20th century. Leaves designed lengthwise in centre, creeper designs all around. Artist Rakhela Khatun.

48. Pillow-cover, 28″ × 14″, Mymensingh, mid-20th century. Embroideries in red, blue, green threads. Tree with three flowers in centre.

49. Asan kantha, 16″ × 15″, Mymensingh, 20th century. Lotus with flowery trees in four corners.

50. Arsilata, 24″ × 9″, Sherpur, 20th century. Designs of leaves lengthwise in centre, creepers. Artist Chhabiran Bibi.

51. Asan kantha, 17″ × 15″, Sherpur, 20th century. Coloured threads used, lotus in centre, circular creeper designs round it. Designs of three leaves in four corners. Artist Chhabiran Bibi.

52. Pan-pachani (to keep rolled betel-leaves), 17″×8″, Sherpur, 20th century. Many coloured threads used to embroider sheaves of corn, stretched flower and leaves in centre. Artist Chhabiran Bibi.

53. Bagli, (small shoulder bag), 13″ × 9″, Jamalpur, 20th century. Spider's web designed with red, blue, green threads. Artist Hamela Bibi.

54. Bagli, 13″ × 9″, Jamalpur, 20th century. Wheel and Kadam flower in centre Artist Hamela Bibi.

55. Dastarkhan, 72″ × 14″, Jamalpur, 20th century. Trees designed on four sides with coloured threads, in the centre lengthwise flower and tree. Artist Hamela Bibi.

56. Bagli, 16″ × 10″, Jamalpur, 20th century. Red and blue threads used for square and 'barfi' designs. Artist Hamela Bibi.

57. Pillow-cover, 28″ × 13″, Sherpur, 20th century. Flowers and creepers made with red, blue, green and yellow threads. Artist Surat Banu.

58. Asan kantha, 19″ × 19″, Sherpur, 20th century. Floral design in centre, stretched flowers on four sides. Artist Surat Banu.

59. Pillow-cover, Sherpur, 20th century Angular designs with red and blue threads, red 'shalu' fringes. Artist Surat Banu.

60. Pillow-cover, 28″ × 17″, Sherpur, 20th century. Red, blue, black threads used to make creeper designs and rows of fish. Motifs of banyan leaf. Rattan basket and tree. Artist Surat Banu.

61. Asan kantha, 16″ × 16″, Sherpur, 20th century. Fringe designs in border with red, blue and black threads. Six trees, two mangoes, sun in centre. Artist Surat Banu.

62. Pillow-cover, $26\frac{1}{2}$″ × 15″, Jamalpur, 20th century. Designs with red, blue, black threads. Kalmilata in four sides and tree with flowers in centre. Artist Chaiadunnesa Bibi.

63. Asan kantha, 22″ × 22″, Jamalpur, 20th century. Embroidered with red, blue, green threads. Round flowers on four sides in rows, hundred petalled lotus in centre, motifs of mango, nutcracker etc. Artist Chhaiadunesa Bibi.

64. Bartan Dhakni, $15\frac{1}{2}$″ × $15\frac{1}{2}$″, Rangpur, 20th century. Designed sith coloured threads. Star-flower in centre, kamranga (sour fruit) flower on four sides, Motifs are, fish, banyan leaf, tree and nutcracker. Artist Ajiran Bibi.

65. Bartan Dhakni, 16″ × 16″, Rangpur, 20th century. Lotus with red, blue and green threads, stretched flowers and leaves on four sides. Artist Ajiran Bibi.

66. Pillow-cover, 35″ × 18″, Rangpur, 20th century. Tree in centre and creepers made with red and black threads. Artist Ajiran Bibi.

67. Asan kantha, 40″ × 25″, Rangpur, 20th century. Red, blue, green threads used. Lotus in centre, stretched flowers, trees in corners. Artist Ajiran Bibi.

68. Asan kantha, 40″ × 25″, Jamalpur, 20th century. Embroidered with red, blue and light coloured threads. Six trees, flowers in centre, kuntilata (creeper) designs. Artist Alema Bibi.

69. Asan kantha, 20″ × 18″, Jamalpur, 20th century. Blue and black threads used. Lotus in centre and on four sides, wheel, sun and leaves. Artist Alema Bibi.

70. Asan kantha, 18″ × 17″, Khulna, 20th century. Black, yellow, green, red threads used. Hundred petalled lotus in centre with bird in middle, motifs of wheel, sun.

71. Asan kantha, 19″ × 16″, Khulna, 20th century. Red, blue, green threads used. Two large and two small banyan leaves round a circle in centre, floral designs around it. Fringe in border. Artist Anwara Begum.

72. Rumal kantha, 19″ × $16\frac{1}{2}$″, Jamalpur, 20th century, third decade. Eight petalled lotus in centre, inside tree and creepers.

73. Rumal kantha, $14\frac{1}{2}$″ × 14″, Tangail, 20th century, second decade. Tree in centre inside betel-leaves, fish, nutcracker, tree. Creepers on all sides.

74. Rumal kantha, $16\frac{1}{2}$″ × 15″, Jessore, 20th century, second decade. Lotus, wheel in centre, inside date-palm tree, fish, three leaves, stretched flowers on four sides.

75. Rumal kantha, 15″ × 17″, Jamalpur, 20th century, second decade. Lotus in centre, tree, pot, inside, creepers on four sides. Written Jerimon.

76. Pillow-cover, 36″ × 17″, Kusthia. 20th century, second decade. Tree, creepers, paddy, amulet designed.

77. Pillow-cover 31″ × $15\frac{1}{2}$″, Kusthia, 20th century, second decade. Designs of lotus flower, tree, creepers, sun, birds.

78. Pillow-cover, 31″ × 17″, Jamalpur, 20th century, second decade. Designs of flowers and creepers.

79. Pillow-cover, 36″ × $15\frac{1}{2}$″, Mymensingh, 20th century. Flowers and creepers designed.

80. Jainamaz, 36″ × 24″, Jamalpur, 20th century, fourth decade. Designs of Kaba Sharif in centre, round which two trees with leaves, four Trees of Life in corners and creepers. Artist Mariam Bibi.

81. Asan kantha, 16″ × 16″, Tangail, 20th century, third decade. Taj Mahal designed with coloured threads.

82. Small Asan kantha, 14″ × 10″, Jamalpur, 20th century, third decade. Designs with red and black threads. Lotus in centre, on two sides two filled designs if flowers, Tree of Life in four corners and creepers. Artist Mariam Bibi.

83. Sujni kantha, 64″ × 51″, Faridpur, 20th century, third decade. Kadam flower designed with red, black, green and yellow threads. Four kadam trees in four corners and rows of kadam flower all around. Artist Rashida Begum.

84. Pan-panchani, 16″ × 8″, Jamalpur, 20th century, third decade. Floral designs with red thread. Artist Ajirannessa.

85. Arsilata, 20″×8″, Nababganj, 20th century second decade. Designs with red and black threads. In the centre two trees with flowers and leaves. Artist Sufia Begum.

86. Pillow-cover, 30″ × 11″, Nababganj, 20th century, third decade. Red, mulberry green, yellow coloured threads used for geometric patterns.

87. Sujni kantha, 62″ × 50″, Pabna, 20th century, third decade. Divided into squares with mustard-yellow and black threads, kadam flower in each square.

88. Asan kantha (for groom to sit on at marriages), 72″ × 70″, Sherpur, 20th century, third decade. Embroidered with yellow, blue, orange threads. Flower, bird, tree designed in middle. Artist Moynar Ma (Moyna's mother).

89. Asan kantha, 32″ × 32″, Faridpur, 20th century, fourth decade. Lotus in centre, mosque on two sides and mosque turrets on other two sides, Trees of Life in four corners, rows of flowers and plants in border.

90. Bastani (small sack) 26″ × 26″, Khulna, 19th century, fifth decade. Lotus and creepers.

91. Bastani, 24″ × 23″, Jessore, 19th century, fifth decade. Lotus in centre, wheels, birds, nut, betel-leaves designed. Geometric patterns around border.

92. Dastarkhan, 60″ × 14″, Mymensingh, 20th century, second decade. Flower, creepers, birds, lamp-holder, nutcracker designed.

93. Dastarkhan, 60″ × 16″, Jessore, 20th century, second decade. Five lotus on the surface, creepers, moon, and stretched designs on four sides.

94. Dastarkhan, 62″ × 16″, Khulna, 20th century, second decade. Fish, kite, four leaves, banyan leaves in four corners.

95. Pillow-cover, 30″ × 16″, Dhaka, 20th century, first decade. Wheel, fish, three lotus flowers and creepers designed on four sides.

96. Pillow-cover, 16″ × 112″, Jamalpur, end 19th century. Tree, mango, creepers (sankhalata and kalmilata).

97. Asan kantha, 32″ × 32″, Faridpur, 20th century, third decade. Sari ends designed on four sides, lotus in centre and floral designs all around. Artist Manikuntala Biswas.

98. Sujni kantha, 64″ × 40″, Jessore, 20th century, fourth decade. Flowers and plants designed lengthwise in centre and on four sides flowers designed with red, blue, mustard-yellow threads. Artist Arjina Banu.

99. Asan kantha, 34″ × 33″, Kishoreganj, 20th century, fourth decade. Flowers, plant, birds, fish designed with red, blue and yellow threads.

100. Asan kantha, 36″ × 33″, Rajbari, 20th century, fourth decade. Geometric patterns embroidered with red, green, mulberry and yellow coloured threads. Floral designs with cross stitch.

Syed Rubi Gaznavi, Dhaka, Bangladesh

1. Nakshi kantha, Rajsahi. Thick lahari (wavy) kantha, designs in red and black threads.

2. Nakshi kantha, Rajsahi, Thick lahari kantha, barfi designs in red and blank threads on white.

3. Sujni kantha, Rajsahi. Known as 'bilyati' (from England), Fine embroidery work on red surface.

4. Asan kantha, Faridpur. Lotus in centre and different motifs round it. Different sari ends design in border. Red and black threads used to fold border.

5. Jaynamaz, Mosque designs have filled up the space. Sari end designs on the side. Red, blue, threads used.

6. Arsilata, tall tree in centre, red, blue, green threads used. Rows of twin fish and eye in border. Sari ends at the end.

7. Arsilata. Red thread on white to design sari ends.

8. Durjani. Embroidered with red and blue threads.

9. Durjani. Embroidered with red and sky blue threads.

10. Kantha made in 1978 by her. A square kantha looks very old. Four types of Tree of Life in four corners. Lotus in centre and motif, man on elephant. Small 'run' stitches inside.

11. In 1982 she got another artist to make a kantha. Artist chose motifs from her imagination and took long to make.

Chandrasekhar Saha, Dhaka, Bangladesh

1. Dorokha, large square kantha, 150 years old. Lotus in centre, Tree of Life in four corners. Other motifs also, sari end designs in border.

2. Sujni kantha of Rajsahi (bilayti). Large kantha and finely embroidered with white thread on red cloth.

3. Sujni kantha, Rajsahi. Lahari (waves) designed with red, light red and light blue threads on this thick kantha.

4. Sujni kantha, Jessore, white thread used on black surface. Run and Ground stitches used. Flowers and trees in four corners. Lotus in centre and also on side. Creeper design in border.

5. Sujni kantha, Jamalpur. Known as 'paar kantha' made on mulberry coloured cloth with white thread.

6. Sujni kantha, Jessore, different motifs. Circular alpana design at centre round which flowers and trees in a circle. Thin angular designs with light mustard- yellow thread. Human figures on horse and elephant back in border. Colourful Tree of Life. Alpana designs in four corners. Red, light green, blue, yellow threads also used.

Album

225. Big Asan Kantha 19th century.

226. Sujni, 19th century.

227. Big Asan Kantha, 19th century.

228. Sujni Kantha, approx. 19th century.

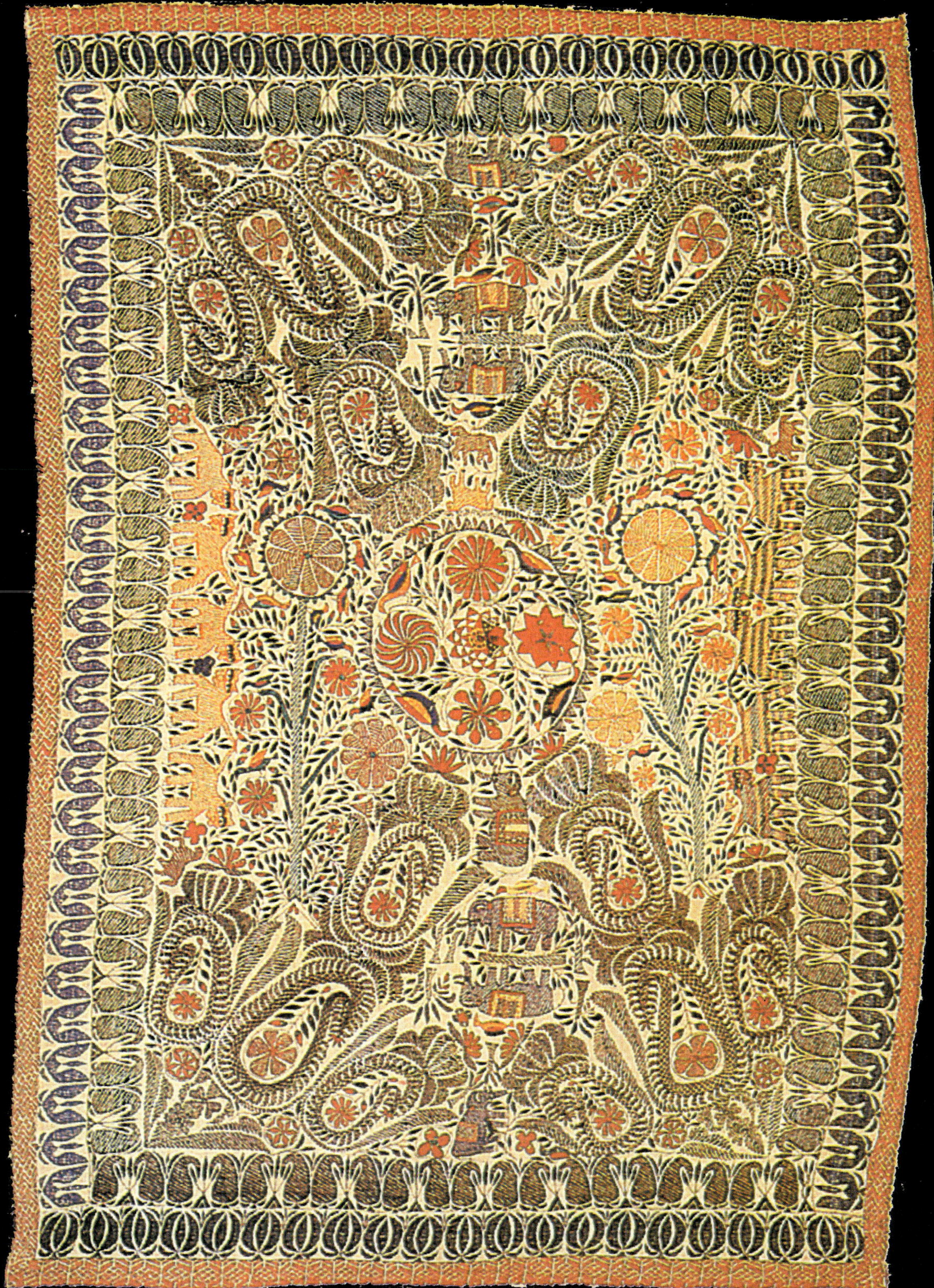

229. Lep Kantha, Jessore, approx. 19th century.

230. Sujni Kantha, Faridpur.

231. Dorokha Sujni, approx. 19th century.

232. Dorokha Sujni, Kantha, 19th century.

233. Asan Kantha, Faridpur, approx. early 20th century.

234. Asan Kantha, Khulna, approx. early 20th century.

235. Sujni Kantha, approx. 20th century.

236. Dhakna Kantha, 19th century.

237. Sujni Kantha, 19th century.

238. Sujni Kantha, approx. 19th century.

239. Sujni Kantha, approx. 19th century.

240. Sujni Kantha, approx. 19th century.

241. Sujni Kantha, approx. 19th century.

242. Betan Kantha, approx. 19th century.

243. Sujni Kantha, Faridpur, approx. 19th century.

244. Asan Kantha, approx. 19th centuri.

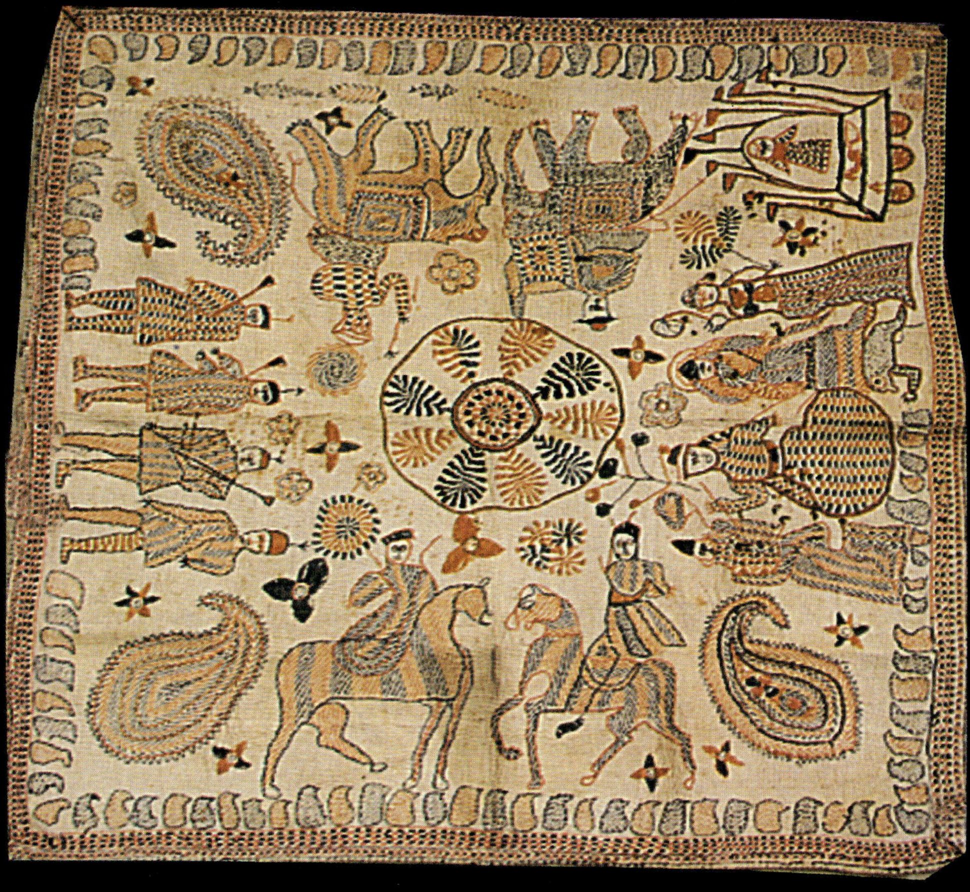

245. Asan Kantha, approx. 19th century.

246. Sujni Kantha, Jessore, approx. 19th century.

247. Sujni Kantha, Faridpur, approx. 19th century.

248. Large Asan Kantha, Faridpur, approx. 20th century.

249. Asan Kantha, Magura, approx. 20th century.

250. Asan Kantha, Kishoreganj, late 19th century.

251. Sujni Kantha, Jessore, approx. 19th century.

252. Sujni Kantha, approx. 19th century.

253. Asan Kantha, approx. 19th century.

254. Sujni Kantha, approx. 19th century.

255. Asan Kantha, approx. 19th century.

256. Sujni Kantha, approx. 19th century.

257. Sujni Kantha, approx. 19th century.

258. Sujni Kantha, approx. 19th century.

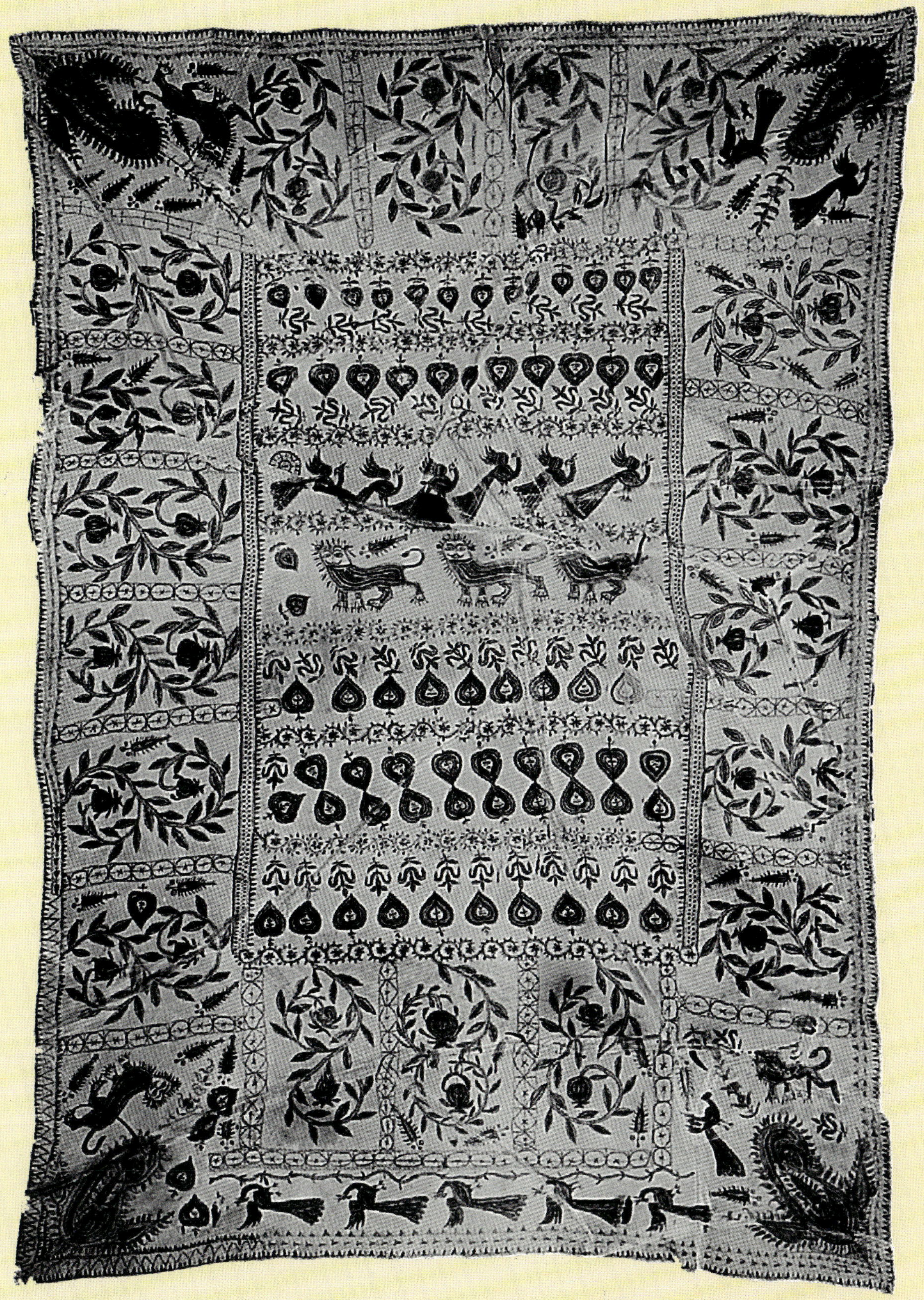

259. Sujni Kantha, approx. 19th century.

260. Sujni Kantha, approx. 19th century.

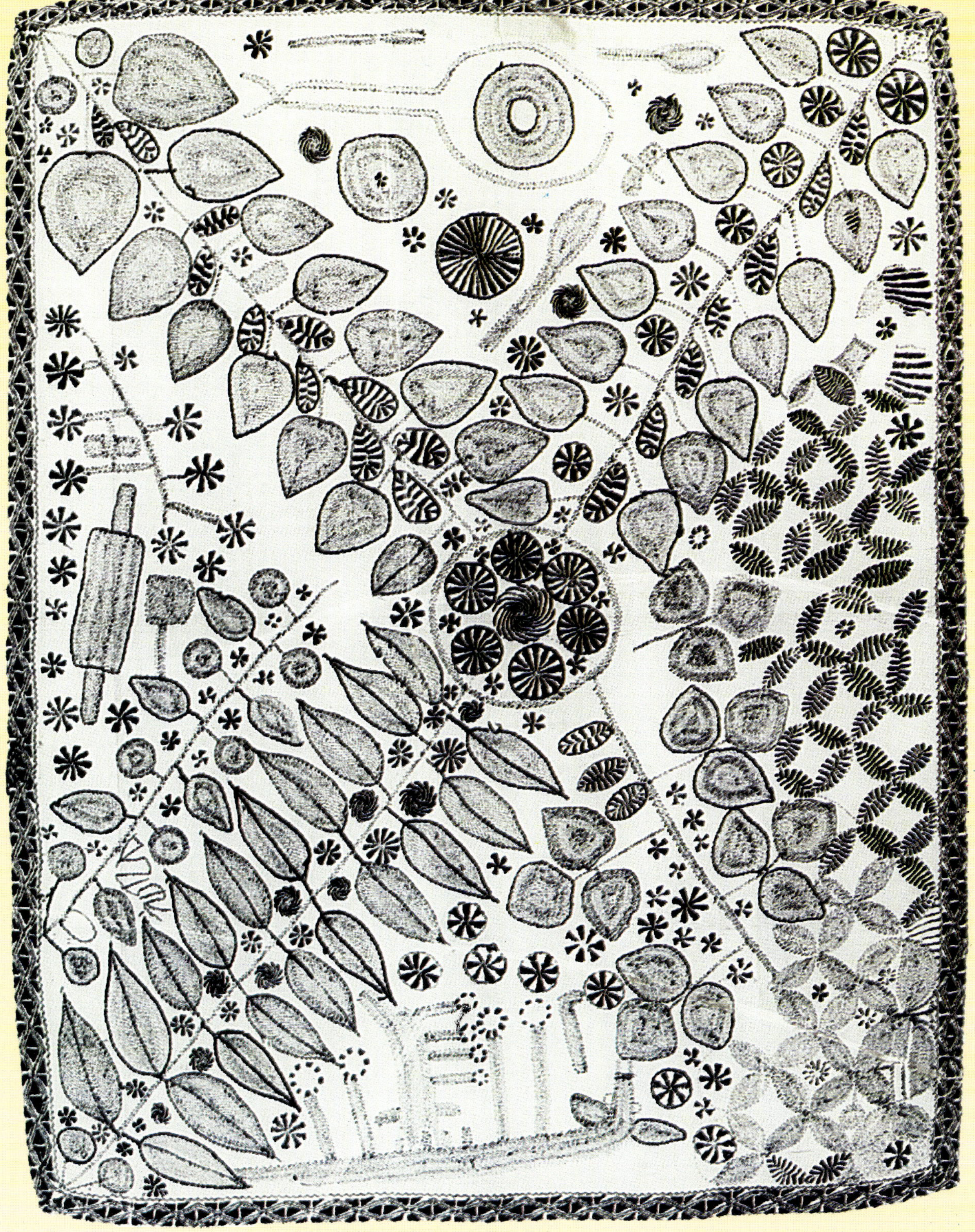

261. Sujni Kantha, approx. 19th century.

262. Asan Kantha, approx. 19th century.

263. Sujni Kantha, Khulna, end 20th century.

264. Sujni Kantha, middle 19th century.

265. Asan Kantha, middle 19th century.

266. Asan Kantha, middle 19th century.

267. Asan Kantha, middle 19th century.

268. Bonchka Kantha, Khulna, middle 19th century.
(Based as bag).

269. Sujni Kantha. Jessore. middle 20th century.

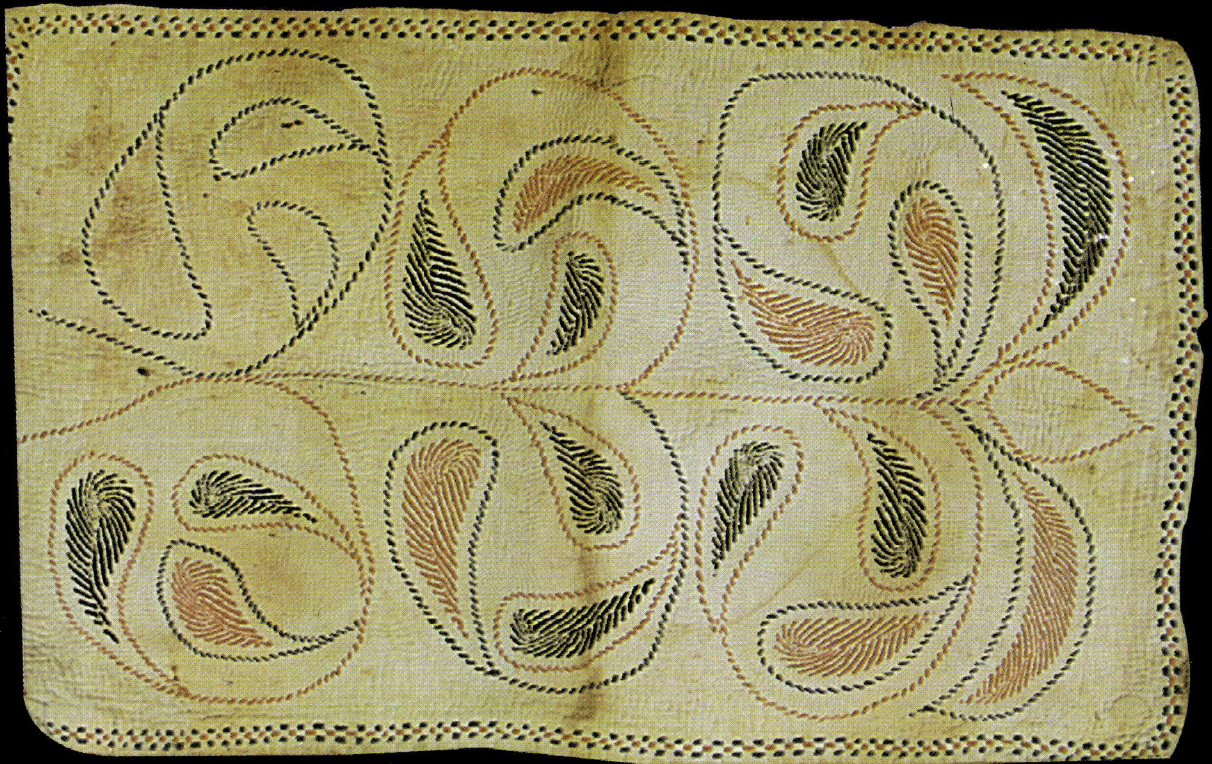

270. Asan Kantha, approx. 19th century.

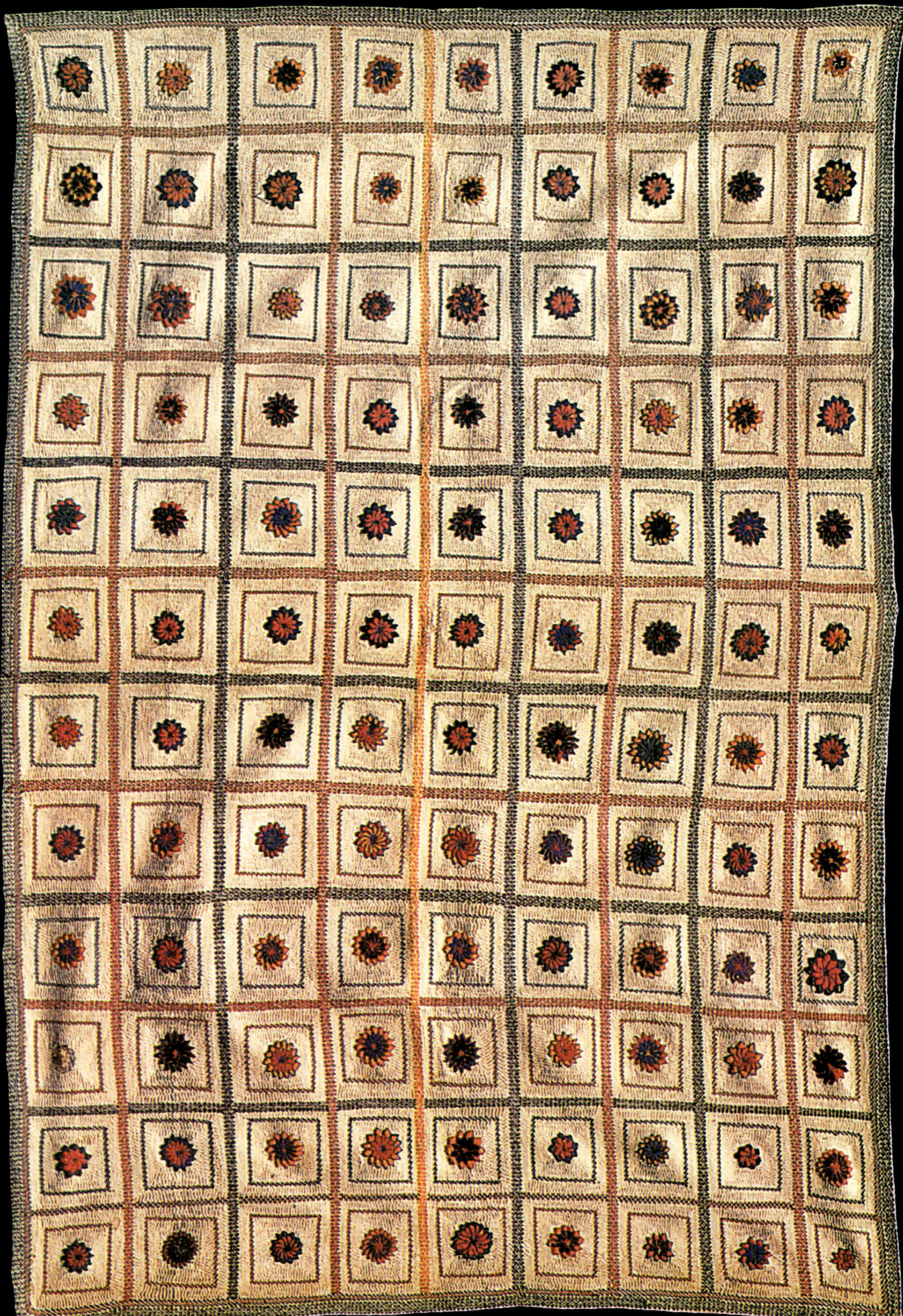

271. Sujni Kantha, end 19th century.

272. Sujni Kantha, approx. 19th century.

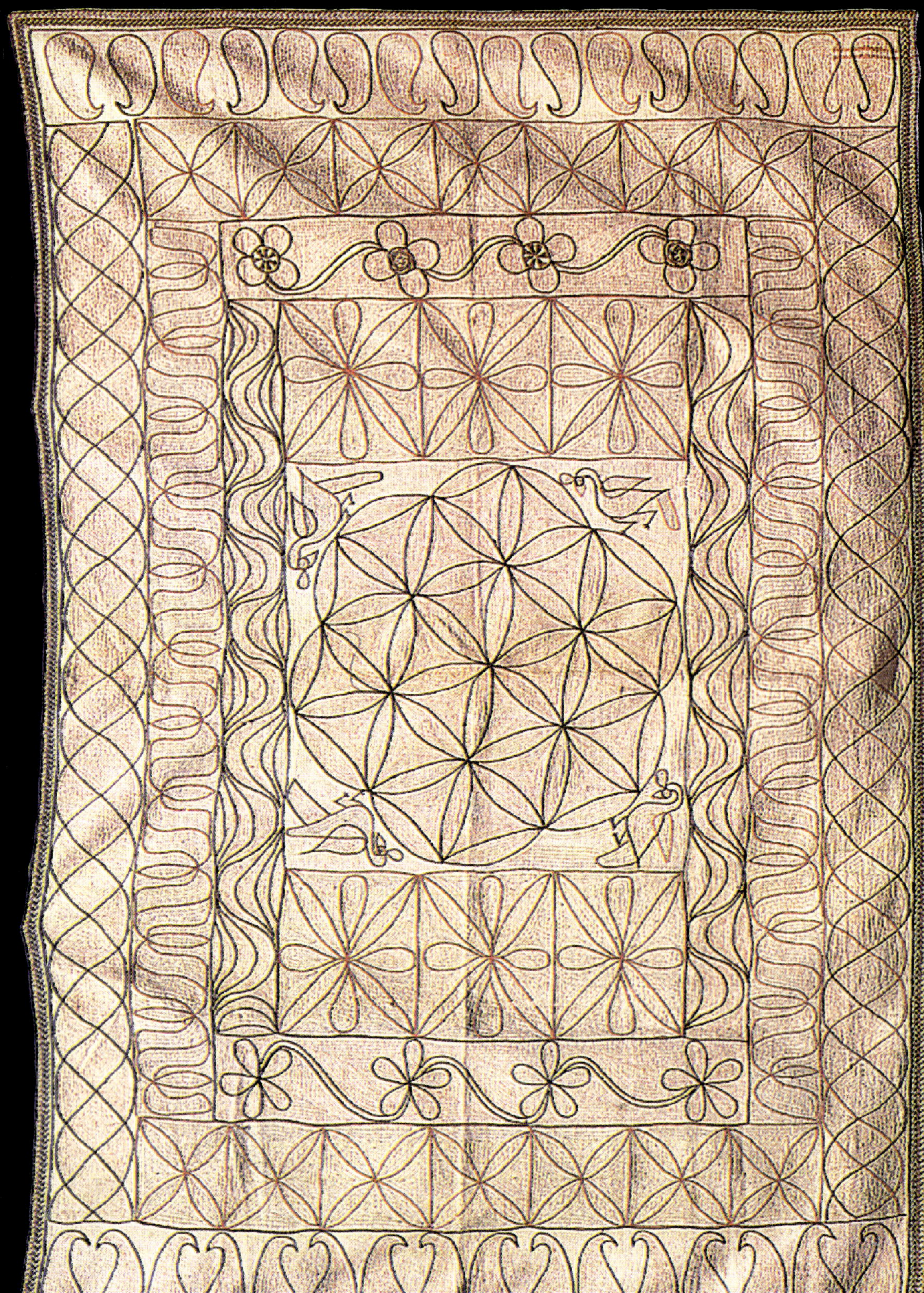

273. Sujni Kantha, approx. 19th century.

274. Sujni Kantha, approx. 19th century.

275. Asan Kantha, 19th century.

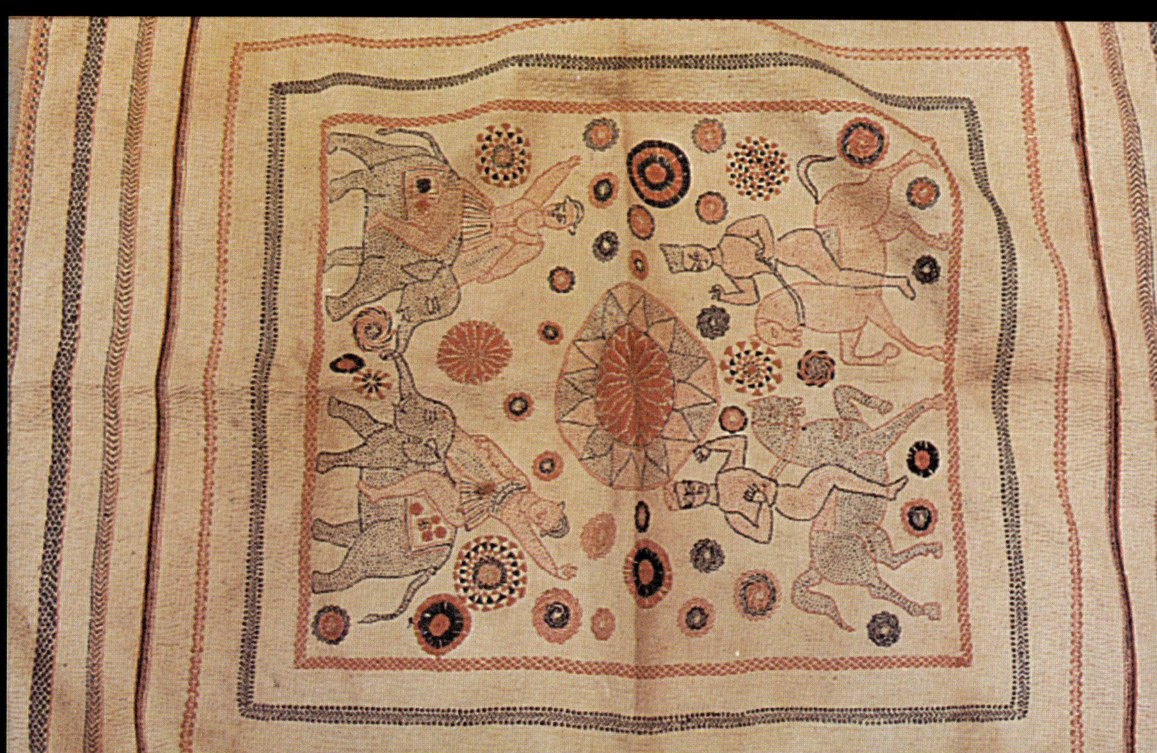

276. Asan Kantha, 19th century.

277. Sujni Kantha, Rajsahi, mid-20th century.

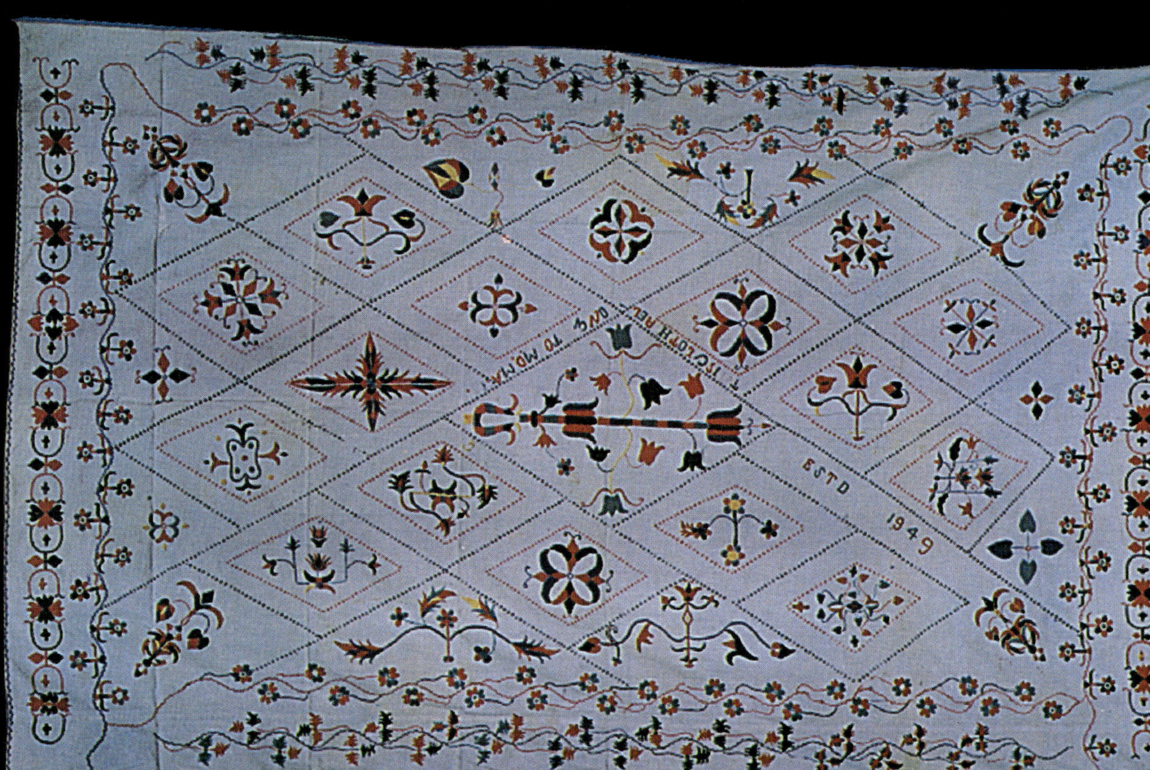

278. Sujni Kantha, Chittagong, mid-20th century.

279. Asan Kantha. Jessore. approx. 20th centuri.

280. Dhakna Kantha, 20th century.

281. Sujni Kantha, 20th century.

282.Dhakna Kantha, 19th century. (For covering furniture etc.).

283. Lep Kantha, 19th century.

284. Sujni Kantha, 19th century.

285. Dastarkhan, Tangail, mid-20th century.

286 .Wall Hanging: Nakshi Kanthar Math, end 20th century. (Jasimuddin's poem).

287. Sujni Kantha, Natore, 20th century.

288. Sujni Kantha, 19th century.

289.Wall Hanging, Sojan Badiar Ghat, 20th century.

290. Sujni Kantha, 20th century.

291. Sujni Kantha, 19th century.

292. Sujni Kantha, Udaypur, Tripura, 20th century.

293. Sujni Kantha, mid-20th century.

294. Sujni Kantha, Faridpur, 19th century.

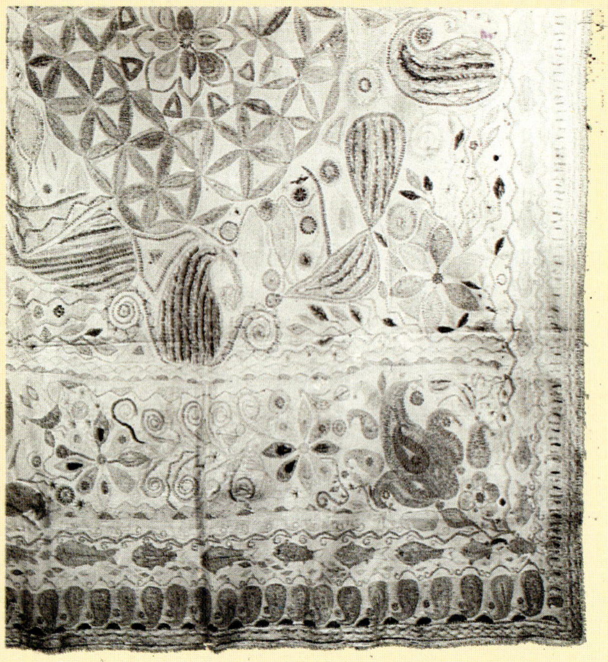

295. Sujni Kantha, approx. 19th century.

296. Sujni Kantha, approx. 19th century.

297. Sujni Kantha, approx. 19th century.

298. Sujni Kantha, Jessore.

299. Large Sujni Kantha, Jessore.

300. Asan Kantha, 19th century

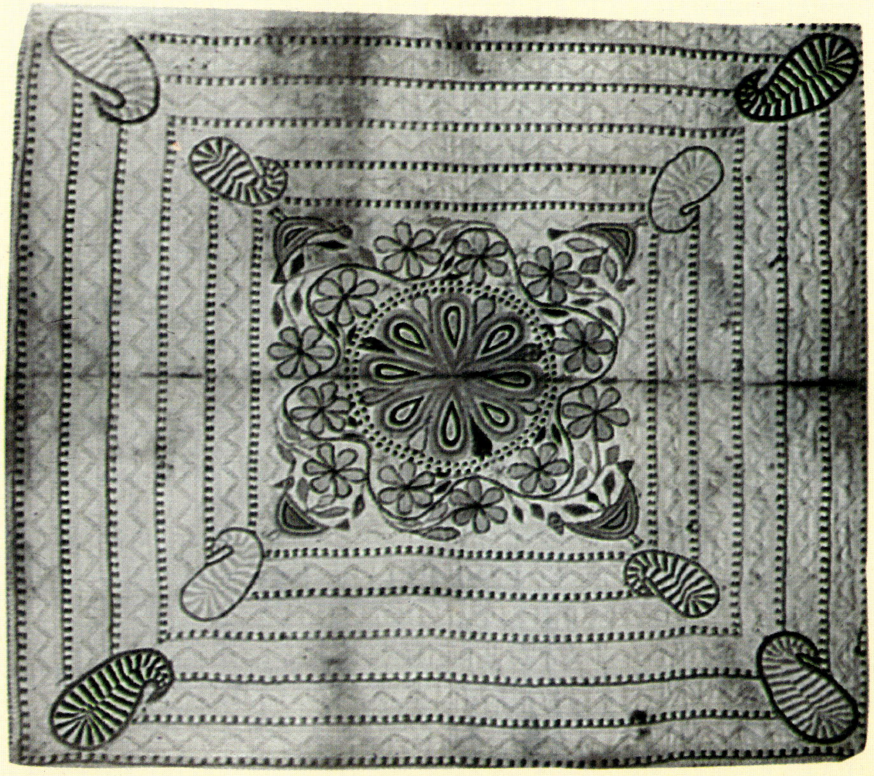

301. Rumal Kantha.

302. Large Sujni Kantha, Jessore.

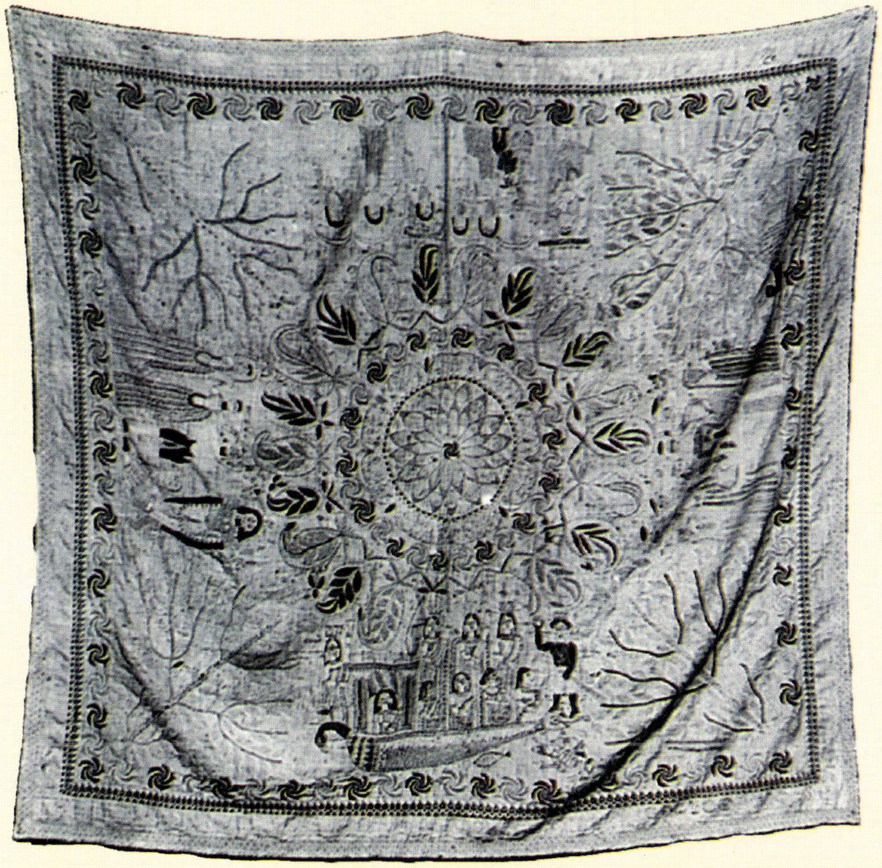

303. Asan Kantha, Jessore.

304. Asan Kantha, Bongaon.

305. Asan Kantha, Khulna.

306. Asan Kantha.

307. Large Sujni Kantha, Jessore.

308. Batua Kantha, Barisal.

309. Lep Kantha.

310. Asan Kantha, Jessore.

311. Rumal Kantha.

312. Large Sujni Kantha, Khulna.

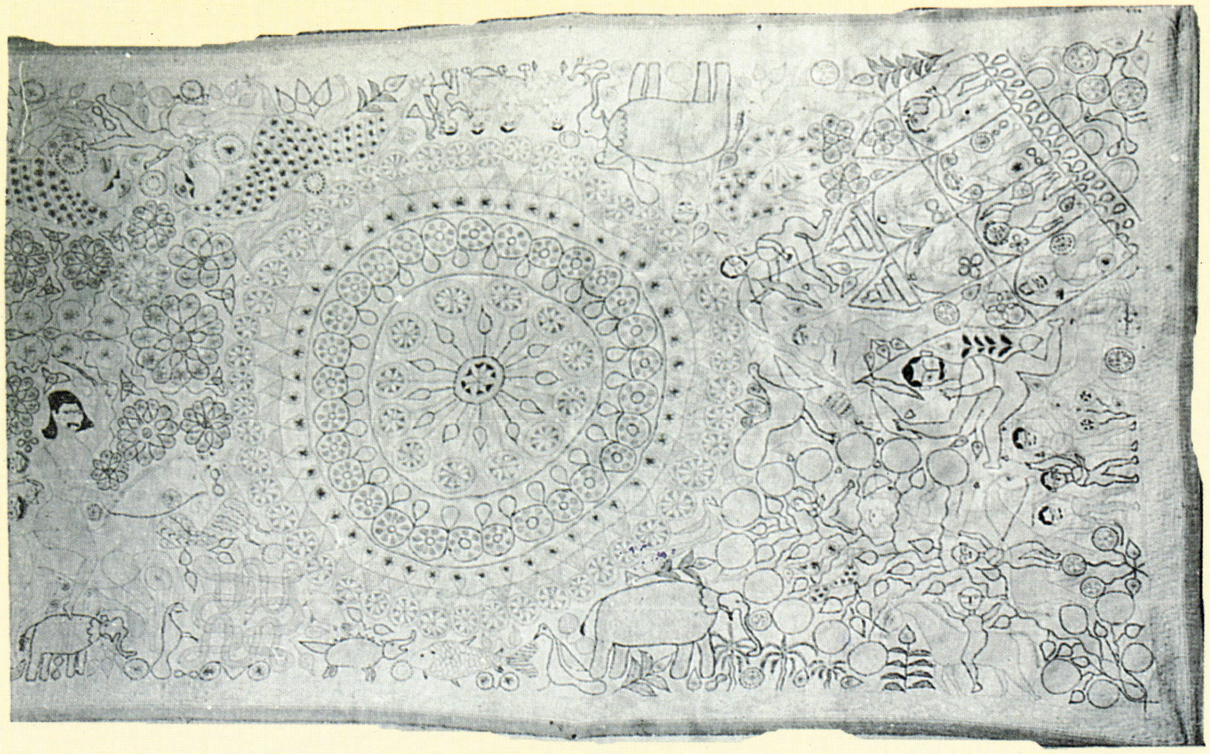

313. Large Sujni Kantha.

314. Betan Kantha, Jessore, approx. 20th century.

315. Cover, Kurigram, approx. 20th century.

316. Palanquin Kantha, mid-19th century. (For spreading in palanquin).

317. Betan Kantha, approx. 19th century.

318. Arsilata, approx. 20th century.

319. Sujni Kantha, end 19th century.

320. Jaynamaz, Tangail, early 20th century.

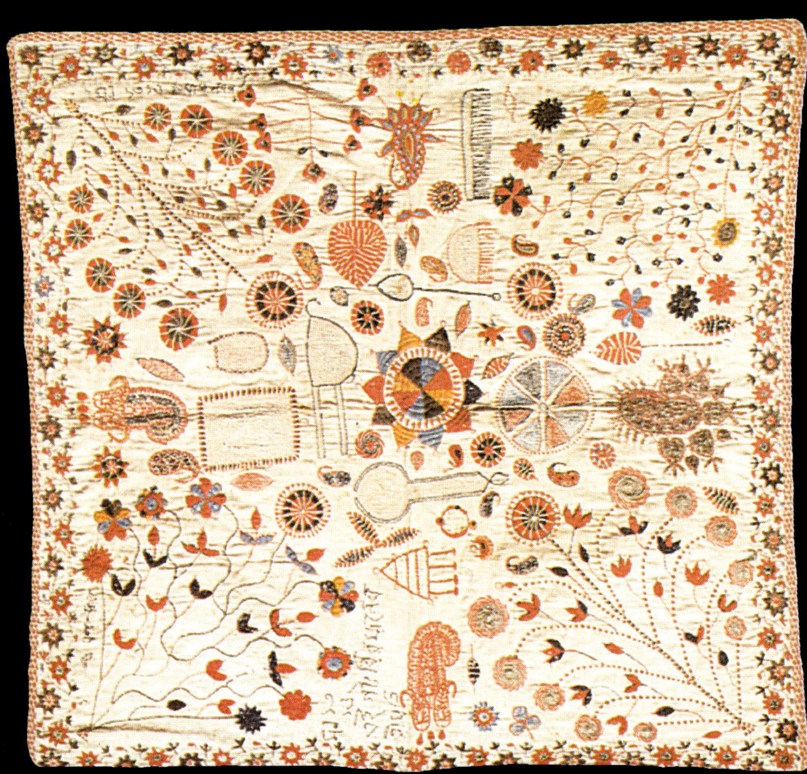

321. Asan Kantha, early 20th century.

322. Pillowcover, Kishoreganj, mid-20th century.

323. Asan Kantha, Khulna, early 20th century.

324.Pillowcover, Kishoreganj, mid. 20th century.

325.Pillowcover, Kishoreganj, mid. 20th century.

326. Wall Hanging: Tagore's Shyama, Dhaka, 20th century.

327. Asan Kantha, approx. 19th century.

328. Asan Kantha, approx. 19th century.

329. Asan Kantha, approx. 19th century.

330. Asan Kantha, 19th cent.

331. Asan Kantha, 19th century.

332. Betan Kantha, Jessore, approx. 19th century.

333. Asan Kantha, Champainababganj, 20th century.

334. Asan Kantha, Faridpur, 20th century.

335. Arsilata, approx. 19th cent.

336.Wall Hanging, Dhaka.

337. Lahari Lep Kantha, 20th century.

338. Lep Kantha, Kishoreganj, end 19th century.

339. Sujni Kantha, Jessore, late 19th century.

340. Dastarkhan, Khulna, late 19th century.

341. Sujni Kantha, Malda, approx. 20th century.

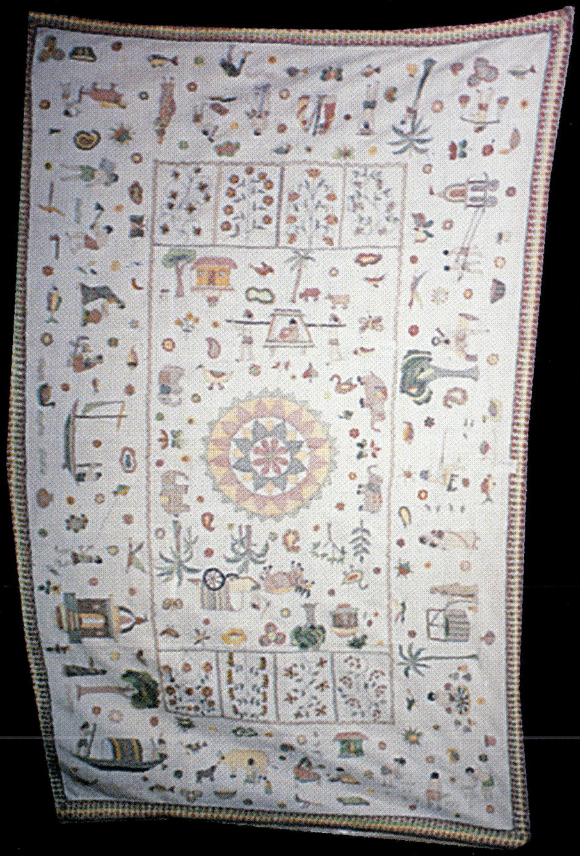

342. Sujni Kantha, Agartala, 20th century.

343. Sujni Kantha, Khulna, late 19th century.

344. Arsilata, Kishoreganj, late 19th century.

345. Dastarkhan, Mymensingh, end 19th century.

346. Arsilata, Jamalpur, mid-20th century.

347. Arsilata, Kusthia, early 20th century.

348. Dastarkhan, Kusthia, early 20th century.

349. Palanquin Kantha, mid. 19th century. (For spreading in palanquin).

350. Asan Kantha, approx. 19th century.

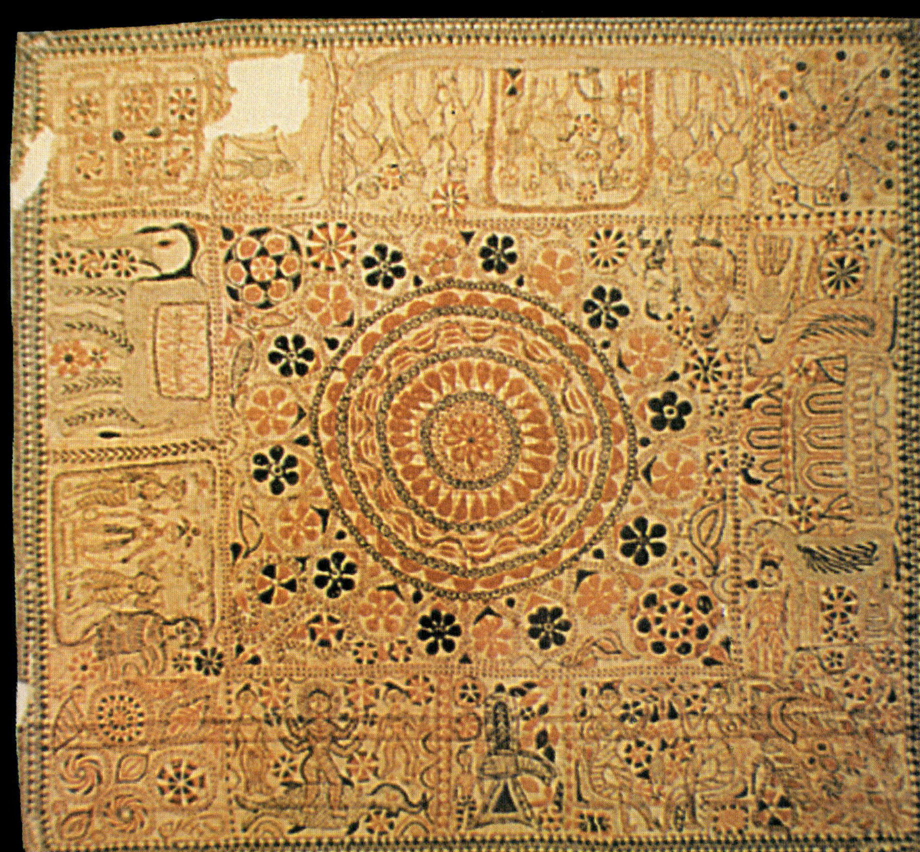

351. Asan Kantha, approx. 19th century.

352. Asan Kantha, approx. 19th century.

353. Asan Kantha, approx. 19th century.

354. Nakshi Bag, early 20th century.

355. Nakshi Bag, Kusthia, early 20th century.

356. Arsilata, Mymensingh, early 20th century.

357. Arsilata, Kusthia, early 20th cent.

358. Kantha-Village women of Bengal

359. Kantha - Bengal in Colonial Period , 20th century

360. Sujni Kantha, Dhaka, 20th century.

Bibliography

Adhikari, Sachindranath : Silaidaha O Rabindranath (Silaidaha and Rabindranath) Calcutta, 1974.

Ahmed, Nazimuddin : Epic Stories in Terracotta UPL, Dhaka, 1990.

Ahmed, Perveen : The Aesthetics and Vocabulary of Nakshi Kantha, Bangladesh National Museum, Dhaka

Ahmed, Tofail : Lok Aitihyer Das Duganta, Dhaka, 1999 (Ten Horizons of Folk Tradition).

Ahmed, Wakil : Banglar Loksanskriti, Dhaka, 1974 (Folk Culture of Bengal).

Alam, Syed Mahbub edited : Lokashilpa Prabandha, Bangladesh, 1999 (Essays on Folk Art) Lokshilpa, Dhaka, 1999.

Ali, Shaikh Akram ed. : Bangladesh Lalit kala, Vol. 2, No. 1, Bangladesh National Museum, Dhaka, 1994.

All India Handicrafts Broad : Handicrafts of India, New Delhi, 1955.

Amalsad, D.M. : Handloom Weaving, Madras, 1961.

Anand, Mulk Raj : Chamba rumals, Marg. Vol. VII, No. 4, Bombay, 1954. : Marg. Vol. XXII, No.4, Bombay, 1969.

Anisuzzaman edited : Sahidullah Rachanabali, Vol I, Bangla Academy, 1994. ; Najrul Rachanabali, 2nd volume, Bangla Academy, Dhaka, 1976

Anonymous : Embroideries, The Imperial Gazeteer of India, Vol. III, Oxford, 1908. : Embroidered vestments, Census of India, 1961, Vol. VIII, vii (a) : Embroidered Tapestries From Bangladesh, Nakshi Kantha, Dhaka, SDUW : Art in Industry, Vol. IV, No. 3, 1953. Art and Crafts, Vikas Publication, Delhi, 1971.

Arts of Bengal : The Heritage of Bangladesh and Eastern India, London, 1979.

Aryan, K.C. : Encyclopaedia of Indian Art, Rekha Prakashan, New Delhi, 1996.

Aryan, K.C. and Aryan, S. : Rural Art of the Western Himalaya, Rekha Prakashan, New Delhi, 1985.

Aryan, Subhashini : Folk Embroidery of Himachal Pradesh, New Delhi, 1992.

Aryan, Subhashini and Datta Gupta, R.K. : Crafts of Himachal Pradesh, Mapin, Ahmedabad, 1993.

Baker, George Percival : Calico Painting and Painting in the East Indies in the 17th and 18th centuries, London, 1921.

Ball, Kathrine M. : Decorative Motifs of Oriental Art, London, 1927.

Bandopadhyaya, Amiya Kumar : Dekha Hay Nai, Calcutta,1386. Banglakshmir Jhampi, Calcutta, 1386 (Have not Seen and Bangalakshmi's chest)

Bandopadhyaya Debnath, ed. : Padmabati — Jaysi, O Alaol, Second Volume, Calcutta, 1985.

Banerji, Adris : 'Phulkaris : A folk art of the Punjab', Marg, Vol. VIII, No. 3, Bombay 1955.

Bangladesh Lok O Karushilpa Foundation : Smaranika, Shilpacharya Jainul Lok O Karushilpa jadughar Udbhodan, Sonargaon, 1996, Lok Karushipla Mela O Lokaja Utsav, 1995 Pratibedan, Sonargaon, 1995. Same occasion, 2000.

Banglar Loksahitya Chhara, Dhaka, 1998 (Bengal's Folk Literature : Rhymes).

Basak Sila : Bangla Dhandar Bishaya Baichitra O Samajik Parichay, Calcutta, 1998 (Bengali riddles and their place in society), Banglar Brata Parban, Calcutta, 1998 (Rituals of Bengal).

Basu, Shibtapan : Barak Upatyakar Lok Sanskriti, Badarpur, 2001 (Folk Culture of Barak Valley). Bengal, Directorate of Industries, Calcutta, 1963.

Bharatiya Adimjati Sevak Sangh : Tribal Art and Handicrafts, 1958.

Bhattacharya Upendranath : Banglar Baul O Baul Gaan, Calcutta, 1388 (Bengal Bauls and their songs).

Bhattacharya, A.K. : Chamba rumal, Indian Museum, Calcutta, 1968.

Bhattacharya, Asutosh : Banglar Loka Sahitya, Calcutta,1962 (Folk Literature of Bengal), Second Volume II, Calcutta, 1963. Bangiya Loka Sangeet Ratnakar, First Part, Calcutta, 1966 and third part, Calcutta, 1977 (Folk music of Bengal).

Bhattacharya, Asutosh ed. : Gopichandrer Gaan, Calcutta, 1965 (Songs of Gopichandra).

Bhattacharya, S.K. : Folk Heritage of India, Varanasi, 1989.

Bhavnani, Enakshi : Folk and Tribal Designs of India, Taraporevala, Bombay, 1974.

Bhowmik, Atul Chandra : Samakalin Nakshi Kantha, Calcutta 1378 (Contemporary Nakshi Kantha).

Bhowmik, Nirmalendu : Banglar Chharar Bhumika, Calcutta, 1979 (Introduction to Bengali rhymes).

Birdwood, G.C.M : Industrial Art of India, London, 1884.

Birdwood, Sir George : Catalogue of a loan exhibition of embroidery of Indian women, (Society for the encouragement and preservation of Indian art), London, 1893.

Boas, Franz : Primitive Arts, Oslo, 1927.

Brijbhushan, Jamila : Indian Embroidery, Div. Govt. of India, New Delhi, 1990.

Bucci, Mairo Miro : Twentieth Century Masters,

Burhanuddin, Khan Jahangir ed. : Baul Gaan O Duddushah, Dhaka (Baul songs and Duddhu-shah).

Campbell, Joseph : Primitive Mythology : The Masks of God, London, 1976.

Caulfield, Sophia F.A. : Dictionary of Needle-work, London, 1882.

Chakraborti, Siten and Bari, Radha Krishna : Handicrafts of West Bengal, Institute of Art & Handicraft, Calcutta, 1991.

Chakravarti, Bimalendu : Lokayat Banglar Chitrashilpi O Chitrakala, Calcutta 1403 (Folk Artists and Art of Bengal).

Chakravarty, Shyamal : Nabanarikunja, Calcutta, 1999.

Chakravarty, Sudhir : Sahebdhoni Sampraday O Tader Gaan Calcutta, 1985 (Sahebdhoni Cult and their Songs). ; Balahari Sampradaya O Tader Gaan, Calcutta, 1994 (Balaharis and their Songs)

Chatterjee, T.M. : Alpana, Ritual Decoration, 1945.

Chattopadhyay, Kamaladevi : Handicrafts of India, New Delhi, ICCR, 1995.; Indian Embroidery, New Delhi, Wiley Eastern Ltd., 1977; Origin and development of embroidery in our land, Marg. Vol. XVII, No.2 (Embroidery) Bombay, 1964.

Chowdhury, Titash : Baisakh O Amader Aitihyar Chetana, Dhaka, 2000 (Our Consciousness of Tradition).

Clavell, Walter : Accounts of the Hugli–Trade, Vol.2. Hakluyt Society, London, 1885.

Coomaraswamy, Ananda K. : The Indian Craftsman, Munshiram Manoharlal, New Delhi, 1989. ; Traditional Art and Symbolism, Princeton, University Press, USA, 1977.

Copper, J.C. : An Illustrated Encyclopaedia of Traditional Symbols, London, 1978.

Crill, Rosemary : Indian Embroidery, Prakash Book Depot, New Delhi, 1999.

Dalton, E.T. : Descriptive Ethnology of Bengal, Calcutta, 1872.

Das Anath Nath and Roy, Biswanath ed. and compiled: Rabindranath Tagore, Abanindranath Tagore, Sangrahita Chhele Bhulano Chhara Calcutta, 1402. (Children's rhymes of Rabindranath and Abanindranath).

Das, Purna Chandra : Kanthir Lokachar, Calcutta, 1978 (Folk customs of Contai).

Das, Sailen, ed. : Loksanskriti: Bankura Loksan-skriti Academy, July, 1999.

Dasgupta, Chittaranjan compiled : Acharya Jogesh Chandra Purakriti Bhavan, Bangiya Sahitya Parishad, Bishnupur Shakha.

Dehejia, Vidya : Devi—The Great Goddess, Mapin, Ahmedabad, 1999. Delhi, 1980.

Deshmukh, P.S. : The Origin and Development of Religion in Vedic Literature, O.U.P., London, 1933.

Dey, Sushilkumar : Bangla Probad, Calcutta, 1401 (Bengali Proverbs).

Dhamija, Jasleem : Kashida, Sujani and applique embroidery, Marg. Vol. XX, No. 1 (Survey of Crafts, Mithila), Bombay, 1966 ; Living Tradition of Iran's Crafts. Vikas Publishing, New Delhi, 1979.; The Survey of embroidery tradition, Marg, Vol. XVII, No. 2 (Embroidery), Bombay, 1964.;

Dongerkerry, Kamala S. : Romance of Indian Embroidery, Bombay, 1951. The Place of embroidery in Indian Crafts, Marg, Vol. XVII, No. 2 (Embroidery), 1964.

Dundes, Alan : Essays in Folkloristics, Meerut, 1978; Folklore Matters, University of Tennessee Press, USA, 1989.

Dutta, Bhabataran, ed. and compiled : Bangla Chhara, Calcutta, 1997.

Dutta, Gurusaday : Album of Art Treasure Kantha (Series One), Gurusaday Museum, W.B.,1995 ; Folk Art and Crafts of Bengal; The Collected Papers, Seagull, Calcutta, 1990.

Dutta, Sarojit : Folk Paintings of Bengal, Khama Publishers, New Delhi, 1993.

Eliade, Mincea : Patterns in Comparative Religion, London, 1958.

Elwin, Verrier : The Tribal Art of Middle India, 1951. Embroidery, Marg. Vol. XVIII, No.1 (Rajasthani Handicrafts), Bombay, 1964. Indian Folk Arts and Crafts, NBT, New Delhi, 1997. Exhibition on Nakshi Kantha organized by Bangladesh Shilpakala Academy and BAC, Dhaka, 1992

Fanelli, Rosalia Bonito : An Indo-Portuguese embroidery in the Bargello, Bulletin of the Needle and Bobbin Club, Vol. 53, Nos. 1 & 2, N.Y., 1970.

Fischer Eberhard and Shah, Haku : Rural craftsmen and their work, (National Institute of Design), Pages 179 to 181 (Embroidery) and 181 to 189 (Patch work), Ahmedabad, 1970.

Fischer, Eberhard and Pathy, Dinanath : Murals for Goddesses and Gods, Indira Gandhi National Centre for the Arts, New Delhi, 1996.

Fisher, Nora ed. : Mud, Mirror and Thread, Mapin, Ahmedabad, 1995.

Frazer, Sir James : The Golden Bough, London, 1963.

Gangopadhyaya, Kalyankumar : Banglar Lokshilpa, Calcutta, 1396 (Folk Art of Bengal).

Ganguli, K.K. : Designs in Traditional Arts of Benga, directorate of Industries West Bengal, Calcutta, 1963.

Ghosh, G.K. : Orissa ; The Dazzle from within : Art, Crafts and Culture of Orissa, Ashish Publishing, New Delhi, 1993.

Ghuznavi, Sayyada R. : Nakshi ; A Collection of Bangladesh, Dhaka, 1981.

Giedion, S. : The Eternal Present ; The Beginings of Arts, Oxford, 1962.

Gill, Harjeet Singh : A Phulkari from Bhatinda, Delhi, 1977.

Gillow, John and Barnard, Nicholas : Traditional Indian Textiles, Thames & Hudson, London, 1991.

Gillow, John and Sentance, Bryan : World Textiles, Thames and Hudson, London, 1991.

Gimbutas, Marija : Ancient Symbolism in Lithuanian Folk Art, Philadelphia, 1958. ; The Language of the Goddess, London, 1990.

Glassie, Henry : Traditional Art of Dhaka, Bangla Academy, Dhaka, 2000.

Goetz H. : An Early Basohli-Chamba Rumal, Bulletin of the Baroda State Museum, Vol. III, Part I, Baroda, 1945-46. Goldstein, Kenneth S. : A guide for Field Workers in Folklore, Pennsylvania, 1964.

Goswamy, B.N. : Experiencing a Museum, Sarabhai Foundation, Ahmedabad, 1998.

Gupta, B.A. : Embroidery, Journal of Indian Art. Vol. II, No. 18, London, 1888.

Gupta, Beni : Magical Beliefs & Superstition, Delhi, 1979. Hamlyn Pub. Group, N.Y., 1970.

Haque, Enamul ed. : An Anthology on Crafts of Bangladesh, Dhaka, National Crafts Council of Bangladesh, 1987. ; Bangladesh Lalit Kala, Vol. I,

Hitkari, S.S. : Phulkari, the folk art of Punjab, Delhi, 1980.

Honda, O.C. : Pahari Folk Art, Bombay, 1975.

Huyler, Stephen P. : Gifts of Earth, Mapin, Ahmedabad, 1996.

Irwin, John : Indian Embroidery, Victoria and Albert Museum Large Picture Book No. 7, London, 1951. ; Indo-Portuguese embroideries of Bengal, Journal of the Royal India, Pakistan and Ceylon Society of Oriental Art, Vol. XXVI, No. 2, London, 1951 ; The commerical embroideries of Bengal,

Journal of the Royal India, Pakistan and Ceylon Society, Vol. XVII, 1949 (Issued in 1952) Reprinted without plates in Marg, Vol. XVII No. 2, Bombay, 1964. Journal of Indian Textile History, Vol. I–VII, Calico Meseum of Textiles, Ahmedabad, 1966.

Irwin, John and Hall, Margaret : Indian Embroideries, Calico Museum, Ahmedabad, 1973.

Irwin, John and Harish Babette : Note on the use of the book in Indian Embroidery, Bulletin of the Needle and Bobbin Club, Vol. 53, No.1 & 2, New York, 1970.

Islam Mazharul : Kavi Pagla Kanai, Dhaka, 1997.

Islam Sirajul edited : Bangladesher Itihas (Vol. III) Asiatic Society of Bangladesh Dhaka, 1992 (History of Bangladesh).

Islam Syed Amirul edited : Journal of Bangladesh National Museum Officers' Samity, 1995.

Jain, Jyotindra : Painted Myths of Creation, Art and Ritual of an Indian Tribe, Lalit Kala Akademi, New Delhi, 1984. Ganga Devi : Tradition and Expression in Mithila Painting, Mapin, Ahmedabad, 1997.

Ganga Devi : Tradition and Enpression in Mithila painting Ahmedabad, 1997.

Jain, Jyotindra ed. : Picture Showmen ; Insights into the Narrative Tradition in Indian Art, Marg publications, Mumbai, 1998. ; Five Contemporary Folk and Tribal Artists of India, Craft Meseum and The Handicrafts and Handlooms Exports Corp. of India, New Delhi, 1998.

Jain, Jyotindra and Aggarwala, Arati : National Handicrafts and Handlooms Museum, Mapin, Ahmedabad, 1989.

Jaitly, Jaya ed. : Crafts of Jammu, Kashmir, Ladakh, Mapin, Ahmedabad, 1990.

Jakaria Abul Kalam Mohammad, ed. : Kabi Shakur Mahmud Birachita Goopichandrar Sanyas, Bangla Academy, Dhaka, 1974.

Jalil, Alamgir : Rajsahir Chhara, Dhaka, 1370 (Rhymes of Rajsahi).

Jaman, Farida : Adhunik Chitrakalay Lokshilper Proverb, Bangla Academy, Dhaka, 1998 (Influence of Folk Art on modern painting).

Janson, H.W. : History of Art, Henry and Abramis Inc, N.Y., 1977.

Jasimuddin : Nakshi Kanthar Maath, Dhaka, 1986 (famous Bengali poem).

Joshi, Indra : Indian Designs in Cross-stitch, Bombay, 1958. ; Journal of Indian Art and Industries, Vols. I to VIII, Calcutta.

Kagal, Carmen ed. : Shilpakar, Crafts Council of Western India, 1982. Kanthas of Bengal, Marg, Vol. 3 No. 2, Bombay, 1949-50.

Kasimpuri Md, Sirajuddin : Loksahitya-Chhara, Dhaka, 1968 (Folk Literature : Rhymes).

Khan, Mubarak Hossain : Shilpakala (Journal), Bangladesh Shilpakala Academy, Dhaka, 1994.

Khan Shamsuzzaman : Bangladesher Lok Aitihya, Dhaka, 1985 (Folk Tradition of Bangladesh).

Khan, Mobark Hossain ed. : Shilpakala (Annual Journal of Bangladesh Shilpakala Academy), Vol. VII, Dhaka, 1995.

Khan, Shamsuzzaman ed. : Folklore of Bangladesh, Vol. II, Dhaka, 1992.

Kramrisch, Stella : 'Kantha', Journal of Indian Society of Oriental Art (JISOA), Vol. 7, 1939.

Kuper, Adam & Kuper Jessica ed. : The Social Science Encyclopedia, New York, 1996.

Leach, Maria ed. : Standard Dictionary of Folklore, Mythology and Legends (in one Vol.), New York, 1984. Lok Shilper Bhubaney, Dhaka, 1994 (In the world of Folk Art).

Loksanskriti O Adivasi Sanskriti Kendra : Lokashruiti, 12th year, Calcutta 1996, 5th volume, 1979.

Lubell, Cecil ed. : Textile Collections of the World, Vol. 3 France, London, Studio Vista, 1977.

Maity, P.K. : Folk Rituals of Eastern India, New Delhi, 1988.

Mannan, Kazi Abdul, ed : Barendra Sahitya Patrika, Barshik Samelan, Rajsahi, 1367. (Annual number, literary magazine).

Marg Publication : Embroidery Issue, Vol. VIII, No. 2, March 1964. ; Rajasthan Handicrafts, Vol. XVIII, No.1, Dec. 1964. ; Bihar Handicrafts, Vol. XX, Vol. 1, Dec. 1966. ; Textiles and Embroideries of India, Bombay, 1965.

Maury, Curt : Folk Origins of Indian Art, New York, 1969.

Mazumdar, Mohitlal : Rabi Pradakshin, Calcutta.

Mehata R.J. : Handicrafts and Industrial Arts of India, Bombay, 1960.

Mehta, Rustam J. : Masterpieces of Indian Textiles, Bombay, 1984.

Memsinkai, S.S. : Survey of Handicrafts in Eight Districts of the Mysore State, Dharwar, 1961.

Miller, Barbara Stoler ed. : Exploring Indian's Sacred Art, Selected Writings of Stella Kramrisch, Motilal Banarsidass, Delhi, 1994. ; Ministry of Information and Broadcasting: Indian Handicrafts, New Delhi, 1956.

Misra, Subhakanta : 'Folk Art of Mithila', Folkore, I, Sept-Oct. 1960.

Mitra Dutta, Devayani : A Catalogue on Phulkari Textiles in the Collection of Indian Museum, Calcutta, 1985.

Mode, Heinz : Indian Folk Art, Bombay, 1985.

Mitra, Ashok : Bharatar Chitrakala, First part. Calcutta, 1995 (Indian Art).

Mitra, Mazumdar Dakshinaranjan : Rachana Samagra, first part, centenary edition, Calcutta, 1386 (Collected Works).

Mitra, Sanat Kumar ed : Loka Sanskriti Gabeshana, Calcutta kartick – poush 1405, Baishak-Asah, Calcutta 1406 Kalkata, 1395 (Research on folk culture).

Mitra, Sudhir Kumar : Hooghly Zillar Itihas, second part, Calcutta 1991 (History of Hooghly district)

Moeller, Marian Estabrook : An Indo Portuguese Embroidery from Goa, Gazette Des Beaux Arts, Vol. XXXIV, New York,1948.

Mohammad, Mansuruddin : Haramony, eighth volume, Dhaka, 1976.

Mohanty, B. : Pata-Paintings of Orissa, New Delhi, 1984.

Mohanty, Bijoy Chandra : Applique Craft to Orissa, Calico Museum of Textiles, Ahmedabad, 1980.; Marg, Vol. XVII, No. 2, Bombay, 1964.

Mookerjee, Ajit : Folk Art of Bengal, University of Calcutta, Calcutta, 1946. ; Folk Art of India, Clarion Books, New Delhi, 1986. ; Indian Primitive Arts, Oxford Book Stationary Co., Calcutta, 1959. Ritual Art of India, Timeless Books, New Delhi, 1998. 5000 Designs and Motifs from India, Dover, New York, 1996.; Kali, Thames and Hudson, London, 1988.

Mookerjee, Ranu : Old Textiles of India, Academy of Fine Arts, Calcutta.

Muhammad, Sirajuddin : Lyrics in Terracotta at Kantajeer Mandir, Makeup International, Dhaka, 1992. ; Living Crafts in Bangladesh, Makeup International, Dhaka, 1992.

Mukerjee, Radhakamal : The Culture and Art of India, New Delhi, 1984.

Mukherji, T.N. : Art Manufactures of India, Indian Museum, Calcutta, 1888.

Mukherji, Tinkari : Phulkari, Roopa Lekha, Vol. XXIV, No. 1& 2, Bombay, 1953.

Mukhopadhyay, Santipriya : Catalogue of Embroidered Textiles from Cutch & Kathiawar in the Indian Museum, Calcutta, 1983.

Naik, Shailaja D. : Traditional Embroideries of India, APH Publishing Co., New Delhi, 1996. ; Folk Embroidery and Traditional Handloom Weaving, APH, N.D., 1997. Nakshi Kantha, Shilpakala, Vol 16, Number One, Bangladesh Shilpakala Academy, Dhaka, 1992.

Narayan, Gita : Crafts India, Crafts Council of India, Madras, 1986.

Nath, Aman and Wacziarg, Francis : Arts and Crafts of Rajasthan, Mapin, Ahmedabad, 1994.

Nicholson, Julia : Traditional Indian Arts of Gujarat, Leicester, 1988. No. 2, Bangladesh National Museum, Dhaka, 1975.

Paine, Sheila : Embroidered Textiles, Traditional Patterns from Five Continents, Thames and Hudson, London, 1995.

Pal, Pratapaditya ed. : Marg, Vol. XLVI, No. 3, Bombay, 1995. ; AFC & Crafts Council of West Bengal: Patua Art, Calcutta, 1989.

Paul, Ashit ed. : Woodcut Prints of Nineteenth Century, Seagull, Calcutta, 1983.

Pischel Gina : The Golden History of Art, London, 1974.

Rahim M.A. : Social and Cultural History of Bengal,1967.

Rahman, Syed Zillur : Shilpakala, Vol. 2, Bangladesh Shilpakala Academy, Dhaka, 1979. ; Shilpakala, Vol. 4, Bangladesh Shilpakala Academy, Dhaka, 1981. ; Shilpakala Vol. 5, Bangladesh Shilpakala Academy, Dhaka 1995.

Rajamani, V.K. : Arts and Crafts of Tamil nadu, Mapin, Ahmedabad, 1992.

Ray, Sudhasu Kumar : The Ritual Art of the Bratas of Bengal, Firma K.L. Mukhopadhyay, Calcutta, 1961.

Rele, J.J. : The art of Rangoli, Hindustan Standard, Vol. 10, 1958.
Rice, David Talbot : Islamic Art, London, 1975.
Rice, Tamara Talbot : Ancient Arts of Central Asia, London, 1965.
Rossi, Barbara : From the Ocean Painting, OUP, New York, 1998.
Roy, Niharranjan : Bangalir Itihas, Adi Parva, Calcutta (history of Bengalis).
Roy, Gopen : Nakshi Kantha, The Indian Society of Oriental Art, calcutta, 1989.
Santra, Tarapada : Paschim banger Lokashilpa O Shilpi Samaj, Calcutta, 2000 (Folk art and artists of West Bengal).
Sarabhai Foundation : Guide to Structural Sewing: Terms and Techniques, Ahmedabad, 1999.
Sarkar, Abdul Matin, ed. : Charukala, first year, second volume, Dhaka, 1994.
Sarkar, Nirjharani : Rachana Sangraha, Calcutta, 1991 (Collected works).
Sarkar, Pabitra : Loka Sanskritir Nandan Tattya, Calcutta, 1996 (Theories on folk culture).
Sarkar, Sarochish, ed. : Bangla Academy, Baisakhi Lak Utsav Prabandha, 1400, Dhaka, 1993 (Essays in journal Baisakhi on folk Testivals).
Sarkar, Jadunath ed. : History of Bengal, Vol. 2, Dhaka, 1948. ;
Schuette, Merie and Sigid Muller, Christesen : The art of Embroidery, 1964.
Sen, Dinesh Chandra, ed. : Purba Banga Gitika, third volume, second number, Calcutta, 1930 (Ballads of East Bengal) Mymensingh Gitika, Calcutta, 1958 (Ballads of Mymensingh) Brihat Banga, first volume, Calcutta, 1935 (Greater Bengal).
Sen, Sukumar, ed. : Krishnadas Kaviraj Birachita Chaitanya Charitamrita, Calcutta, 1983 (Life of Chaitanya by Krishnadas Kaviraj) Brindabandas Birachita Chaitanya Bhagabat, Calcutta, 1991 (Also on Chaitanya).
Sen, Probhas : Crafts of West Bengal, Mapin, Ahmedabad, 1994.
Shah, Shampa ed. : Tribal Arts and Crafts of Madhya Pradesh, Ahmedabad, Mapin, 1996.
Siddiqui, Ashraf : Loka Sahitya, first volume, Dhaka, 1994.
Singh, Puran : Some Rumals from Chamba, Rupam, No. 32, Calcutta, 1927.
Stevens, Helen M. : The Myth & Magic of Embroidery, David & Charles, U.K., 1999.
Swarup, Shanti : Arts and Crafts of India & Pakistan, Bombay, 1957. ; 5000 years of Arts and Crafts in India and Pakistan, Taraporavala, Bombay, 1968. ; Ritual Decoration in India, Modern Review, February, Calcutta, 1950.
Tagore, Abanindranath : Banglar Brata, Calcutta, 1402 (Rituals of Bengal).
Tagore, Rabindranath : Rabindra Rachanabali, Centenary edition, West Bengal Govt., Vol. I and Vol. VII.
Tagore, Abanindranath & Kramrisch, Stella ed.: Journal of the Indian Society of Oriental Art, Vol. XVII, Calcutta, 1949.
Taylor, James : Descriptive and Historical Account of the Cotton Manufacturer of Dacca, 1851, pages 103 to 107 (notes on Bengal embroidery).
Thomas, Mary : Mary Thomas' dictionary of embroidery stitches, London, 1934.
Unknown India : Ritual Art in Tribe and Village, Philadelphia, 1968.
Vankatachalam, G. : Mirror of Indian Art, Chapter on Rangoli, Bangalore, 1929.
Vatuk, Ved Prakas : Studies in Indian Folk Tradition, New Delhi, 1979.
Victoria and Albert Museum : The Indian Heritage: Court Life & Arts under Mugal Rule, London, 1982. ; Indian Embroidery, London, 1951.
Walker, barbara G. : The woman's Encyclopaedia of Myths & Secrets, New York, 1983.
Walton, J. : Man in India, Vol. XXV, 1945.
Wartson, J. Forbes : Textile manufactures and the costumes of the people of India, 1866.
Watt, Sir George : Indian Art at Delhi, Official Catalogue of the Delhi Exhibition 1902-03, London, 1904.

Index